GETTING THE PROPERTY SOUL'D

A BREAKTHROUGH SYSTEM FOR SUCCESSFUL

STRESS-FREE BUYING AND SELLING

PAULA PAGANO

Getting the Property Soul'd
A Breakthrough System for Successful Stress-free Buying and Selling

Published by New Voices Press
315 W. 70th Street Suite 6C
New York, N.Y. 10023
Send feedback to jkatzcreative@aol.com

ISBN: 978-0-9883591-2-3

An application to register this book for cataloguing has been submitted to the Library of Congress

1. Business 2. Real Estate 3. Real Estate Training
4. Self Help 5. Sales 6. Sales Training

Disclaim & Legal Notices
Some names of people mentioned in this book have been changed to protect their privacy and preserve broker-client confidentiality. The opinions expressed are those of the author, and she will not be held liable for any damages, real or perceived, resulting from the use of this information.

This book is not intended to be used as a basis for any specific business or other legal decision, and the author assumes no responsibility for any such decisions made in connection with reading this book.

Book editing and artistic direction by Judy Katz, www.ghostbooksters.com
Cover photo by John Arbuckle, www.JohnArbucklePhotography.com
Hairstyle and makeup by Steffon Mateo, steffon@episodesalon.com
Cover and graphic book design by Tony Iatridis, www.nycartdirector.com

Printed in the United States of America

Dedication

I dedicate this book to my beloved husband, Gralen Britto, who has given me what I craved the most: the unqualified, limitless respect, acceptance and love I so desired as a child. And isn't that what we all want, and need, at any age?

This book is also dedicated to my father, Peter Pagano, who has grown beyond measure as a very special human being and as a father. I love you Dad.

Thanks also to all the people in my life who have supported and/or challenged me throughout the years. Thank you for caring, and for sharing. I am the richer for it–in all the ways that truly matter.

And let me not forget to also dedicate this book to my often delightful, sometimes challenging but always colorful clients–who are at the very core of this book.

Acknowledgments

Deep thanks to all those people in my life who have supported or challenged me throughout the years. My mentors: Bette Mae, Sue Bates Pintar, Mary Moeller. My managers: Joe and Jay Costello, Paul Newell, Tim Brown, Tim Murray, Bill Jansen, Charles Moore and Linda Carroll. And those who gave me speaking opportunities: Aldo Congi, Betty Walton, Cathy Scharetg, Charlie Krackeler, Dana Wellington, Eileen Mougeot, Eric Lofholm, James Caldwell, Joanna Philips, Isle Cordoni, Mark Best, Ruth Tralonga and Sonia Gomez.

For inspiration to keep me plugging away I thank my gurus, Mark Hopkins, Barbara Corcoran and Mike Larsen, whose writing group was the organizational structure I needed. Also thanks go to the other supportive organizations to which I belonged: NSA, National Speakers Association, NAWBO, National Association of Women Business Organizations, SFAR, San Francisco Association of Realtors, Santa Clara Power Training and WCR, Women's Council of Realtors.

Many thanks to all my dear friends and colleagues, who were the best cheerleaders anyone could ever have: Andrew Schulte, Anna Girod, Ann Tamminen, Azeb Clark, Barbara Erickson, Dan and Barbara Friedman, Cathy Clancy, Charlene Cogan, Debbie Cucalon, Dena Ashlanian-Williams, Diane Deiters, Diana Kirk, Dr. Stan Yantis, Doug Wink, Elaine Larkin, Ellie Kravets, Garey DeMartini, Jillian Alderson, Katey Shinn, Kathleen McIntosh, Kathleen Deggelman, Lee Bender, Louise Chegwidden, Lynne Dantzker and Craig Johnson, Lynn Fraley, Lynne Hillock, Mary Lou Myers, Michael Peck, Mindy Noble, Rebecca White, Sandra Hughes, Summer Simonton, Valerie

Sadler, Yvonne Meyer, Valerie and Harry Thurston and Danny and Vicky Faria.

Most thanks to Lisa Bass for your unwavering support throughout this whole process. Also, special thanks to Larry Cogan and Jean Marie Romeo whose encouragement, I remember so fondly, though their souls have left this world way too early.

Thanks also to my personal assistants for the last fifteen years who have worked so hard on my behalf: Karmen Tang, Jennifer Zheng and Euncie Ma. You gals are my favorites! And all my students, who took my classes seriously, especially those who became SuperStars: Katherine Holland, Danielle Lazier, Dennis Otto, Edie Narrido, Heidi Rossi, John Solaegui, Sara Werner Costa and Ron Sebahar.

For the help of constructing my website I want to thank Jeff Brock, Tony Iatridis and Diana Concoff Morgan. For the help getting this manuscript ready, I want to thank Tony Iatridis for his eagle eye, creativity and emotional support. Also thanks to Carol Adrienne, Frank Jordan, Gini Grahm Scott, Maureen Simonton, Joyce Maynard and Ray Brown–you all told me I could do this. I also want to thank Ellen Roberts of Where Books Begin, who started me in this process.

A special shout-out to my editor, Judy Katz of Ghostbooksters. Judy has been at my side throughout and culled my manuscript into the masterpiece I always envisioned. I have found her generosity, expertise and tenaciousness invaluable. Her input on creating a title that would sum up my message was especially helpful. I didn't have the strength or persistence to do it myself and I needed her steadfast guidance to steer me through the mysterious worlds of writing, marketing and publishing. Thank you, thank you, Judy, from the bottom of my heart for pushing me to be the writer I always aspired to be. I really truly could not have done this without you!

On a more personal note, but just as worthy: I want to acknowledge my beloved niece and nephews, who are the children I never had and who I love beyond measure: Mike and Matt Pagano and Cam and Holly Cogan. And thank you Aunt Betty, for finding those typos and who, sadly, just passed away two weeks before her 108th birthday. What a life she had, but that's another story.

Finally, last, and certainly not least, my wonderful husband, Gralen Britto, whose patience and love exceeds that of all the saints and angels above.

There are others who have touched my life, personally and professionally. To those I have not mentioned, forgive the oversight, and please accept my humblest apologies. Even if you are not on this page, I love you.

Testimonials for Getting The Property Soul'd

"Don't learn how to sell (or buy) real estate the hard way! Take advantage of the stories, experiences and sage advice put before you by Paula Pagano. They will help you shortcut your way to success in this exceptionally important and sometimes overly emotional area."

– Tom Hopkins, 40-Year Real Estate Trainer and Guru,
Best Selling Author of Master the Art of Selling Anything

"Bravo Paula! What a mirror! The real stories in *Soul'd* dramatically demonstrate to every one of us – buyers and sellers as well as industry professionals–how our reactions to one another can affect the sale in a positive or negative way. Read this book before you venture out–or proceed at your own risk!"

– Hon. Ellen Tauscher, Former Congresswoman and
Under Secretary of State for Arms Control
and International Security, and Client of Paula Pagano

"I took coaching classes from Paula Pagano who helped me succeed in this very competitive business. She has been a top producing salesperson in San Francisco for 30 years. She often wondered how she–self-described as overly analytical, impatient and often emotional–succeeded in this tough business. The answers are all in *Soul'd.* I could not put the book down. I was entertained, educated, amused and enlightened: a lot of value for the money and time!"

–Danielle Lazier, Broker Associate and Co-Founder,
San Francisco Keller Williams Office,
Ranked Top 0.01% of San Francisco Realtors® (per MLS)

"Paula is a passionate storyteller. Along with priceless real estate insights and lessons learned for salespersons, buys and sellers, she provides life lessons that will help anyone persevere in the life they were born to live. *Soul'd* is truly inspirational!

– Mike Larsen, Literary Agent and
Author of Guerrilla Marketing for Writers

"For me, Paula Pagano was a caring mentor and coach. The stories and insights she shared were invaluable to all of us: agents new to the profession as well as those wishing to take their craft to the next level. Learning from her was the high point of my budding career and I use the tools I learned from her every day. If you too want Paula's wisdom, generously offered between two covers, read *Getting the Property SOUL'D!*"

– Ron Sebahar, Broker Associate, MBA,
Hill & Co's #2 Top Producing Agent

"I loved reading about all the different situations Paula went through, the emotions involved and how she learned to control them to gain success. *Soul'd* is a great book for anyone who needs help acknowledging and changing the way they think."

– Marcia Copeland, CEO Copeland Creative Café

"Through riveting anecdotes that explore the real stories of how deals are made or broken, Paula Pagano shares her own personal saga: how she went from medical researcher to top producer in the challenging San Francisco real estate market. Her raw honesty and introspection is refreshingly humble. She is a great storyteller and everyone can find inspiration and valuable insights on dealing with others while understanding how to best optimize their own strengths and weaknesses."

– Tracy O'Neill, Co-Active Leadership Coach

"*Getting the Property SOUL'D* is an excellent handbook in organizing your business and understanding how to measure its effectiveness. It's written in a down-to-earth and interesting style, and tells the ins and outs of not just surviving but thriving in the real estate market. Paula understands the challenge of being a real estate agent and has included lots of secrets that have made her so successfully through her career."

– Valerie Sadler, HR Executive for CBS

"Just finished reading *Soul'd.* I thought it was fantastic, and not just for Real Estate professionals. I am a salesperson in another field, and found Paula's secrets very helpful. I especially enjoyed the way that she wove her secrets into a most interesting life story. I read this in one weekend. Each and every chapter was a new learning experience and an adventure. A great read that I highly recommend."

– Sandra Hughes, Entrepreneur, Cazenovia, New York

"In *Soul'd,* there are practical real-world situations that everyone, whether in sales or not, will relate to at least fifty percent of the time. The book doesn't claim to be scientific with a formula to win the world! Instead, the author shares her intimate and personal experiences in an accessible, fast-moving and entertaining fashion, with insights that could be applicable in any life situation. Thank you, Paula!"

– M. Clarke, Financial Advisor

“Ms. Pagano makes her business come alive with all ranges of emotion, from anxiety to joy. Mixing in lessons learned with appropriate anecdotes makes this book a page-turner. I'm not a Realtor® but I am in sales for a different industry, and I found this book refreshing, informative and a genuine feel-good experience!

– Mike Wild, Automobile Sales Executive

“This book is a rare combination of information, inspiration and entertainment. The author writes with feeling and her insightful professional advice is delivered with warmth, energy and humor, not a clinical ABC approach. While real estate is the obvious focus, and the lessons reflect the author's successful experiences, the book is also loaded with thought-provoking messages that could have wider application. An excellent read.”

– L. Hillock, Bechtel Executive

“I thoroughly enjoyed reading *Soul'd.* It was refreshing to learn how one woman's journey into successful business was shaped by her understanding of her emotions and ability to use that knowledge to her advantage. Unique for what is essentially a business book; Paula went to the heart of the matter as she shows you how working WITH your emotions in business and not against them can make you successful beyond your wildest dreams.”

– Sue Bates Pintar, Retired Real Estate
Broker Associate, Seattle, Washington

Contents

INTRODUCTION

Discovering What Makes You Great In Real Estate

It was obvious from the beginning of my sales career that I was not a natural-born salesperson. I came into real estate not having any business experience, so I had to endure humiliation and heartache. By recounting my struggles for success in this book, I hope to spare others from suffering a similar fate. I also wish that learning from my experience will help smooth your path to a successful sales career.

I believe that many people, like me, have a plan. Usually, however, it is not one's plan but an unexpected opportunity that ultimately shapes career choices. After graduating from college, I became a medical researcher. It was not until I had to experiment on animals, and actually kill them, that I realized I needed to find another profession. I traveled to California looking for some answers. When someone suggested real estate, I thought it would be a good fit because my father was an architect. I also loved architecture, but was that passion enough to make me a success?

Nevertheless, passing the licensing test and getting hired by a company turned out to be fairly easy. But I quickly learned that real estate was not really about houses. It was about sales and those sales came out of solid relationships. I was a young, immature biologist with few communication skills, little life experience and an emotionally challenged Irish-Italian background. Was I capable of assisting people in one of the most important investments of their lives? No way!

My customers were making important life decisions and I

had nothing to offer aside from my impatience. (Oops! I forgot to mention that the Native American Mohawk ancestry on my mother's side only adds to my impetuous nature.) The truth was, my clients' anxieties, their dawdling and indecisiveness and their occasional emotional outbursts drove me crazy.

Although there were plenty of books and seminars available about systematic business plans, scripted sales techniques and ramped-up positive thinking, they did not show me "the underbelly" of sales–how to get along with anxious clients, their overprotective friends and family and pushy colleagues. What I needed–and what I believe most struggling salespeople need as well–was an understanding of how to set and hold boundaries, communicate effectively and change limiting belief patterns. And sure enough, these skills can be learned just like contracts and building codes. Changing negative habits is hard work, but it can be done.

As a scientist, I understood something about human physiology that I believed I could apply to human psychology. For instance, the process of changing the neural pathways of learned behavior, like impatience and worry, offered a similar choreographic model for changing my career and succeeding in a new one.

First, I had to identify my negative habits and understand why I was addicted to those behaviors. Then I had to let those negative habits go and replace them with positive ones. For example, I learned to talk to myself soothingly when clients whined at me. I learned to have faith through the weeks and months a buyer waffled indecisively about putting a realistic offer on a property. Similarly, I learned that if I assisted incompetent mortgage brokers and title officers in getting their job done, the escrow would eventually close. And I learned that if I listened patiently while a seller railed incessantly about not getting the price they hoped, we forged a trustful, bonding relationship that could last for a lifetime.

Each time I faced up to challenges, I always got something positive in return, such as my client's repeat business and their recommendations. With this arsenal of skills for controlling my old emotions, I enhanced my self-esteem and became the number one top producer in my office during a recession marked by 17% interest rates. I remained highly successful for three decades.

It took emotional strength, personal awareness and courage to deal with people's roller-coaster emotions–and some empathy, too. Their new house would change their lives. It was the biggest investment they would ever make, so of course they were stressed out! A new agent at one of my seminars said it the best: "I knew that my clients would be emotional. What I didn't consider was my reaction to all their emotions." It is my intention to explain in these pages exactly how to develop healthy and creative ways of communicating and connecting with clients through a wide variety of changing and often unpredictable situations and circumstances.

In this book I reveal and discuss all of the virtues necessary to be a top producer, as well as identify the detrimental behavioral practices, or "vices," to avoid. Because my case histories are about actual people (although the clients' names have been changed to protect their privacy), the reader will be able to see and understand how much our personal issues color our interactions with others. For instance, remaining upbeat, positive and helpful around the office can result in a referral from an over-booked colleague. Congratulating even the most arrogant of agents can mean you are first in line to hold their best available open house. Observe the nuances of what customers say and you can discern the real players from the unmotivated. Take this a step further and stay in the present moment to develop your sixth sense of intuition, which will help you prepare for any challenge.

The practical tools mentioned within these pages will help you close transactions, make more money and make your life easier. For the best results, go slow. Perhaps you might want to read only one chapter a week and take the time to integrate the Lessons Learned into your business practice. Or you might want to read the whole book and go back over each chapter, one at a time. If you want to delve even deeper, there are detailed success exercises on my teaching website, www.paulapagno.com.

In spite of all the stress and drama, sales can be tremendously fulfilling–emotionally, intellectually and financially. I urge you to join me on my journey of personal transformation as I grow as a person, expand my business savvy and make my lifelong dream a reality. I wish the same for you.

1

CLARITY

Determining What Matters Most

Finding My True North Star

My carefully laid plans of a career in medical research had turned into a bit of a disaster. Not only was it isolating–I was stuck in a dark, dank laboratory most of the day–it was also heartbreaking. When I was not reading research articles, I was hunched over furry little hamsters doing all sorts of terrible things to them. Sometimes I had to slit their throats to collect blood samples. Other times I had to implant cancers into their cheek pouches, wait for the tumors to grow and then irradiate them. When co-workers saw me crying, they scolded me as if I were a little girl, "Paula, if you want to be a scientist, you are going to have to learn not to be so emotional."

As my colleagues shrugged their shoulders and continued torturing small animals, I had violent nightmares. I hated walking up the six flights of stairs to the floor where they housed the doomed mice, rats, hamsters, guinea pigs, rabbits and monkeys. Each time I climbed those steps, I clutched the handling gloves tightly to my chest and said a prayer, knowing that the animal I chose could die. I kept thinking my frame of mind would change; I would become hardened and strong like the rest of them. But I didn't. Every new day was as hard as the first, which is still seared into my memory:

When Dr. Nelson, one of the PhD's in the Radiology Department, instructed me for the first time to collect a hamster for an experiment, I was more eager than afraid. I had been reading research articles for a month and wanted some hands-on action. I felt I was ready and he agreed.

I was halfway down the hallway when he called to me. "Paula, aren't you forgetting something?" Dr. Nelson held up a pair of gloves.

"Oh, I don't need those," I said, remembering my neighbor's sweet cuddly ball of fur.

He walked over to me and gave me two canvass-covered hand protectors. "Trust me. You will."

When I unclasped the lock to the cage, the cute little animals inside shrank en masse to the farthest corner and stood on their hind legs with front claws drawn, baring pointed front teeth and letting out such a collective screech that I was jolted backwards. "Damn," I yelled as I rammed my hand on the metal cage, trying to get out of harm's way. Gloves were a definite must. I put on the bulky contraptions, making sure none of my flesh was showing.

As I reached inside, the high pitched screaming started all over again. I was forced to withdraw. Remembering how well I connected to animals, I started talking to the small creatures in a low, soothing voice. I slowly slid my hand in again, but lost confidence when the animals rushed toward me, apparently determined not to let me take one of their own.

Dr. Nelson insisted that animals did not have emotions, but these animals seemed pretty angry. I had always been a big proponent of medical science, thinking that experimentation on animals was necessary for the benefit of mankind. Now I was not so sure. Didn't Hippocrates preach, "First, do no harm"? Or did he just mean no harm to us, the most highly evolved species (theoretically) on the planet? And did scientists really believe we were the only living beings on the planet with emotions? Or was it because it was easier or more convenient to think that way in order to do this work, just as it is sometimes easier for us to deny our own emotions? Granted, emotions are complicated, often irrational and difficult, if not impossible, to measure, but does that also mean they don't exist?

The reason I got my BA in biology was because of my love of all living things–there they were again–those damn emotions! Being a doctor or veterinarian was out of the question. I did not have the funds or the commitment, and no way did I want to be a nurse and push bedpans. Full of optimism and hope that I would be part of a team who would discover a breakthrough cure for cancer, I told myself medical research was the job for me. Now I was forcing myself to get out of bed every morning. I hated my life. So when Ted Martin, my boyfriend at the time, received a job offer to teach at the University of California campus in Irvine, California, I decided to move with him. Just like The Mamas and the Papas, I hoped "I'd be safe and warm if I was in L.A." Without any further thought, I left the cold, blustery winter days in upstate New York behind. California, I believed, could be my ticket out of hell.

Escape to Laguna Beach

Starting over, I chose Laguna Beach, a small artistic beach town, as my new home. The golden sand at Laguna reminded me of the French Riviera, except there were no pebbles to hurt my feet, few men in bikini Speedo trunks (thankfully) and no topless women. This was the United States after all. It felt like a slice of paradise.

The town center had the usual coffee shops, restaurants and stores, city hall, fire and police departments, and a library. Unlike the polished, very sophisticated nearby beach towns of Newport, Corona del Mar and Balboa Island, Laguna was quaint and charming, nestled between grass hills and the Pacific Ocean.

There were no high-rises on the beach (the hotels had been built in the twenties and thirties) and not a chain store in sight (except for an Albertson's tucked away from the city's center, where people bought their groceries). The houses surrounding the town center, where I was looking for a rental, were mostly small beach cottages, some of which had been renovated and expanded into more substantial homes. However, even the smallest cottage was too expensive for us. I found a tiny one bedroom apartment in a fourplex located on a busy commercial corner. It was curtainless, dingy and in desperate need of a paint job, but since the beach was so close, none of that mattered.

Bette Mae became my inspiration; she told me her remarkable story of how she was widowed, twice, before she was thirty and left with three young children. She invested the money she received from her husbands' life insurance policies and bought two houses–one for her family and the other for income. Real estate had literally been her savior. Perhaps it could be mine as well.

I knew nothing about business, sales or dealing with the public. I was new to California and a complete stranger. Yet sales was enticing because my success would depend entirely on me. On days that I had surplus energy, which I often had, I could work as long as I wanted and had a good chance of benefiting directly from the fruits of my labor. The harder I worked the more income I stood to make.

"Ambitious salespeople are amply rewarded for their success," Bette Mae said. "It actually helps being a woman, because the average person trusts us more than the fast-talking men."

I had been in the medical field long enough to know that the men got the promotions. Coming in early, willingly filling in for my less ambitious colleagues, and working on weekends to finish an experiment all got me nowhere. No overtime pay. No bonus. No extra day off. No acknowledgment. Not even a pat on the back.

In sales, I could be my own boss and come and go as I pleased. The freedom would be liberating. No more feeling boxed in by a life that was not harmonious with who I really was. No more living someone else's dreams. Hadn't I done enough following others orders rather than taking the time to find out what I wanted?

In my youth, voices had echoed in my ears, "Get a science degree. You can always do something with that." I heard it said to me over and over. It reminded me of the advice, "One word: Plastics" given to Dustin Hoffman in The Graduate. My mother, in particular, had some rather specific criteria for what represented a "respectable" profession. I, on the other hand, would call them narrow-minded.

Why was it so necessary that I please others and not myself? Ironically, I might just as easily have wondered why I hadn't chosen sales in the first place, because it certainly was in my genes. My great-uncle's real estate firm, Pagano Real Estate, had "For Sale" signs everywhere in Delmar, a small suburb outside of Albany, where I grew up. And although I was not the most popular girl in school, everyone always commented on how beautiful our house was. And indeed for good reason, because my father was an admirer of Frank Lloyd Wright and an architect himself, who designed and built our postmodern ranch high on a full acre parcel fronted by a row of regal pine trees. A hand-laid stone walkway cut across to the front door, and a four-foot retaining wall encircled the house, of which both masonry structures were ingeniously lined with bright ornamental shrubs, roses and colorful long-stemmed flowers.

The focal point was a huge picture window with flagstone siding bordering each side. The house door and under-hanging soffit were painted turquoise. This was a daring choice on my father's part, which might have seemed gauche, but he knew the bright iridescent color against the flagstone would be spectacular. It was the one obvious thing I could boast about my family. The rest of the stuff I'd just as soon keep to myself, though perhaps nothing could be more revealing than the conversation–if one could call it that–in which I announced my new and exciting career choice to my parents.

Telling them I was leaving the medical field was not easy. Any conversation, other than the weather, had always proved to be a test of wills. No wonder I had moved so far away. Maybe Dad would understand, especially if he thought his work inspired me. Without analyzing any further, I grabbed the phone. Mother picked up.

"I have some exciting news to tell you," I gasped, enthused. "Is Dad around?"

Mother called for Dad to get on the other line "I know–you're finally getting married! I hope not to that Ted person. His head was always stuck in a book. But I guess something is better than nothing. At least you won't be an old maid."

"No, Mother. Something much better! I've found a new

profession! Something I think I'll be really good at–real estate! I'll be selling houses, meeting new people, always on the go and doing something I enjoy. You've always said how I can't sit still. You know, I hated being cooped up in a laboratory all day, doing one rote experiment after another. It's so boring." *Plus, I won't have to kill animals.* But I didn't say that.

"Paula, your father is an architect, which is a respectable occupation." Mother enunciated the syllables of the last two words so I would really get the point. "That's a whole lot (again more enunciations) different than selling houses." In her most critical voice, she added, "Life isn't always fun and games–you need a *real* job."

"But selling homes is a real job," I countered. "I'll be writing contracts, finding people their dreams, negotiating offers. Every day there will be something new to do, to learn, people to meet…"

I heard a loud sigh on the other side of the phone and prepared myself for the emotional backlash. Her voice raised an octave higher. "So you want to be a common salesperson, after all that money and time spent on getting your BA in biology? What a waste!"

Yeah, but it was my money I used for college and it was not working out. I didn't say that, much as I wanted to. Instead, I said, "Sales is something I feel aligned with–it suits my personality better. Since I will be working as an independent contractor, my success will be measured by how well I do my job. You know what a hard worker I am, and as a medical researcher, I never got recognized for all my accomplishments. All the promotions went to the men. My real estate success will depend solely on me."

Mother kept on talking as if she had not heard a word I

said, trying to convince me to continue living my life of quiet desperation and despair. Perhaps Dad would understand. I turned my attention to him, recalling all our Sunday drives looking at the different architectural aspects of the homes in our neighborhood. His predictable response: "Listen to your mother."

I had to live my own life, I told myself as I hung up the phone, wondering why the many miles between us could not give me the emotional distance I craved. I turned on my stereo and chose a record album to match the raw emotion I was feeling so I could get the clarity to decide what to do next.

When I told Bette Mae of my decision to get my real estate license, she cautioned me about the fate of other people she knew who had tried to be salespeople and failed. "First of all you need a minimum of a year to two years of savings in the bank." I checked my finances. I had a good nine months and, if I was frugal, a year–enough time to get my business rolling.

She then explained that being in sales was cyclical. "You have to be prepared for the dips and valleys. Real estate is 100% commission-based. If you don't make a sale, you don't get paid. Not one dime. And you see those successful real estate agents driving around in their fancy cars? Most of them live on the edge–just one step ahead of creditors. They make a sale and then they spend, spend, spend, thinking that the good times will never end. But they do. My question for you is–do you have the courage, tenacity, discipline and confidence to hang in there when things get tough?"

I walked to the beach with a notepad in hand to think this all through. Finding a place of solitude, I let the soft golden sand sift between my toes as I made two columns on my paper. I closed my eyes, concentrating on the soothing, lapping sound of waves on the sand. I felt the healing rays of the sun on my face and opened my eyes only to write.

I knew the analytical life of a scientist was not for me; there was nothing else on the horizon, and I may very well have had the qualities it took to be a salesperson. I certainly did have the drive and self-discipline. I had been working since I was sixteen. I wrote that down. Plus, I put myself through college and believed I had the determination and tenacity necessary to hang in there. I felt comfortable around people, and I had just moved 3,000 miles, so I must have had some confidence–and ample courage as well. I had been stuck in a suffocating role too long. Having a boss tell me what to do only irritated me. I liked my independence. I could do sales my way on my terms. The thought gave me a liberating feeling inside. I felt my heart opening wide–the possibilities enticing. For me it was worth the gamble to give sales a try.

Bette Mae lent me the Anthony School Instruction Book, which she had gotten for her older son Mark, hoping he would choose a more steady career than just washing cars, and she assured me the material was not all that hard. I told her I was not worried. If I could pass my Organic Chemistry final, I could take just about any test. For the next month I spent my days and evenings at the library. Escrow, trust deed, amortization, equity, leverage: those were all words I had never heard before, but I studied hard and passed the test on my first try.

The interview process was more difficult. Bette Mae gave me the names of the two best firms in town. I made the appointments, dressed the part and talked myself into being calm. "It's a piece of cake," I told myself. I laughed–always the sweet eater. The first firm was Nolan Real Estate, which was within walking distance of my apartment.

A secretary ushered me into a private office where I was to wait. It was only a few minutes, but it felt like an entire afternoon. It was hot and stuffy with the sun beating through the windows in the middle of the day and, as the minutes crawled by, I started to perspire and grow increasingly uncomfortable. Finally, a middle-aged man with a brisk manner and obvious high self-esteem walked in, shook my hand and took a seat at the desk opposite my chair.

My hands were folded neatly on my lap. *No fidgeting,* I told myself. *No dramatic talking with the hands. Speak slowly.* He asked me the same question I had asked myself. "Where will you get your clients? You just moved here. You have no sphere of influence."

"What's a sphere of influence?" I asked. I did not catch that phrase while studying for my real estate exam.

"A sphere of influence is all the people you know–family, friends, past business associates, your doctor, lawyer, hairdresser, and then all the people they know. To get started you need a minimum of one hundred contacts. Then each of them has a hundred, and so on. Real estate is a contact business. Your success depends upon who you know."

"I just moved here," I said.

He thought for a moment. "We find that many of our successful women agents meet their contacts through their children's schools. Do you have any children?" Before I had a chance to answer, he said, "I'm sorry. I should ask first–are you married?" When I said no, he ended the interview and gave me the "good luck" handshake.

The second company was Lingo. Within minutes of meeting me, the sales manager asked me what model car I drove.

Proud to even own a car, I answered, "A Chevette," and was immediately told that the company had no desk currently available. He ushered me out the door, saying he would call if anything changed. Needless to say, I wasn't going to wait around for that call. For them, a Realtor's® image was very important, in fact critical. I figured it was not just the car; I was too young, inexperienced, unconnected and poor.

When Bette Mae's suggestions didn't pan out, I realized I needed to make my own plan. I decided to try Newell Associates, the real estate office on Pacific Coast Highway, which had helped me find my rental. Okay, so it was not the most prestigious office in town, but it did have a good reputation. Moreover, it was an established family-run business with a high-visibility location.

On the day of the interview, I convinced myself this was my lucky day. I took my time getting ready, choosing my best dress, pulling on my pantyhose–though it was again warm outside–and heels. I carefully applied my make-up–not too much rouge or lipstick or dark eyeliner, but enough to look mature.

I checked myself in the mirror, doing a quick turn-around. Not bad for someone who was not into fashion. As I looked at my reflection, I said: "Today is the day," convincing myself the third interview was the charm. All I needed to do was believe in myself. I waltzed through the door, smiling with anticipation.

Paul Newell, Jr., the owner's son, was a Laguna native, an amber-tanned well-dressed man in his mid-thirties who had a perpetual smile. I guessed that he had a lot to smile about if his family owned a real estate firm on Pacific Coast Highway. We got in his immaculately kept, champagne-toned Cadillac

Seville with cushy leather seats. This was the nicest car I had ever ridden in. I regarded Paul's invitation to lunch as a good sign. He chose the historic Laguna Hotel right on the water. As soon as we pulled up, a valet opened the car door for me.

I acted like I did this every day. I got out with the graceful ease of a model. For that day, I had decided, I was the queen. The hotel had a restaurant deck which overlooked an azure blue ocean overspread on that day with a blazing indigo sky. We sat beneath a green-and-white striped umbrella. I noticed all the wealthy vacationers enjoying themselves–women in oversized sun hats and dark glasses sipping strawberry daiquiris while athletic men with bulging biceps downed ice-cold beers. Over the railing I could see surfers gliding atop the waves despite the fact that it was the middle of February! I was feeling relaxed, confident and assured. I just assumed I had the job.

When Paul said, "We haven't hired you yet," I ignored his comment and kept proceeding forward as if he had. He was the type of person, I surmised, that had a hard time saying no to young attractive women. After a lingering lunch, we went back to the office. My charm, my courage and my chutzpah paid off. He showed me my desk and I joined Newell Associates that afternoon.

Lessons Learned from Chapter 1:

- RESEARCH YOUR OPTIONS If you are thinking of real estate as a career, try to start talking to people who work in the field. Ask them how they got started—what made them successful and how long it took.
- EVALUATE YOUR FINANCIAL READINESS Since real estate is commission-based, you need to have enough money to work without income for a year. You also need to know how to live frugally at the start without getting discouraged. As Bette Mae said, "You have to be prepared for the dips and valleys. Real estate is 100% commission-based. If you don't make a sale, you don't get paid. Not one dime."
- RECOGNIZE THE PITFALLS OF A SALESPERSON Being in sales depends on the state of the economy at the time. You must save for the downtimes. Ask yourself, do you have the courage, tenacity and confidence to hang in there when things get tough?
- ARE YOU COMFORTABLE RELATING TO PEOPLE OF ALL PERSONALITY TYPES? A sales career is not for the timid. Do you have an outgoing personality? Do you have the ability to deal with all kinds of people?
- RECOGNIZE GOLDEN OPPORTUNITIES I found that the best way to make important life decisions was through the physical process of writing everything down on paper. The hand-eye-brain coordination unlocks hidden answers that using a computer can not.

2

COURAGE

Making Changes

Early Lessons in Real Estate

After I spent several months learning the basic tools of the trade, Paul Newell thought I was ready for a referral. The client was a high-profile lawyer, who was recently divorced and had two teenage sons. At the time he was staying in a short-term rental–all the signs of the perfect buyer–financially qualified and under a time restraint. When he walked through the door that Monday afternoon, I was taken by surprise. Stunningly handsome, tall and lean with dark almond eyes and a bronze-toned complexion, this man had the same exotic look as Omar Sharif in Dr. Zhivago. I almost tripped over myself as I extended my hand. So much for a graceful introduction.

"Paul Newell tells me you are new to the area," I said, "Why don't we step into our conference room and you can tell me more of what you are looking for?" I attempted to pour each of us some coffee. The cup made it to him, but not without some of the hot black liquid dribbling down the side. "Sugar?" I asked, willing my hands to stillness.

His voice was soft and sultry. He took his coffee black. Silently I bet myself he didn't eat quiche and in the bedroom he....

"I need a three-bedroom family home for my two sons," "Omar" said, interrupting my lust-filled daydream.

"Two children make only two bedrooms," I said, chuckling at what I thought was a good joke, "but then I was never very good in math."

Omar's facial expression was unchanged. I wondered if he was already on to me. This was my first face-to-face meeting with a client. Switching to my most professional mode, I asked, "What else is important to you?"

Omar put his coffee down and looked me straight in the eye, serious and businesslike. "Whatever it is that teenagers need–a yard, a garage big enough for their sports stuff and a good school district."

"All the schools in Laguna are pretty good," I said. "Anything else? View? Fireplace? Architectural preference?"

"All nice to have, but not essential. Of course, we'll want our own bathrooms and an additional half bath for guests."

"That's it?" I asked.

"That's it," was his reply. *Boy, if being a real estate agent was this easy*, I thought, *I am going to love this job!*

"By the way, did Paul Newell tell you I'm a trial lawyer? I do not have a lot of free time for going around looking."

"That's fine," I said. "I can preview all the houses that meet your criteria ahead of time."

Omar pulled himself away from the table, said goodbye and was gone in a flash. I probably forgot to ask half the questions I should have, but I was flying-the-sky thrilled. I fantasized about being taken away on a white horse to Arabia or wherever he was from and living a life of excitement, travel and luxury. To expand on the fantasy, I reminded myself that my boyfriend, Ted, was nothing more than a poorly paid professor who was difficult to live with. And I was definitely not in love with him. What could be more serendipitous than an encounter with such a well-qualified, good-looking client! I guess you could say that I wasn't exactly focused on the career-oriented task at hand.

Regardless, I faced the grimmer facts of life when I paid for my groceries the next day. Ted was insistent we go half on everything. Nothing like a quick glance at my bank balance for a reality check. Peanut butter and jelly looked like my main fare until I sold something. Forget romance with handsome strangers.

I previewed several different neighborhoods and included all architectural styles–Spanish, Contemporary, Craftsman, Bungalow, Ranch–as long as the floor plan was suitable for families. The most popular family neighborhood was located on the top ridge of the Laguna Hills called Top of the World. These ranch homes were built in the sixties with large yards, two car garages and good square footage–certainly enough for a family. Some even had ocean views, so I showed these, receiving a lukewarm response from my client.

Another possibility was the more expensive remodeled beach community in the center of town. These homes were my favorites–charming, well-kept bungalows with lovely manicured front lawns within walking distance of schools, shopping and restaurants. Surprisingly, Omar was not impressed, and I was perplexed. Perhaps because they were too small? He did not explain and naively, I didn't ask. Then there were those few precious homes located right on the beach on the other side of Pacific Coast Highway. Forty or fifty years ago these paradise estates were built within steps of the ocean. Equally prestigious were the newer gated communities of Emerald Bay, Irvine Cove and Three Arch Bay, again right on the beach. Those he loved, but he still did not write an offer. Next

I showed a contemporary home in Bluebird Canyon, which seemed to appeal to Omar, but once he learned the area was prone to landslides, he changed his mind. I would need to expand the search to the surrounding townships.

At the time, South Laguna was composed of long-ago vacation cottages with poorly planned additions and referred to in the business as "fixer-uppers." Too funky for Omar. Laguna Niguel, a fairly new suburban development further south was also a No.

Omar's reaction to all the houses I had shown him had been one of polite disdain. Since he was so quiet and reserved, I was afraid to pry. I dealt with my client's apparent lack of interest by continuing to show him whatever new family homes came on the market, hoping he would make up his mind soon. Days turned into weeks, weeks into months. "Find a house as soon as possible" was just not happening. I was slipping into negativity and half-believing the words I had overheard from my cynical office mates: "Buyers are Liars and Sellers are Storytellers."

Paul Newell was too busy with his own clients to help me, so I approached Sue Bates, one of the more successful agents in the office. Files piled high on her desk, she was on the phone, taking copious notes while another call was on hold for her. I walked by her desk several times, trying to catch her eye. Another phone call came in. I went home, discouraged. Mission unaccomplished.

Knowing I had to salvage this deal for my financial survival, I got to the office early the next day and caught her before she started her day. Sue got straight to the point. "Have you asked your client why all the houses you have shown him didn't work?"

Confident that I had followed the correct protocol, I told her we had a counseling session before we even went out to look at properties.

"How long ago was that?" Sue asked.

"About four months ago, and he still hasn't bought anything! I thought he was a motivated buyer."

"Most clients do not know what it is they want," Sue said. "As their agent, you have to continually ask questions to help guide them. Did you ask the client for feedback throughout your showing process?"

"I'm sure I must have asked if he liked the neighborhood, floor plan, amenities, you know, things like that."

"All those questions require simple yes and no answers. You need to get to the meat of the problem–which is why he is not buying. Ask opened-ended questions. Questions like: 'How do you think today's house tour went?' or 'What are your feelings about the houses I've been showing?' Then he has to give you a more detailed answer. That will require some inner searching on his part. And better feedback for you." Sue paused. It was me doing the soul searching now. She continued, "Personally, I like to use the word *feel.* That way I am addressing the client's emotional right brain. It is especially important with high-powered people as they often are not in touch with their emotions." Sue pointed to her chest. "Home is where the heart is."

I was glad I asked for help! I would never have been able to figure all this out on my own.

She then asked, "Do you think perhaps you are afraid to use open-ended questions? Are you afraid of the answer–that maybe he won't buy?"

"I'm not sure," I said, beginning to doubt myself.

"Okay, so we do not have any verbal answers as to why your client is not buying. Tell me–how does he react when you show him houses?" Now Sue was using this open-ended question technique on me! I did not have a simple, easy answer to give her. This was a good start though, because it was forcing me to get to the meat of the problem. Sue continued, "Check out body language, facial expressions, even what your client does not say. Is he avoiding any questions? Non-verbal cues are just as important as what clients say–sometimes more so, because the body does not lie."

"Ah, so buyers do lie?"

Sue explained. "Not on purpose. Most people have no idea what it is they want. They have a hard time deciding what to order from a menu, so how can you expect them to make a decision when it comes to committing to a big purchase? That is why they need professionals, like us, to help guide them. You say your client is divorced? Perhaps he wants to be perceived as a family man, but underneath he may really be a Bachelor Babe. If that's the case, you are showing him the wrong type of house, regardless of what he says he wants to see."

I decided to put Omar to Sue's test. On my next tour, I included a contemporary townhouse located in Arch Beach Heights. No yard to speak of–instead, lots of decks with stupendous ocean views. The master bedroom was the only one with a door–the other two bedrooms were lofts. The windows were two stories tall–not really a house for kids–instead, the epitome of a bachelor pad.

As soon as Omar stepped into the living room with the exposed rafter ceiling, wood-burning fireplace and wet bar, his facial expression softened. His eyes scanned every detail.

A broad smile formed underneath his black moustache when he stepped onto one of the redwood decks and noticed sailboats with their colorful jibs dotting the waves. He clasped his hands together as if to say, "This is what I've been waiting for."

Yep, my family man really was a Bachelor Babe.

It was late in the afternoon on a Friday. I had been planning a sailing trip to Catalina Island for weeks. Of course, Omar decided he wanted to write an offer that night! This was the same guy I had been taking around for months without the least bit of interest in buying anything. I figured if he waited this long, he could wait another few days.

"The Barracuda Way place has been listed for a month," I said. "I have plans this weekend, so why don't we wait till Monday to write the offer?" Omar agreed. I left for Catalina.

When I walked into the office Monday morning there was a hushed silence as I approached my desk. A sickening feeling grabbed at my stomach. I attempted a feeble, "Good morning" but my mouth was dry from embarrassment. All eyes shifted downward as people addressed whatever paperwork lay in front of them. Paul Newell approached my desk with short quick steps, motioning me to meet him in his office. He shook his index finger in my face. "Mr. Farad wanted that house you showed him on Friday and you left him in the lurch! How could you just go off for a weekend and not have anyone cover for you? Boy, are you lucky he is a loyal client and called me to write the offer."

I hung my head in shame, knowing I made a colossal error in judgment. I let a task that had been dragging on and on fall to the bottom of my to-do list when it should had stayed priority number one. "No one told me this information before," I said, looking down at my hands, which were beginning to tremble. "This is my first sales job, you know."

"Buying a home is emotional and spontaneous. A hot buyer can cool quickly and the opportunity to make the sale can be lost. Like doctors, real estate agents have to be available 24/7."

"But Mr. Farad just didn't seem that motivated," I said. "I've been taking him around for months and he hasn't liked anything."

"He liked what you showed him the other day, didn't he? He did tell you he wanted to write an offer, right?"

"Well, he said he did, but he also told me he wanted a family home and that is certainly not what he bought," I said, knowing I was merely protecting my position, and lamely so.

"Did you ever ask Mr. Farad why he did not like the houses you were showing him?" Back to asking those damn questions! "I want you to read this sentence in bold above the signature line of the real estate contract."

My throat was parched and raspy. I opened my mouth, but no audible words came out.

"Louder," he said, his voice elevated and stern.

I swallowed hard, "Time is of the essence."

"What do you think that means?" Paul asked, lowering his voice.

"Act immediately–as soon as the buyer is ready," I said, still not willing to look up.

Paul continued, "Okay. Important lesson learned. Next time a client says they want to write an offer, do not take the weekend off. You drop everything and write the offer, understand?"

As I made my way back to my desk, I tried to integrate the impact of my manager's last comment–that he was taking half my commission for all the work he did to keep the deal together.

I figured the math in my head–the whole commission is 6%. Since Lingo was representing the seller and Newell Associates was representing Mr. Farad, our office's portion was 3%. Since I was a new agent, my split with Newell Associates was 50/50 or 1.5% of the sales price. But now Paul Newell was taking half of that, so all I ended up with was 0.75% on $150,000. How could I survive on $1,125? I had not had any income for eight months! Ted expected me to pay my share of the rent, the groceries, the utilities and gas for the car. I felt like going back and telling Newell Associates how unfair all of this was.

Maybe I would quit. That's right–I didn't have to put up with this injustice! I'd go back to a salaried job. That would show Paul Newell! Then I remembered the lab with the furry little hamsters, the men getting all the promotions, and the boss constantly leaning over my shoulder. I took a deep breath, grabbed my things and went for a walk. I needed to think all this through. Maybe it was true what Paul Newell had said. If he had not been available, Omar would have found another salesperson to write the offer and I would have ended up with nothing. At least I was getting something.

It had not been a year since I left my familiar East Coast surroundings and moved here. That took some guts. I also had the bold courage to put myself through college when my parents gave me no emotional or monetary support, probably hoping I would take the easy marriage route. After graduation I procured a job in a city which was unfamiliar to me. More guts.

Sales offered me the lifestyle I wanted–independence,

lots of interesting learning experiences and an opportunity to do well financially. I told myself that gratification was not going to be instantaneous in this line of work. I may not be a natural-born salesperson, but I still graduated with honors despite the fact that I was not a natural-born student either. Believing I had the courage, tenacity and confidence to be successful, I decided to give sales another chance. Or maybe it was to give myself another chance at sales.

It's a Dog-Eat-Dog World Out There

Rachel Simmons swept into our office like a whirlwind. Wispy, shoulder-length, strawberry hair framed her angelic heart-shaped face as she gave everyone a wide engaging smile. Her tall angular body and long legs reminded me of one of those New York City runway models. She extended a gracious hand as she was introduced around the office and gave the impression that she was more a VIP than a new agent. Whereas my self-esteem had been earned through hard work and accomplishments, hers was apparent by the way she moved. How nice it would be to be accepted by just being you and not having to prove anything.

I showed her around, took her on tour, and helped her with the basic questions all new agents have. We went to the title company parties together, not only to have fun as Paul Newell suggested–his belief being that, "a happy salesperson is a productive salesperson"–but also to start forming our team of professionals of title officers, escrow coordinators, lenders and contractors whom we would rely on during the sales process.

"The best way to choose who you wish to work with is to meet them in person," Paul advised. "Besides, networking with other agents is essential so you know your competition up close."

I should have suspected something was amiss when we attended our last office meeting. Paul Newell lauded my praises to everyone present for getting my first sale. Rachel did not sit with me at the meeting, which was our custom and purposely shunned me when I approached her. I told myself she would get over it. It all seemed so high school. Then came the inevitable day when we both had clients for one of our office's hot new listings. Rachel planned to show the house first, promising she would leave the key underneath the mat. (The listing was so new that the lock box had not even been installed yet).

I arrived shortly after with my client, James Wallace, a fellow I met at an open house the week before. He was thrilled when I described this house over the phone. It was in a perfect location for him, close to his family, friends and his job. Also, it was in his price range. Since this would be his starter home, he did not mind that it was small and needed work. He was ready to move. He had been diligent in saving his money for the down payment, so I had a willing and able buyer who had already been preapproved by a bank. Besides having saved 20% for the down payment, he also had another 3% saved for closing costs, such as title and escrow fees and building insurance. He also had a 33% debt to income ratio and a good 760 credit rating. As I fumbled for the key underneath the mat, James told me how appreciative he was that I found something for him so quickly. He stepped around to the side of the house, rubbing his hands together, eagerly anticipating what was inside.

"It needs a little work like I told you, but it's really charming," I said brightly, hiding the disgust I was feeling as gritty dirt was now underneath my newly polished fingernails. I reminded myself to remain upbeat, calm and collected. This was a great house and I had the perfect buyer. So what if I had to get a new manicure?

I looked up from my awkward kneeling position with a happy face. "You will not be disappointed, I assure you. Just give me a moment." *Where is that damn key?* Throwing polite decorum to the wind, I tossed the welcome mat onto the grass, intensifying my search. "It's got to be here somewhere," I said.

"Paula, are you sure your friend said the mat? Let's look under the plant boxes," James said, trying to be helpful. The key was not there, either. Next we tried the back door mat and the frame above both doors. Then we got the brilliant idea of trying to break inside. We checked out all the windows, hoping to find one unlocked. There was not. James tried to pry one open, but I was afraid he would break the glass and told him to stop. Looking for a solution, I pointed to the small dog door in the back. "Do you think either of us can fit through that?" I laughed, trying to see the humor in a disastrous situation which was making me more uncomfortable by the minute.

"Paula, I'm really disappointed. I had to call in sick today and left my boss short-handed. It is really difficult for me to get off time from work. Can't you do something?"

"I am sure there has been some misunderstanding. Let's go back to the office. Perhaps Rachel forgot," I said, making sure I remained positive. I hopped in my car, praying that I had misunderstood Rachel somehow. James followed in his car as we drove back to the office. No key there and no Rachel either. I asked around the office, checking if anyone had seen her. No one had. I left a message for her at the front desk and one at home. I shrugged my shoulders as James gave me a reproachful look and headed out the office door. "Call me as soon as you find out," he said.

"I promise," I said with a smiling, wilting farewell, wondering if this was the last time I would ever see him.

Rachel never called me back. The next day I asked about the key when I saw her scurrying around the office with paperwork flying here and there. My suspicions were confirmed when she said, "My client wanted to write an offer so why should you bother showing it–it would have been just a waste of time!"

I felt the blood rising to the top of my temples and turned away lest I say something I would regret later. *That's it!* I thought. *I don't care how pretty she is–our friendship is nothing more than past tense!* With Paul Newell's permission, I moved my things to another desk and asked him to do something, hoping for some sort of compensation. "I cannot undo what is already done, Paula. The house is sold. Money has already been placed in escrow. Remember, as agents, we are not officially part of the contract; we are only the bridge between the buyer and the seller."

"But what if my buyer wanted to pay more?" I said, exasperated over this unfair treatment of my client.

"That's unfortunate. But to tell a seller that now might mean a lawsuit involving not only two of my agents, but also the listing agent. A lawsuit would be a black mark against our company and you wouldn't want that, would you, Paula?"

"Of course not," I said. "I just feel like I've been screwed–especially after all the help I've given her." Maybe I should not have been be so explicit with my wording, but I was upset and I wanted Paul to know that.

"Be more careful next time and call the listing agent directly. I will say something to Rachel, but keep in mind she is young and inexperienced."

"That's not the point. What she did is unethical."

"That's conjecture only. She told me she was so excited that she just plain forgot about leaving the key." I looked up, trying not to show my pain. Paul got up from his chair and gave me a warm handshake and an encouraging wink. "Fine–it's all settled then."

James did not return my calls for several days. When I finally reached him, he told me he had found another real estate agent who was more reliable. I was back pounding the pavement, looking for business to replace the sale I lost. I walked my neighborhood, held open houses, sent out mailers and got as much floor time as I could. I tried my best not to get discouraged–remembering past successes. I realized there were those salespeople who would do anything to make a deal–kind of like cheating in college. I had learned that I could not expect management to get involved with what they consider petty problems. From then on I would be much more vigilant in observing other people's behavior and, honestly, be more wary of their motives.

So the sharks stayed and the rest of us fish tried to either keep out of their way or, better, to be a bit more clever in order to stay one step ahead of them.

Lessons Learned from Chapter 2:

- SEEK HELP FROM EXPERTS Confident people know it takes time to become an expert in any field. There are a lot of successful business people out there. Gather up your courage—swallow your pride if you must—and ask for help.
- PRIORITIZE Realize that you may have to make choices between work and your personal life to be successful. Do not procrastinate or put off tasks because they are time-consuming, stressful or daunting. When you are not available for a client, ask a trusted colleague to help you.
- BE BOLD – ASK QUESTIONS Listen carefully to what your customers tell you, but do not stop there. During the sales process, ask probing, open-ended questions. Remember, circumstances are always changing, so be open to the answers, which may surprise you.
- FACE REALITY HEAD-ON There are unscrupulous people in all businesses. A pretty smile, flattering words and an aura of self-importance does not give a person character. Learn to discern who you can trust and who you cannot.
- GO AFTER WHAT YOU WANT Do not allow other people's visions to get in the way of your success. You are the only one who holds the key to creating the life you want.

3

TENACITY

Overcoming Obstacles

Doing the Homework, Accessing the Experts

Real estate sales are based on a sink-or-swim mentality. Paul Newell was a competing manager and did not have the time or the inclination to teach me much. I had to learn by observing the other agents. I listened to how agents spoke on the phone, how they set up appointments and closed deals. Once I understood the process, I practiced doing these tasks myself. To help take the guesswork out of the equation, I joined the local Multiple Listing Service (MLS). Now when I was introduced to a potential home buyer, I could search the MLS system and retrieve information about all homes for sale in a given area and price range. This entitled me to weekly updates to help me determine market prices and fluctuations for both buyers and sellers.

Every week I religiously toured the new properties on the market. I walked the neighborhoods to get a feel for what they had to offer. I attended the weekly sales meetings, took notes and asked questions. I familiarized myself with the forms in the office file drawers. Still, it was not enough. So when Sue Bates asked if anyone would like to accompany her to a sales seminar, I volunteered. The cost was two hundred dollars and, although it was beyond my budget, I knew I needed to get my business rolling. Sue told me the speaker, Tommy

Hopkins, was the best in the business–a multimillionaire producer who truly shared his secrets. Hopkins' main premise was that selling is a learned skill. In his last year as a real estate agent in California in the 1960s, he sold 365 homes–one a day for an entire year!

Like any motivated buyer, I was ready, willing and able to do whatever was necessary to get what I wanted–success as a top-producing real estate agent.

I can still remember that stuffy auditorium in the City of Angels, bursting beyond capacity with over five hundred people. Certainly no fire marshals here, just rows and rows of eager salespeople wanting to improve their game. Sue and I finally found two seats together in the middle of all this madness. We were forced to climb over people's legs to get seats, juggling our coffee containers like accomplished trapeze artists. We stretched our necks over people's heads to get a glance of Tommy, striding from one side of the stage to the other, bellowing out his sales techniques. I was mesmerized. Tommy Hopkins was so full of charisma, so confident, so enthused, that I knew if I followed what he said, I would be successful.

A few nuggets of wisdom: We had to get clients to like us first. Only then would they consider doing business with us. We could do that by building on whatever we have in common–whether it is playing tennis, raising children or going to church.

Next nugget: Sales is a numbers game. The more people you connect with, the better chance you have of landing a buyer or representing a seller. Not every person you meet will be a prospect, not every prospect will become a loyal client and not every loyal client will result in a sale.

Third nugget: Sellers are golden, because they must sign a written contract with you. This Exclusive Right to Sell, or Listing Form, as it is informally called, states that you will be diligent toward finding a buyer within a specified amount of time. "It does not mean that you personally have to find the buyer," Tommy said. "Instead, you market the property to the real estate community and cooperate with other sales agents. The cooperating agent and his/her office get a percentage–usually half–of the fee. Like most salespeople, you get paid only when the deal is finalized.

"With buyers, it is a free-for-all. They pretty much work with whomever they choose. They like being free agents and not committing to anyone. You can work with them for months and they can jump ship on you and buy through someone else." "For instance," Tommy warned, "if your client buyers get carried away with emotion at an Open House, they could write an offer right then and there. You need to explain to them how the sales process works–that you get paid on commission only. The best way to do this is right at your first face-to-face meeting. When you feel you have connected with them, ask if they would like to work with you."

Tommy also suggested asking clients to sign a Buyer Retainer Form to get their commitment in writing, which, he said, is a good way of weeding out the "Lookie Loos" from the serious buyers. He emphasized that most experienced agents require this, because they get paid only on closed transactions, not on the amount of hours they spend showing people properties. "In any case," Tommy said, "at minimum, you will gain valuable insight into their psyche by asking them to sign a commitment. And if you choose to work with a buyer who is unwilling to sign anything in writing, you better be

90% sure they will work with you. If not, find someone else who will."

To make his last and most powerful point, Tommy was jumping up and down on the stage like a jackrabbit. "What is most important to a person working on commission?" he shouted. BIG PAUSE. "Understanding *Time Is Money*!"

A whole new world of sales was opening up for me. Pumped up after the seminar, I requested more floor time. This meant I was spending more time at the front desk where I got first dibs on all inquiries–people calling in or walking in off the street. These uninitiated potential clients most often came to us simply because they had seen our newspaper ads or a *For Sale* sign on a property or, perhaps, the most "qualified" ones were referred to us through a previous satisfied customer.

With the sales skills I learned from Tommy Hopkins, I hoped to make more appointments and turn potential buyers into paying clients. Hopkins had indicated that the statistics were one in eight of getting the first appointment and then one in four of turning that potential client into a sale.

A popular way of acquiring new clients was the Open House. Again the statistics sounded discouraging–one in ten. Despite these numbers, I knew I was much more engaging face-to-face than over the phone and made myself available on the weekend. Making the choice to go to Catalina had been costly. I had learned my lesson to put business before pleasure.

Pursuing a Cold Call–And Getting Burned

Cold calling on listings that never sold was an even better role of the dice, one in seven, Tommy said. These are the properties which appear in the Multiple Listing Book as Expired. Few agents have the courage to call someone they have never met. I had heard horror stories of rude customers, even hang ups, but I was not deterred. I figured, hey, the odds are more in my favor–so why not give it a try? Doing something others are afraid to do could mean money in my pocket.

I perused The Multiple Listing Service Book and noticed several expired listings. One in particular stood out: a three bedroom house located in the Top of the World neighborhood. Since I had gotten to know this family neighborhood during my intensive search with Omar, I felt fairly knowledgeable. These basic, no-frills, boxy tract houses were not the renovated beach homes I drooled over, but for me, a beginner, it was a good place to start.

I stopped by the Multiple Listing Office and got more information on Top of the World–the school district, public transportation and neighborhood activities. It was the only subdivision in Laguna, so any home located outside of this area would not be a statistic I could use. I could hear the well-worn phrase, *Location, Location, Location,* echoing in my head. Location was what Anthony School, Paul Newell and Tommy Hopkins all stressed when determining what a property was worth. Only after a location had been valued did other factors come into play, such as the condition of the property, square footage, room count, architectural style and amenities–view, fireplace, updated systems, such as air conditioning and thermal pane windows, just to name a few.

I compiled the data of three-bedroom houses in this neighborhood. My analysis had three components: houses which had sold over the past six months, those currently on the market and the ones whose listings had expired. The first figures gave me the range of actual sale prices; the second, the competition we were up against; and the third, homes which were conceivably overpriced and thus did not sell. Since there were so few houses for sale in Top of the World, I checked out four-bedroom houses as well. I also went further back by including sales made over the previous year. Once I had data on six to ten homes, I would be ready to talk to the owner.

From the tax records I found that the owner was Margaret Burns. Another woman seemed not so threatening for my first call. I looked up her telephone number and sure enough, it was listed. I reviewed the cold call sales script that Tommy Hopkins recommended, took a deep breath, and dialed the number.

"Hello, Mrs. Burns. My name is Paula Pagano. I noticed that the listing on your property has expired. I wonder if I could stop by and tell you what Newell Associates has to offer."

"Who is this again?" The voice on the other end sounded suspicious. Or was it just my imagination?

I repeated what I had just said. "Hello, Mrs. Burns. My name is Paula Pagano. I noticed that the listing on your property has expired. I wonder if I could stop by and tell you what Newell Associates has to offer."

Mrs. Burns said now was not a good time to talk.

"When would it be convenient for me to call you back? I have important information I would like to share with you," I said, knowing persistence was key.

"Anytime, but not right now," she said, and hung up the phone.

At least Mrs. Burns did mention I could call another time.

Maybe she was just trying to get me off the phone when she said it–but maybe not. Tommy said you have to hear the word "No" at least five times before you give up on a sales prospect. Most agents give up after only three.

I gathered up my courage once again the following morning. I was clear on what needed to be done. The worst she could say was "No." "Words do not hurt a person," I told myself. *But rejection does*, my mind answered. I asked myself, "Do you want to be a successful entrepreneur or a medical researcher?" My answer: I want to be a successful entrepreneur. Then I needed to go over Tommy Hopkins' script once more. I even recited it aloud to gain more confidence. My notes also said: "Do not stay on the phone too long and do not give away all your expertise. Give only enough to keep them interested and wanting more. Remember, you want your clients to need you. Come across as the expert." I made the call. Mrs. Burns answered. Her voice sounded bright and light. I took her lead and tried to match her speech pattern.

"Mrs. Burns, this is Paula Pagano, calling from Newell Associates. I called yesterday. I would like to share some information with you, which can help you with the sale of your home."

"Yes?" she said.

I found myself stumbling for words. "May I come by and take a look at your house? No cost or obligation, of course." I had heard one of the other agents say that and it sounded good. But obviously not good enough. Mrs. Burns told me she was busy and hung up the phone.

My call felt like a dismal failure, almost a slap in the face. I was so unprepared for the rejection I felt that I gathered up my things and went home. I stayed in bed for two days, watching reruns of *Dr. Kildare* and wondering if medical research might still be a possibility for me. I actually spent a day looking through the classified job opportunities for another career. Seeing nothing, I reflected on whether sales was the right profession for me after all.

I knew I was ambitious, independent, eager to learn and quick to get bored–perhaps a little too quick. Becoming a successful salesperson would mean I might be rejected occasionally, but, nevertheless, this job offered me the lifestyle I wanted. I felt that it was worth the sacrifice and the heartache. I also understood, though I had to constantly remind myself, gratification was not going to be instantaneous. I would need to acquire tenacity and some grit if I wanted to make a career in sales work.

"Don't take everything so personally," I said to myself, realizing I was speaking out loud. I smoothed out the script in front of me and noticed my hands trembling. Still shaking, I picked up the phone and dialed Mrs. Burns' telephone number once more.

"Good day, Mrs. Burns! Paula Pagano from Newell Associates. We talked a few days ago. I want to share some interesting sales statistics with you and wondered if now would be a good time?"

"Oh, yes, Paula. I remember you. I have had quite a few calls from agents this past week. Everybody wants the listing, but I'm not sure if I want to sell now or not." (Tommy said this might happen). "What exactly is it you want to share with me?"

"Mrs. Burns, it sounds to me like you have a bit of an accent. Where are you from originally?"

"Dorset. Dorset, Vermont. I'm surprised you noticed. I've lived in California over twenty-five years."

"Well, what a coincidence! I'm from that part of the country myself–upstate New York," I said, happy to find a common thread, no matter how slight.

"Mrs. Burns," (I made sure to use her name a lot in the conversation), "most of the homes in your neighborhood sold, but yours and one other did not. I think there may be a connection."

"Really? How so?"

Now I had her interest. "I would like to meet with you in person so I can explain in better detail what the commonality is."

"You can't just tell me over the phone?"

"I'd prefer not to if that's all right with you. I promise I won't pressure you in any way." I took a long measured breath. Hopkins maintained that real rapport could only be established face to face. "Guaranteed you will find the information I have most helpful. Is it all right if I come by sometime today to show you what I found?"

"Today does not work, but why don't you swing by later in the week? I'm home most days. Gotta go now, Paula."

I stopped by her house several times. On my third attempt I found her there. Margaret Burns opened the door in jeans and a worn apron. She was older than I expected, her brown hair tinged with gray, her soft blue eyes surrounded by deep-set wrinkles. She remembered our phone call and invited me in. In the living room, she kept glancing at my marketing packet. I was glad I took the time to get a manicure to cover up the nail biting I'd been doing the past week.

"So, Paula, what is it you wanted to share with me?"

I opened my booklet and handed her a copy of the comparable listing. "This is the other house that did not sell," I said, handing over the sales sheet. "Like your house, it has only a bath and a half. The other properties that sold in your price range had two full baths."

"So? I can't do anything about that," Mrs. Burns said.

"No, but maybe a buyer can. That is why I wanted to stop by and take a look at your house, if I may."

"Oh, I see. Why don't I show you around then?" She ushered me inside. *Clients want to do business with people who they like and trust,* echoed in my mind as she began the tour of the house.

"Mrs. Burns, you certainly have a knack for decorating. I love the paint color you chose here in your living room." She gave me a wide smile. I made sure our eyes met. I scanned the room, looking for something else positive to say. I did my best not to focus on the floor where a mustard shag carpet offended my aesthetic senses. I didn't want to lie, but needed to say something. She might think I was being insincere if I praised the rugs or the drapes, so I pointed to some photos on an end table. "And who–may I ask–are these little people?"

"My grandchildren. Do you have any kids?"

"No, but my brother and his wife just had identical twin boys. What a joy children are." I remembered to emphasize, not our differences, but what we had in common. Thank you, Tommy! But the effect was not as dramatic as I might have hoped. "Ummm," was all she said.

"So what are your children doing now?" I asked.

"They are long gone, living their own lives." She looked tired. This could be my segue into getting the listing, relieving her of the stress of selling her house.

"Why do you think your agent wasn't able to sell your house?" I remembered Tommy telling us to ask that question. I did not want to make the same mistakes the first agent may have made.

"I don't think he ever really liked my house. Besides, he was pretty busy. He had a lot of houses for sale in the neighborhood."

"Did he advertise on a regular basis and hold open houses?" Mrs. Burns was vague and noncommittal.

"Well," I said, "I have a marketing plan that will knock your socks off!" (Again, a line I heard a senior agent use.) "Newell Associates and I will give you copies of all our ads so you are aware of exactly what we are doing to market your home."

The other agent was a man, so maybe I could use being a woman in my favor. "It also sounds to me like you need a female's touch," I said. "Plus, right now I am in between listings." I quickly added. "Your house will be the only house I'll be marketing."

"That's a relief," she said, as she showed me the half-bath.

"A buyer could easily put a shower here," I said, as I pointed to the linen closet next to the bathroom. "In fact, I think there used to be a shower here. Look at this! " I showed her the patched dry wall.

"There was. It kept leaking, so when the kids moved out, I thought it better to just take it out and put in a closet."

"Well," I said, "I think we just solved the main problem of why your house did not sell. This is an easy fix. It is likely that the buyer for your home will have children, so they will welcome an additional full bath."

I let Mrs. Burns lead the pace of the conversation while she showed me the rest of the house. Although it did not show that well, she was immensely proud of her home. The drab earthy tones and oversized furniture were making me claustrophobic. She offered me a cup of tea and motioned for me to sit down on her overstuffed–and over-worn–green couch. From the living room I could see the avocado appliances in the kitchen. Well, she certainly loved that pea green color. In spite of all the drawbacks of this home, I couldn't help but think what a nice lady Mrs. Burns was.

This sales job was not that hard. In fact, I was beginning to like being an entrepreneur. Noticing I was beginning to drift, I gave Mrs. Burns an engaging smile, wondering when to ask the million-dollar question–"How about signing with Newell Associates?" I needed to tap into my courage and was about to do so when Mrs. Burns broke the silence.

"Paula, I really like you, but both my sister and I are owners and she is away for the weekend. What shall we do?"

Without a thought, I said, "Why don't we wait until your sister gets back? I will leave my marketing plan here for you to review. You can show it to your sister and I will call you Monday morning." My plan was to bring the Exclusive Right to Sell Agreement–the contract which employed me and my agency to market the house–when we met again.

I was starting to feel a bit queasy. I had to get out of there and get some fresh air. Like a robot I got up and headed to the door. It was all I could do to get my key into the car lock.

I knew I should have brought the form with me, but so much had happened leading up to that day, and to this critical (and for me, tense) first face-to-face meeting, that I was actually feeling relieved that I did not have to fill out forms at that moment, especially in front of Mrs. Burns. I did not want her to think that I did not know what I was doing. When I reached the office however, I was having second thoughts. Surely Tommy Hopkins would have signed her up. Even without her sister. What happened to the assertive courageous nature I took such pride in? I had Mrs. Burns in the palm of my hand and blew it. Was it because I did not have enough confidence? Did I feel that I didn't deserve another sale? Was I afraid of success? When I confided to Paul Newell the details of the presentation, he rolled his eyes in disbelief. "Paula, I want you to hightail it back up there and get the listing agreement signed–one signature is better than nothing."

I called several times over the weekend, but Mrs. Burns' telephone just rang and rang. I stopped by twice, but no one was home. On Monday morning, when I called as I had promised, Mrs. Burns told me how sorry she was, but her sister had another agent in mind.

So What if the Furniture Doesn't Fit?

From the moment I requested more floor time from Paul Newell, I often found myself manning the front desk while everyone else was enjoying Laguna's gorgeous weather. Most likely, they were all down at *Las Brisas* having piña coladas and feeling the soft tropical breeze off the ocean. So on yet another sunny picture-perfect day at the beach, I was alone at the office.

Tired from a full week of touring houses and answering the endless phone calls, I was tempted to close early and go home. But in spite of my fatigue, another part of me was determined to make this job work. A few minutes before five, a short balding man in his forties pushed through the door. He was muttering under his breath about all the real estate offices being closed this Friday afternoon. He introduced himself as Alan Davenport, and he was curious about home prices.

He and his wife were moving to the area with their three kids in six weeks. He was unsure whether to buy or rent. Luckily the rental agent was not here–otherwise she would have swept him up like a whirlwind. Now, at least, I had a chance. I sat Alan down for a quick counseling session, asking him about his new job, the size of his family and their basics requirements. (Tommy said to be sure you qualify your clients before you show them houses).

"What about your current home do you like? Anything you don't like? If money were not a problem, what would your perfect home be?" While asking all these questions, I was taking copious notes. Once in a while I looked up and nodded for that personal connection.

Doing my legwork for Mrs. Burns' house was going to pay off, I thought to myself. Researching all those three and four bedroom family homes in *Top of the World* the previous month had made me an expert. I could hear Paul Newell's words every Wednesday if he caught an agent in the office. "Why aren't you out touring houses? You can't sell something you don't know."

I zeroed in on two possibilities that I could show Alan immediately. "They are both located on the flat part of the ridge overlooking the ocean. It's a fabulous family neighborhood called *Top of the World,* and each has four bedrooms, three baths and a large yard. Plus, the best school district we have here in Laguna."

Alan talked slowly, rolling his vowels as he spoke. "Well, you see my wife is not with me." Certainly a valid objection, but I was not giving up quite yet. Margaret Burns was ready to sell without her sister. Maybe Alan Davenport was ready to buy without his wife.

"Didn't you say your wife sent you out here to find a house?" I asked.

"Yes, but we were thinking of renting first." There was a long pause, as he looked over my shoulder at the Multiple Listing book. "...unless, of course, you have some special deal."

I showed him the photos in the Multiple Listing Book. Luckily I knew the market. "This house just came on this week. I hear the seller has been transferred and needs to sell quickly. A house priced this well does not last long." When he did not respond, I asked, "What's the harm in looking?" I flashed him my best smile. He nodded in agreement. Love those subtle body language cues!

I knew he was vacillating between buying and renting so I needed to emphasize the advantages of owning on our ride up the hill.

1. *Paying a mortgage is better than a savings account, because you can't withdraw it easily.*
2. *Rent money is money down the toilet–you will never see any of it again.*
3. *You will save additional money by getting significant tax breaks.*
4. *You can modify and decorate the home to meet your needs.*
5. *80% of your investment is being financed by a bank.*

We toured the more expensive house first. That way he would understand the value he was getting with the lower priced home. With both houses I made sure that I pointed out all the positive features while asking his opinion:

"What do you think about the remodeled kitchen? The back yard?" Remembering Sue's advice, I then targeted the more emotional part of his brain: "How do you *feel* about the layout of the two houses?"

Alan told me both floor plans work, the closets were large enough and the flat yards were perfect for his three kids. I noticed, though, that he took more time in the second home, closely examining the amenities in the kitchen, because, he said, his wife was a gourmet cook. Plus, this house had all the other amenities as in the first home which was priced higher.

Now that I had a *feel* that the second house was a match for Alan, I would use Tommy Hopkins' Tie-Down approach. Although these Tie-Down Questions are posed for simple yes and no answers, the sales strategy is to get a buyer to keep saying yes, reinforcing the positive feelings he had about the house. I began with the most obvious questions, anticipating a yes to all.

"It's a perfect family neighborhood, don't you think?"

"Wouldn't your kids love this yard with the swing set?"

"It's a lovely view of the canyon, wouldn't you agree?"

"Can't you imagine having great barbecues on this deck?"

He took the bait and answered in the affirmative each time, each response bonding him more and more to the property. I was literally "tying him down." *Yep, I am on my way to selling Alan a home!* In the car driving back to the office, I was strategizing. I decided a direct, open-ended emotionally driven question was the best close.

"So, Alan, what are your *feelings* about the last home I showed you?" He did not answer right away. I started to speak and stopped myself. A salesperson's biggest mistake was talking too much, Paul Newell said.

"I'm concerned that my wife is not here with me. I think she'd like the second one we saw–it seems like a great deal. But buying a home is a big decision."

This was a legitimate objection and might be the stumbling block for me in making this sale. I tried the *Alternative Close* by asking, "Which would be worse–to have no home at all or one that is not quite perfect?" Using "or" in a question gives the client a feeling that he or she has a choice. However, it's really a bit of a set-up, because I only gave him two choices, with one of them–to have no home–being particularly bad, or unsatisfactory at minimum.

"No home at all, of course," was his answer.

"We can't have that, can we?" I said, using another *Tie-Down* question. As we walked up the steps to the office, my mind was working hard on how to get Alan's signature on the contract. "With your permission, I am going to borrow Ben Franklin's negotiating method for just a moment."

As one of the founders of our country, Franklin often made tough decisions by listing the pros and cons of an argument. He was such a good negotiator that he was able to convince France to join us against the English in the Revolutionary War. Without the French, we would never have won our independence. If Franklin could convince a country to go to war using this pro-and-con method, I reasoned, then I certainly had a good chance of using it to sell this house to Alan. Besides, this method had been effective for me when I used it to make some pretty big decisions in my own life.

I now started to list the positive features of the home:

1. *The good school district*
2. *The large yard with jungle gym*
3. *The sundeck*
4. *The gourmet kitchen*

I stopped mid-way, remembering that Tommy Hopkins said it was even more powerful when you let the prospect do it themselves. In that way, you learn what features were the most important to them. What I felt was important might not be the same as what a client felt was important. I handed Alan Davenport the pen. "Here, why don't you jot down what you specifically liked about the house." He took the pen from my hand and wrote down the following:

1. *Four bedrooms on one floor*
2. *Two and a half baths*
3. *View*
4. *Large two car garage*

"Anything you wanted to add in the negative column?" I asked, offering no suggestions this time. Tommy said clients did not need any help with this part. They already have enough of their own reasons not to buy. Of course, if there was something I needed to disclose about the home, it was my legal–and moral–responsibility to do so. And since I planned on having a career in sales, it was also to my benefit. I wanted Alan as a repeat client and I wanted his referrals, and for these reasons, I wanted him to believe that he could put his full faith and trust in me. But in this case I saw no indication of any structural problems, so I said nothing.

When Alan told me he thought the master bedroom was a bit small, I asked how important that was to him. He told me he was concerned about fitting in all of his furniture. "Are you saying you don't think your furniture will fit?" This is the Hot Potato or Porcupine Close–you throw the objection the client voiced back at them. This way they may reconsider whether their doubts are well founded, or even whether those doubts are that significant in the big picture.

"Well, some of my furniture would fit, but I don't think all of it."

"Which is more important–buying a house which meets your needs or fitting in all your furniture?" I asked. Alternative Close once again.

Alan pondered that thought for a moment, then said he did not like the carpet. He wrote this objection in the negative column.

"Well, changing the carpet is easy," I said. "We can either ask the seller to replace it or ask for a credit."

When Alan was finished writing, I asked for the paper and went back to emphasizing the positives of what he just told me. "Let's not forget the family friendly yard you can enjoy all year round. And the ocean view–I bet you don't have views like this in Minnesota, do you?" Alan had to admit he did not. I was hoping he was thinking that the size of the bedroom and shade of the carpet were not deal breakers. Who wouldn't love it here? It was probably ten degrees below zero back where he was from!

"This is typical weather for us," I said, as I pointed outside to the swaying palm trees. "It is almost eight o'clock in the evening and still balmy warm weather. You don't even need a sweater, and since we're by the beach, it hardly ever gets too hot. A real paradise, don't you think?" He nodded. Those *Tie-Down* questions are invaluable!

It was time for me to ask for the order. "So as far as an investment you could not do better. Laguna Beach is very special because there's strong demand and a limited supply of four bedroom homes. I would hate to see you lose an opportunity." Raising the specter of Loss of Opportunity is always a good final closer. So is reminding buyers, when appropriate, that historically, buying a home in the area has been an excellent investment. In this case, I had to acknowledge that the market had gone down somewhat over the past few years, but that it was sure to rebound. He nodded again.

I then mentioned another benefit of home ownership.

"And once you own your home, you will have complete control of your destiny. You won't be at the mercy of some landlord who gives you and your family a thirty day notice to move out and find someplace else to live."

"I get only thirty days?" His calm demeanor suddenly shifted to serious concern. "I travel a lot–what if I'm away on business?"

"Only thirty days. That's it." I had hit a sensitive issue with Alan so I continued. "Who wants to be at the mercy of some fickle landlord? Personally, I do not think it is worth the risk–with a family and all."

Alan was eerily quiet. I waited a few moments, then responded with even more ammunition, "Plus, paying rent is like flushing money down the toilet. You will never get any of it back. And even if Laguna property never appreciates, which is highly unlikely, you will get most or all your money back when you sell." Now was the time for the Assumptive Close: my favorite, because one does not have to say anything. I simply opened my briefcase and started filling out a purchase contract.

"What are you doing?" Alan asked.

"Filling out some paperwork," I said in as neutral a voice as I could muster. I was doing exactly what Tommy Hopkins told me to do. Never say contract, signature or anything technical. Keep it light and simple "I'll need your approval, of course. Why don't you help yourself to a cup of coffee while I finish? It will only take a minute or two."

Not surprisingly, price is the biggest objection for most buyers. I showed Alan some comparable homes with higher asking prices, which had nonetheless sold. He was still hesitant. I tried a contingency close. "If you could get this house for $10,000 less, would you be willing to give the seller a bid today?"

"Okay, but I won't pay a penny more."

"Mr. Davenport, please don't tell me what you will or won't take. During the negotiating process, anything can happen. Let's just take it step by step, okay?" I smiled as I said this. I didn't want him fixated on any particular price. We could close this sale, if I could keep him open to the negotiating process. He still seemed a bit shell shocked, so I added, "Keep in mind too, that our offer is dependent on you getting a loan and also on your approval of the contractor's inspection report. This is still far from a done deal." On making a big decision such as this, buyers want to feel that they have a chance to change their minds. Plus, as I mentioned earlier, full disclosure on the condition of a property is essential.

"Okay, then. Where do I sign?" A little back and forth with the seller over the weekend, and Alan Davenport was the proud owner of a new home in Top of the World, Laguna Beach. His wife could not have been more pleased.

Lessons Learned from Chapter 3:

- COMMIT TO A PLAN Do whatever is necessary to make your dream a concrete reality. Make daily, weekly and monthly goals, fully understanding what actions need to be done to consummate a sale. Analyze your success ratio and chart your results.
- DEVELOP PATIENT PERSISTENCE Do not let disappointments discourage you. Keep looking for a solution while you model the qualities of clarity, courage and tenaciousness. Each day is an opportunity to succeed.
- GO FOR THE YES You need to be willing to hear the word No at least five times before you make a sale. Most salespeople give up upon hearing the word No only two or three times. Be the exception. And remember to ask questions that encourage your clients to say Yes.

4

PASSION

Loving What You Do

Itching to Find My Niche

Two years had passed, and even as I felt the soft crystal-lized sand shifting between my toes, the warm tropical breeze against my face and the taste of the ocean's salt between my lips, I still felt unsettled inside. I looked above, noticing the mesmerizing blue sky with its fluffy marshmallow clouds which I could almost reach up to touch. Yet I was so un-happy. I thought, "What is wrong with me?" I hand-picked this charming beach town in Southern California because I thought it was the closest thing to paradise. It was me who decided that we should settle in Laguna Beach, not Irvine, the new industrial planned community where Ted worked. Ted had to commute twenty miles back and forth every day to work and never complained. But I did.

I put on my sundress over my lavender crocheted bikini and gathered up my pink and purple towel. I bought them for their bright, joyful colors, but the new purchases, the beauti-ful setting around me and my new job in real estate were not making me feel satisfied. I think that perhaps it was because I felt out of place next to these blonde beach beauties with twig-like bodies in their teeny-weeny bikinis. Like them, I was in the prime of my life, but their sole ambition is to be a model, get in the movie business or marry some rich toad. I wanted something more. With an inquisitive mind, adventuresome spirit and big ambitions, a beach town with lots of expensive gift shops offering items I couldn't afford is not what I needed. Even the easygoing locals eyed me suspiciously, as if I had just stepped off the plane from Mars with my over-the-top excitement, loud voice and Italian-style hand gestures. So when I went to a party and met Maria Gonzales, with her reddish brown ringlets, rosy cheeks and quick smile, I listened when she told me about her hometown, San Francisco. I had been to the "City by the Bay" once on vacation. I had loved its diverse culture, people and turn-of-the-century architecture.

Maria confided to me that she was thinking of leaving her boyfriend, Lew, and the superficial Los Angeles area and returning to the bustling activity of San Francisco, which she considered a cultured city. She told me about the exciting classes one could take on everything from holistic health to creative writing to ballroom dancing. And the food–the popular Californian-cuisine restaurants, charming Italian outdoor cafes, authentic French bistros and inexpensive Asian take-outs. Any night of the week you could pick your venue of what to do–a play, stand-up comedy, poetry readings. She spoke of her extravagant evenings at the opera, ballet and symphony, making me envious of those who had the extra money to spend.

"And it isn't all about money in San Francisco like it is in L.A.," Maria insisted. "San Francisco is different. It is a city filled with artists, intellectuals and entrepreneurs. Of course, they still have the high society crowd and business people, but they all mix together with the gays, the poets and other minorities. It has been an open liberal city from its beginnings in the heyday of the Gold Rush. You know it's funny, but more people know about the Summer of Love than know that the United Nations was founded there."

Maria suddenly lowered her voice to a quiet whisper when she noticed Ted and Lew approaching. "I have to be careful. Lew doesn't know of my plans just yet. I don't plan to tell him till everything's all arranged. No muss. No fuss. That's the best way."

"Promise me you'll keep in touch," I said as we turned our attention back to our dates. Like Maria, I wasn't expecting to stay with Ted much longer either and was looking for a way out.

True to her word, Maria gave me her address when she moved. She called me several times from San Francisco, telling me she made the right decision and how happy she was. And I needed to get out of this monotonous town which felt like it was closing in on me. As soon as I found a discount plane fare I was on my way.

I remember that trip as if it were yesterday: Pulling my suitcase behind me, I take in the moist cool air through both nostrils so different from the sunburnt air I am used to. I feel my energy shift as I breathe, expanding my chest in nervous excitement. I hop on a shuttle headed downtown and hand the driver a crumbled piece of paper with Maria's address, where I'll be staying. I find the key underneath the mat, let myself in and grab a sweater, some money and good walking shoes.

I take a long walk through the old red brick Cannery which has been converted into a score of gift shops and small restaurants. Even though I am in a touristy mood, I cannot get excited about a string of cheap beads a local vendor is selling. I ask the couple next to me, "What's the big deal?" The man's bulky frame, cowboy boots and hat and the woman's bouffant hairstyle, pancake makeup and stretch pants tell me they may be from Texas.

"Weren't these beads popular during the Swinging Sixties?" he asks, giving me a wink. He then grabs this woman's amply endowed buttocks, brings her closer to him and plants a big kiss on her lips. They burst into uncontrollable laughter and I join in. Well, San Francisco seems to attract all kinds, I say to myself. And that is what this city is showing me–all kinds. Besides the assorted artists and musicians, the street people and the punk rockers, the blue collar workers and the business men, there are the wealthy couples flaunting 14-carat gold pendant necklaces (more the men than the women), the love-struck couples walking hand in hand (again, more the men than the women), and the typical wide-eyed tourists like me. This, I think, is what America is supposed be.

Feeling the stomach pangs of not having eaten, I buy a circular loaf of sourdough bread filled with creamy white clam chowder at Alioto's Grotto. I take it to go and plop myself down on a nearby wooden bench, making sure I am not too close to the strong-smelling fishing boats, but close enough where I can watch the sea lions. I take a taste of the soft and chewy bread, which practically melts in my mouth, and, combined with the slightly salty soup, it is an epicurean delight. I am in heaven, for, as I eat, I hear a sea lion barking, taxi horns and conversations humming around me. I notice a majestic red-gold bridge across the water, which I surmise is the famous Golden Gate Bridge. I remember reading about its innovative suspension design and its construction in the thirties–ahead of schedule and under budget. I strain to see the affluent tourist towns across the Bay–Sausalito, Tiburon and Belvedere. Maria has told me that they are quaint, like

Laguna, and I might want to take a ferry over to visit. But I don't want to–I love it here! So many things to see and do here. Quaintness is just not on my agenda. I have had enough of quaintness after living in a beach town for two years. I find myself dawdling, vainly hoping to hear San Francisco's fog-horns–though today is unlikely because a crystal clear blue sky hangs overhead.

It is time for me to explore some more. I continue on along the pier, looking up at a tall circular building on a steep hill; it has funny shaped windows up top. I check my guide-book, never having seen a building shaped like that before and learn that Coit Tower was allegedly built in the shape of a fire hose nozzle as a memorial to the San Francisco firefight-ers after the 1906 earthquake. Amazing! Wanting to get clos-er, I walk the European-flavored neighborhood with its nar-row streets, hillside gardens, pedestrian alleys and secluded staircases through Russian Hill to the top of Telegraph Hill. Here the architecture is more a blend of old-fashioned flats, Edwardians, Art Deco fifties and contemporary style–some boring and some cutting-edge modern–most, I imagine, with superb views of the bay and beyond. It feels like I am walk-ing in a living museum.

Out in the damp cold, the bellowing sound of the fog-horn I had been hoping to hear comforts me as I stamp my feet and rub my hands together to keep warm. An amateur guitarist strums the oldies hit, *Dock of the Bay*, hoping for a tip. He is off-key, but I give him a dollar anyway. I figure he is adding to the whole ambience I am experiencing. I sing along in my head, changing a few words: *Three thousand miles I've roamed to make this place my home. Sitting here on the dock of the Bay* (I'm only a few blocks away) *wasting time. My loneliness* (or is it yearning) *just won't leave me alone.* San Francisco has been pulling on my heartstrings all day. Could it be Southern California, like Upstate New York, is not a suitable match for me? Could not being in the right town be one of the reasons my business has not been humming along?

I notice how I keep comparing San Francisco to my Italian-Irish heritage–their love of food and wine, art and architecture, beauty and design, their connection to nature and the robust engaging way they live their lives. I feel like I belong here–like I found a long lost love. Is that why after just a few hours I feel a lift in my spirit, a heightened sense of aliveness and an appreciation of life I have never felt before? San Francisco stimulates me, motivates me, and inspires me. I realize happiness is within oneself but isn't it also about knowing who we are so we can make good life choices–like choosing a fulfilling occupation and being in surroundings which resonate with who you are inside? Shouldn't things like that increase one's happiness quotient?

If I chose San Francisco as my home, I believe I could be that independent, financially secure and personally fulfilled businesswoman I have always wanted to be. I know no one here except Maria, but I have made up my mind. Yes, San Francisco, you are just what I need.

Searching for a Mentor

It was a week before Thanksgiving when I got in my car with a small collection of personal belongings to make the nine-hour drive from Laguna to San Francisco. I was a bundle of anxieties when I arrived. Although I knew San Francisco and I were a fit, would I be able to be successful here in the big city as a salesperson? The Tommy Hopkins one-day seminar helped, but it was not nearly enough. I knew I would need to develop a sphere of influence. I would also need a better support system so that when a sale falls through I wouldn't fall apart.

Saxe Realty was a family run office across town in the Mission District, which was a colorful fusion of Latino and American culture. The working class, the artists, the feminists and the freelancers lived here because of the low rents. Its busy streets were lined with aromatic burrito joints, Spanish tapas bars and prolific produce markets. However, it is not exactly among the imposing grand mansions of the superrich and famous which I initially thought I wanted.

I did not like the graffiti, litter-strewn sidewalks and pick-up trucks in the driveways, but the close-knit families with their adorable chubby-cheeked children won me over. I figured that the love of family and food was a big enough connection to my Italian-Irish heritage. Also I was realistic. I was not socially or financially connected to San Francisco's upper echelon and this would be just a first step among many. I did not have to stay here forever. And since the homes were reasonably priced, the agents less formidable, and the support system at Saxe Realty better established, there was a better chance of making it here than in the more affluent districts of town. So I said "Yes" when Tim Brown, a new and upcoming manager with a stellar reputation, offered me a desk.

Eileen Maxwell, a modish looking gal, appeared to be the whiz kid of the office. Her thick dark hair was pulled back in a tight bun, which was accentuated by her super-large black-framed glasses and tightly fitted pin-striped suits. I learned she graduated magna cum laude from Berkeley and read *The Wall Street Journal, The Washington Post* and *The San Francisco Chronicle* daily.

At first, I was impressed with all her learning. She knew all about the Consumer Price Index, Gross National Product, Unemployment Rate, and the Dow Jones Industrial Average and how it affected the real estate market. After a month or so, I realized she was not doing as much business as I thought. She knew a lot, that's for sure, but in the results department she came up short. She was spending all her time analyzing economic trends instead of pounding the streets and closing real estate deals. On any particular day I could hear her saying, "Did you notice that San Francisco passed a rent control initiative? Now it will be next to impossible to sell income units. Too much of a legal hassle. Who wants to get sued?" Or, "Did you read that Alan Greenspan is raising the prime rate again so interest rates will be at 18%! He claims inflation is still too high so he has to take action. Who is going to afford those mortgages?" Or, "Look at our high unemployment rate. We will be in a full-blown recession before you know it. Maybe even headed for a depression."

Confused, I asked Tim Brown, the ultimate pragmatist, his opinion. He firmly believed real estate was the best investment one could make–in any economic climate. "People have to live somewhere. When you rent, all that money goes down the toilet. You can't recoup any of it. At least when you own a home, there is substantial tax savings and the possibility of appreciation. Also remember, these so-called experts are not in the trenches like we are. Each one has his or her own view on what's happening. I suggest you stay away from the news and their predictions of doom and gloom. It will only bring you down. Focus your attention on your goals, and remain upbeat and confident instead."

I was clear what my goal was–to be a top salesperson,

and I was getting more confident all the time. I went home that day and canceled my newspaper subscription. I switched the television channel if anything negative came across the screen, including Ted Koppel's *Nightline* covering the Iranian hostage crisis that was ongoing at the time. I decided not to accompany Eileen on house caravans.

I also knew that I could achieve more confidence by becoming an expert in my field and I didn't need to reinvent the wheel. All I had to do was model a successful salesperson's behavior. So I continued my search for a mentor–someone who could help me to make it in this business. I came across three possibilities–all top producers exhibiting maternal instincts that could work in my favor: Mary Francesca Moeller, a heavy-set Italian woman who carried herself with a subtle panache; Nettie Dieves, a confident, spectacled slip of a woman; and finally, Heidi Carter, a very blonde Swede with a thick accent and midriff to match. When I learned Heidi had been the number one agent for the last two years, I decided to approach her first.

Heidi must have been from a small town in Europe, because she dressed like a country bumpkin with huge fluffy hats in varying shades of red, orange and purple. She was also a bit full of herself–in spite of her preferred attire–so I learned quickly she consequently was not well-liked in the office. But I ignored what other people thought and purposely stayed away from gossiping colleagues. I was not going to let their negativity get in the way of my success. She was getting results and I wanted to know why.

I complimented her when she got a new listing or a new hat. Occasionally–so I was not too much of a nuisance–I asked her advice. I noticed that she had a monthly newsletter and managed to squeeze a copy out of her. She was flattered by all my attention and told me that she personally delivered the newsletter every six weeks to her surrounding neighborhood. Saturday and Sunday afternoons were best, she claimed, because people were home. Not only did she give her neighbors timely real estate news, but she also included a recipe and a discount coupon to a local establishment.

Heidi helped me choose a neighborhood to canvass. I improved on Heidi's ideas by choosing a more professional layout for my newsletter and had it printed on better quality paper with my own personal flair. The sale colloquialism for this activity was "farming." I never thought I would end up being a gardener like my Dad, but that was exactly what I was doing–nurturing relationships. Every weekend, even when I didn't feel like it, I walked the neighborhood, remembering Tom Hopkins yelling over the loudspeaker–"Just do it!" So I did.

I must have made some sort of impression on Mary Francesco Moeller, because she asked me to cover for her during the summer when she visited her relatives in Italy. Perhaps it was just a maternal instinct to help a new fledgling like me. Or maybe she noticed that after eight months, I already had a few sales under my belt. Mary, like Bette Mae, was my mother's age. (Was this a subconscious need or what?) She was personable, fun-loving and a smart dresser. She wore jewel colored coordinated suits that complimented her Mediterranean olive skin and what looked to me like professionally applied makeup. I welcomed the help as Heidi, in spite of her best intentions, was difficult to be around. Mary's connections were also with a higher echelon clientele who could afford more. Being Italian myself, we had a special bond and soon we paired up going on tour together and lunch afterwards. I finally had found my mentor.

A Client Who Needed to "Get out of Dodge"

The first of a series of well-qualified buyers Mary referred to me was a couple who lived in Berkeley. She gave me the tantalizing scoop before she left: Justin, a long-standing tenured professor at Cal-Berkeley in his mid-forties, had just left his wife for Diane, an attractive, will-go-far graduate student in her late twenties. Mary blushed as she told me, "How shall I say it… they need to get out of town and fast!" then quickly added, "They want a Victorian with a view and a garage."

Didn't everybody?

It was with this knowledge that I got ready to meet my first reasonably affluent clients. I already knew that they were real buyers, and, since they were a referral, they probably had not talked to anyone else. If I could show them that I was professional, knowledgeable and honest, hopefully they would be loyal.

I had only driven across the Bay Bridge once or twice before and had no sense of direction. I planned ahead by getting an early start. I went over the instructions on how to get to their place one more time, put on my newly purchased red power suit and a touch of soft rose lipstick. I made sure I brought my listing book and calculator to help prequalify them. I stopped at the local car wash and requested "the works"–inside and out–just in case they wanted to start looking today.

I double-checked my map one more time and, taking deep, long breaths, I prepared for the nerve-racking drive across the expansive five-lane bridge. I was on a constant lookout for the merging traffic while I did my best to locate the exit. After a few wrong turns, I finally found the correct address off University Avenue and rang the doorbell–full of optimistic enthusiasm.

Justin and Diane were pretty much what I expected–academic, well-off hippies. They offered me some herbal hibiscus tea while I led them through a property qualifying process that I had learned in my sales training class. I gave them each a blank piece of paper and had them individually describe the home of their dreams. Next they were to rank the characteristics they wanted most. Once they prioritized their wants I had them compare their lists. There was usually some negotiation between partners at this point. It was here I acted as a facilitator by asking open-ended questions. Justin and Diane were pretty much in agreement. They wanted a three bedroom, two bath Victorian with a two-car garage, a small yard (Diane said she liked to garden), a fireplace and a view of downtown.

During the counseling session, I asked lots of questions to translate the *features* (the physical characteristics of a property, such as the number of bedrooms and baths, yard, garage, neighborhood) into *benefits* (pride of ownership, prestige, convenience, safety, investment). Once I understood what was important to them, I could serve them better. For instance, Justin and Diane may have said they wanted three bedrooms, two baths, a view and a two-car garage, but I needed to find out why.

"Diane, you said that you want three bedrooms–do you mind me asking what you plan to use them for." My pen was ready. Being young and single, I made sure I paid most attention to the woman to eliminate any jealousy. Besides, it would be her making the final decision–whether she contributed financially or not.

"As you probably know, it is just Justin and me. We don't plan on having any children, but we both do a lot of work at home and want our own separate offices."

Asking that one question gave me a lot of information. I continued. "If I am able to find a house which has two bedrooms and a study, would that work for you?" Diane gave a quick glance to Justin, who nodded.

"And how about bathrooms? If I find a great house which has only a bath and a half, would you be willing to add a shower later?" Since I did not want them to feel like they were being interrogated, I added, "The reason I am asking you all this is because if you are flexible on your criteria, you will have a larger selection of houses to choose from." I wanted to establish a realistic expectation level for them. No one ever gets 100% of what they want–not even multimillionaires. I then explained that a two-car garage in San Francisco was practically unattainable in their price range. They decided it was an unnecessary luxury, but did need additional space for storage.

"So do you think an attic, basement, or even a large laundry room could work?"

I opened my listing book, which had descriptions of the current houses available, to show them the possibilities. Since price was always important, I could now give them a wider range of possibilities–some of which were only two bedrooms with a bath and a half. Others had no garage.

The view was a whole other issue. Almost every client who initially looked in San Francisco said they wanted a view, but views of the bridges and downtown were pricey.

There were, however, other views which they might find appealing, so my job was to pin them down to what benefit they were seeking–whether it was aesthetics, prestige or a brighter, open environment.

I was also fortunate in being able to gauge what Justin and Diane might want from a visual perspective by observing their current surroundings. Their rental was an Arts and Crafts bungalow amidst a yard full of blooming plants. To get a clearer sense of Justin and Diane's taste, I asked them to give me a quick tour. Their interaction with their home would tell me a lot. Putting them in an unimaginative sixties box, for instance, would never do. The flower generation had great imagination and music, but the people building houses at that time, coming out of the Depression era, held values centered more around saving money, so it was no surprise that the fifties and sixties homes were known for their practical simplicity.

I made sure I mentioned that they would be lucky to get the top five items on their wish list. If they were particularly frugal buyers, they might only get the top three. Again, I was doing my best to keep their expectations realistic. If they aimed too high, they would get disappointed and maybe blame me, which might cost me a sale. Since we seemed to have established a good rapport, I asked them to sign an agency disclosure form. This form described the fiduciary duties of a buyer's agent, seller's agent and a dual agent, opening up the discussion of how real estate agents got paid. If the potential buyers failed to sign the form, then they became a B client–someone I would work with only when I had no other business.

The counseling session took almost two hours. We were

all emotionally spent. We decided to wait until the following week to start looking. As I waved goodbye from the walkway, I knew the meeting has been a success. The next step in the sales process was a good follow-through by sending them a handwritten thank-you note for choosing me as their real estate agent. I wanted to keep that cozy, warm emotional connection. As this was the beginning of our relationship, I needed to be in constant communication. When they mentioned they could look on their own that Sunday, I insisted that we set up private appointments instead. I did not want any high-pressured salesperson to lure them away from me.

After three visits to San Francisco, Justin and Diane put an offer on a sprawling three bedroom, Craftsman style home in Liberty Heights. The house had a sweeping view of surrounding vintage homes, trees and hills–not a view of downtown as they originally hoped–but all wishes did not come to pass. On the plus side, it did have more space than they thought they could afford. At close to $350,000 ($2.5 million today) this was the highest sale I had made so far.

No need for peanut butter sandwiches for dinner or having to decline theater and dinner invitations any longer. Success was sweet!

Lessons Learned from Chapter 4:

- EXAMINE YOUR VALUES What is it you secretly crave? What is your most cherished dream? What does success mean to you? Values represent who you are as a person–what principles you hold dear to your heart– what gives your life meaning? Reflect on what is most important to you.
- FIND YOUR NICHE To be the best you can be, it helps if your surroundings are congruent with your personality strengths, goals, and what is most important to you. Take the time to find an environment that will support you on your journey.
- SURROUND YOURSELF WITH SUPPORTIVE PEOPLE Start making friends with people who are more knowledgeable, powerful and established than yourself. Just being around these experienced people will teach you aspects of business that you cannot learn from a book, and it will greatly shorten your learning curve.
- LET PASSION MOVE YOU FORWARD When you want something, let your joy, excitement, and inspiration propel you forward. Then take the action steps necessary to achieve your goals. You will find that taking action is no longer hard work, but a source of pleasurable fulfillment. The cliché, "Do what you love and money will follow," is a rule I practice every day.

5

CONFIDENCE

Developing a Strong Sense of Self

Maxwell Maltz and the Self-Image

Working with Mary Moeller gave me more confidence. As a result, I doubled my efforts. Imagine my excitement when I got a call from Rex Whitworth, asking me to help him find a home on the recommendation of Grace Elliot, a fellow agent from Concord in the East Bay. I had met her at a Relocation Seminar and given her my business card, following it up with a short note a few weeks later. A simple thank-you note had gotten me a client! It certainly was something to remember in the future about the importance of connecting with out-of-town agents–an important resource of referrals.

Rex and his boyfriend, Sandy Quinn, were both good-looking, charming and financially approved by a bank. If they were straight, I would be happy to date either of them. Rex, a city urban planner, looked a bit like Michael J. Fox, but more fit because he got up early every morning to row with his crew. Sandy was older, probably in his mid-forties, dark complexioned, well-built and bearded.

I could hear my girlfriends saying, "What a waste–too bad they're gay!" Being from a straight-laced Catholic upbringing, I was forced to learn about the gay lifestyle on the job, because so many of the professional men drawn to California were homosexual. When I met Rex and Sandy for our counseling session, they told me they wanted a two-unit building.

"Looking at your combined incomes, I don't see that you have to limit yourself to a multifamily building. You can also afford a single family home," I said.

"It is not because we need the income," Sandy said in his sexy baritone voice.

"What is the reason then?" I asked. They both shifted uncomfortably in their seats and shared an intimate glance. I realized I have asked a question that has intruded on their privacy. I was perceptive enough not to intrude further.

Finally, Rex piped up. "We don't want our families to know we are living together."

"Oh well, in that case... " I mumbled, "Let's only look at duplex units then." I opened up the Multiple Listing Book. I forged ahead, knowing I had important information to help them locate their dream home. We identified some possibilities and started our search.

Rex and Sandy were particular in what they wanted, but I was determined to sell them something no matter what. Several rejected properties later, I found a two-unit in the Upper Market neighborhood on the periphery of the Castro–the predominantly gay area of San Francisco–that met all their criteria. I called Liz McEvoy, the listing agent, to find out all the particulars: How much action the property had had, why the seller was moving, any pertinent disclosures or inspections and the length of the escrow period. Liz answered all my questions, letting me know that she would be presenting an offer later that afternoon. Lucky I called.

When there are multiple offers, closing a deal can be a footrace–the first agent who produces the signed acceptance wins. If I had not checked with the listing agent ahead of time, we might have written an offer on a property that had already sold. I did not want to make that mistake!

Knowing that someone else also wanted this property gave Rex and Sandy the confidence to move forward. I took out the contract (which I now always carry with me) and wrote it on the roof of my car. When Rex asked if they had to go to full asking price, I asked, "How badly do you want this house?"

His response–"We *really* want it."

"Then we have to show the seller we are serious," I said.

"So that means we meet their asking price?" he asked.

"We meet their asking price and we offer good terms."

"'Good terms' means what?" Rex asked.

"Twenty percent for a down payment, with three percent up front as earnest money. You did bring your checkbook, didn't you?"

"Of course. Anything else?"

"A short timeframe on inspections and for approving any disclosures the seller may give us. A seller wants to know he has a sure deal. Is all that all right with you?"

"To give three percent right away seems like a lot," Sandy said.

"It is and the sellers will be impressed," I said, "which is what we are trying to accomplish. If you can swing it financially I recommend you do the three percent." I turned to Rex.

"Make the offer as strong as you can," was his answer. Sandy agreed.

I asked Sandy and Rex to come with me as I drove to Liz's office. This not only was to be my first independent sale since Alan Davenport, but my first independent sale in San

Francisco. I hoped they didn't notice the perspiration pouring from my body, soaking the blouse underneath my jacket, and the beads of nervousness on my forehead. Why was I feeling so insecure? I wasn't exactly a newbie in the business anymore.

I instructed them to wait in the car while I presented the offer. I did my best to pull myself together, talking calmly to myself as I walked up the steps to meet with Liz. I stumbled through the presentation with lots of ums and ahs, but got through it, knowing I would have to deal with my self-confidence issues later.

Since Liz had already had reviewed one offer with her clients already, they were quick to respond, telling me they were going with the first offer. Liz explained that the first set of buyers had written a seamless offer, one with no loan or inspection condition. Plus, the couple wrote a handwritten letter to the owners with snapshots of their family, assuring them that they would take good care of their home. I had never thought of doing that! With slumped shoulders, I shut the door behind me. Rex and Sandy stumbled out of the car, wanting to know what happened.

"The other party got the house," I said.

"Really? How come?" Rex, as usual, was his calm low-key self in spite of the disappointing news. Sandy started to get indignant. "They wouldn't even respond to our offer and ask us to come up in price? That's downright rude!"

"Sellers can choose how they want to handle offers," I said. "They can counter both or accept one on the spot. They chose to accept the first offer."

"But we gave them their asking price and good terms!" Sandy shook his head in disbelief. Rex talked to him in a low soothing voice.

I did my best to respond with a smile and a calm voice, but inside I felt sickened with fear that I was going to lose these buyers. "We came into this listing late, and the other buyers had more time to prepare," I said, still amazed that we were knocked out of negotiating so fast. Then remembering what Liz said, I added, "Even if we came in higher I don't think we would have gotten the house. These buyers got all the inspections done ahead of time and wrote a letter to the sellers, telling them how much they loved their property. They even included snapshots of their family."

"You're kidding! Why would they do that?" Sandy exclaimed, still in shock over losing the property.

I decided to impart the valuable lessons in this dismal turn of events. "Next time we will be better prepared," I said." We will get prequalified with a bank, have the inspections done ahead of time if possible and write an introductory letter to the seller. Sometimes a sale is not always about the most money. If sellers have sentimental memories of the house they are leaving, they often want to sell to someone they like. Someone who loves the house the way they did."

Wanting to get them to recommit, I added, "Let's keep looking. This won't be the only property you will fall in love with."

Before I called them back with more possibilities, I knew I needed some help with my self-esteem issues, so I asked Mary out to lunch for a boost. We picked a family-owned Mexican restaurant with the Christmas decorations brightly lit and still hanging–although the holiday was long past. As we munched away on chips and salsa, she handed me a name of a client she wanted me to contact.

"Thank you," I said and took the piece of paper in my hand. I was careful not to look disgusted at the lumpy pea green concoction the waiter just put on our table.

"Haven't you ever had guacamole?" Mary asked, as she took a huge helping.

"I guess I've heard of it before," I said, "but I never imagined it would be so green or so... er... mushy looking."

"Give it a try–you may like it. It's kind of like sales," she said with a laugh. "It seems kind of strange at first, but then you acquire a taste for it and you can't imagine living without it."

I took a chip and dipped it in, opening my mind for another new experience. "You know," I said, as I took another taste, "I think you're right. It has a bit of fullness and zing to it." I gave Mary a wink. "Just like real estate!"

We both started to giggle. I was giddy with delight at having a new friend. I gathered some courage and asked the question I had been pondering for the last few days, "Why did you choose me over the other sales people in the office to cover for you?"

"Paula, you know what you want and you go after it. Plus, you have a gusto for life which I find refreshing. Sure, most of the other people in the office have more experience, but they take their business for granted or they're too busy to really enjoy what they're doing, so guess what? They are not going to connect to my clients as well as someone like you, who is tenacious, enthusiastic and confident."

I was grateful for the kind words and told her so. "Any advice you want to give me as a new salesperson starting out?" I asked.

"Before selling real estate, I worked for Sarah Coventry Cosmetics. I learned the importance of making a good first impression, establishing rapport with your clients, and how to close a sale, but that's not enough to last in this business. We are dealing with people who are making the most important investment in their lives–both emotionally and financially. To deal with them, you have to have a strong sense of self."

I remembered Bette Mae's similar advice, but was curious about what she meant by that, more specifically. Mary took a moment to answer. "I would say a truly self-confident person is a person who embodies a balanced blend of giving and receiving. Being an ingratiating people pleaser won't work in sales. By giving without constraint your clients won't respect you and the other sales people will walk all over you." She continued, "Of course, the polar opposite is the self-absorbed narcissist, who can't give at all. When you are truly confident, you do not need to brag, put people down or act high-and-mighty. It is interesting to watch when these people's external accomplishments are taken away. They deflate like pinpricked balloons–their self-esteem blows off into thin air."

She lifted her glass to mine. "When you come up against an obstacle, rely on your strong inner core of confidence to get you through. And, of course, surround yourself with upbeat, positive people who appreciate you."

I followed, clinking my glass against hers. "Here's to our new business partnership," I said. Noticing that the guacamole bowl was empty, I motioned the waiter to come over. "Could we have some more please?"

Mary gave me a wide smile. "I know you're going to be a big success–just wait and see."

As my mentor, Mary recommended a book for me to read that she felt would help me with my self-esteem issues. I was quite skeptical, of course. A book was going to restore my self-confidence? Against my better judgment, I went to the bookstore, found the paperback and read the blurb on the back. The author was a doctor. Well, that's good news–at least it was written by an educated professional. I read further. He was a cosmetic surgeon. Not a likely book for a young woman who wanted to be successful in breaking into sales in a new city. What could this guy possibly teach me about success? It would turn out to be one of the most important books I have ever read.

In *Psycho-Cybernetics,* Dr. Maxwell Maltz wondered why, after successful surgeries in which he improved people's appearances, many of his patients returned unsatisfied, complaining they still felt ugly. If only he did one more small adjustment, they pleaded–a lift here, a tuck there, a slightly smaller nose, a fuller chin–all would be well. But doing more surgeries did not change how people saw themselves. Even when Dr. Maltz took before and after pictures and had concrete evidence of vast improvements, many patients still could not see a difference. Hundreds of case studies later, Dr. Maltz concluded that improving people's exterior appearance was not enough. In order for people to feel better about themselves, they needed to be repaired from the inside out. They needed to build a stronger self-image.

Self-image is a mental picture that each of us has about ourselves–a summation of strengths and weaknesses. Our beliefs might be completely inaccurate, but what matters is that we believe them to be true. Like Dr. Maltz's patients, I realized my reality was based on some erroneous perceptions. Coming from a highly critical, unsupportive family, I often felt like I was not good enough. Now this negative thought pattern was getting in the way of my success. It did not have to be that way. I could build up my self-image by changing how I viewed myself. I could focus on my strengths of tenacity, courage and passion.

If At First You Don't Succeed, Let Confidence Be Your Guide

With that positive shift in attitude, I showed Rex and Sandy a Spanish style home, solidly built in the 1930's, with several subsequent additions. This particular property had been on the market for months. In the real estate business, this was called a sleeper, because it had been on the market so long. So it was either overpriced or seriously flawed. Very unlikely that Rex and Sandy would be outbid on this one.

Lesson learned, Rex and Sandy wrote a personal letter to the seller and had a prequalified letter from a bank. With no other bidders in sight, we made a contingent offer–one that was subject to an inspection of the property's condition before the buyer proceeded with the loan. I brought a bottle of champagne along to the inspection, figuring Rex and Sandy would be celebrating the sale with me before I headed back East for vacation. Another assumptive close.

All the galvanized plumbing had been replaced with copper. The wiring had been updated to circuit breakers with 220-volt service in the kitchen and laundry room. The foundation of the house was sturdy. The pan-and-cover barrel roof with its dark crimson clay tiles passed with flying colors. So far so good. We got to the kitchen which had been extensively remodeled. The listing agent had assured me that although the seller did not get permits for some of the work, it was not important. Now I wanted the opinion of an independent expert.

"You don't need permits for these simple renovations, do

you?" I asked, feeling a little nervous, but not like the last deal.

"Sure do," Ed Stephens, the contractor, answered matter-of-factly.

"It's my understanding that if appliances are just replaced you don't need a permit," I persisted, wondering where Rex and Sandy were. Probably placing their furniture in the living room.

"That's true. But in this case there had been extensive remodeling."

"Really?" I said. "How can you tell?"

"All you have to do is trace the electrical and plumbing routes." Ed tapped the end of his pencil on his temple a few times.

"Oh," I said, happy Rex and Sandy were not around to see this exchange.

Ed proceeded downstairs to the second unit, which was now becoming a looming concern for me. If the seller did not get permits for the kitchen, would he have gotten the permits for the two-bedroom garden apartment? I followed Ed down the creaky back stairs. I called to Rex and Sandy to follow. As awful as the outcome may be, they needed to hear all this for themselves. The good and the bad. Looking at the second unit this time around, it did feel like an impromptu addition. Ed did not say anything, but scribbled unintelligible notes on his pad. I was too intimidated to ask what he was noting. Besides, I told myself, I would find out soon enough. I shifted my attention to Rex and Sandy who were still smiling ear to ear. I joked about what a great Christmas present they were getting for each other.

Then Ed asked for the permit history. I handed him a copy of the building record. Now I wished I had taken the time to review the material with my manager. Then I'd understand more what the permit history revealed about the legality of the unit. Ed took his time to read it thoroughly. My suspicions were confirmed when Ed announced in his brisk non-personal style, "It is not just the kitchen and bathrooms that don't have permits, but the whole second unit. I hope the city doesn't get wind of this." Ed handed the paperwork back to me as he prepared to make his exit.

I turned to Rex and Sandy. "Maybe we should talk to one of the city inspectors directly?" Rex gave me a disgruntled look which I took seriously, because he was usually so agreeable.

"I don't need a second opinion," he said.

Huh? I was mystified, but asking questions was the name of the game in sales. I might be uncomfortable, but it wouldn't pay for my rent or my vacation, which I had been planning for months. "You are not going to let the fact that the unit is illegal get in the way of buying this property, are you?" I asked, making sure I smiled. Both Rex and Sandy were quiet. I continued, "We can always ask for a credit from the seller. This property is such a great buy."

Rex's jaw was tight and his voice deliberate as he turned to face me. "Paula, I do not want to buy a property which may require us to make corrections for possible code violations. Not only would it be a hassle for us logistically and financially, but it could jeopardize my standing with the City Council. It is just not worth the risk."

I turned my attention to Sandy, asking him what he thought.

"I am so sick of living in my small apartment–can't we make some sort of deal with the city?"

I looked to Rex. The silence was deafening. His voice was

low and his demeanor steadfast. "This is not the property for us, Paula. We are not approving the contractor's inspection. Draw up the necessary paperwork."

Although this property was a No, I wanted Rex and Sandy to continue working with me. "Shall we continue looking then?" I asked.

"Paula. We are more interested than ever."

I did my best not to let another failed transaction get me down as I canceled our escrow, postponed my trip back East and continued my search for another property. It was close to the holidays, so there was little inventory. Finally, I had motivated clients, who were ready to go, but no property to show them. I didn't want them getting so discouraged they would end up going to another agent. I had to keep moving this process forward. Desperate, I needed to look beyond what was currently listed in the Multiple Listing Service.

With the help of a title company and the reverse directory, I got the names and telephone numbers of owners of two-unit buildings which had been up for sale in the last year, but never sold. Some were *For Sale by Owners* (FSBO'S) and some were *Expired* (like Mrs. Burns' home). I spent the next two days making cold calls.

It was worth all the effort when I finally found an owner who wanted to sell his three bedroom Victorian home with a separate carriage house. Richard Epstein and his family had already moved to an inland suburb for a better school district. Although he just found some tenants to rent his property, he had not signed the lease yet. "Let me talk to my client before you sign anything," I told him. Barely able to contain my excitement, I called Rex and Sandy with news of this property that was perfect for them. The only other caveat, I explained, was that Mr. Epstein wanted full price. "So?" Rex said. "If it is a good property, we are ready, willing and able to buy."

Rex and Sandy were perfect buyers to have, like ripe apples ready to be picked off a tree. They were so anxious to move that they made room in their schedules to see the property the very next day. We were not disappointed. Understanding the importance of time, we met at a nearby coffee shop to write up the offer. (Traveling with all my forms had proven to be a great boon to my business). Wanting both parties to sign on the dotted line as soon as possible, I drove to Mr. Epstein's house. It was almost a two-hour drive away in some nondescript sleepy bedroom community, safe for his young children, but too boring for me to even remember its name.

Richard Epstein was a classic anal retentive personality, who found two tiny changes he must make in the pre-printed contract. I made all the necessary changes. He also insisted on having the changes initialed by tomorrow because, as he said, "I can't put my tenant off any longer." It was close to midnight when I called Rex and Sandy.

They picked up immediately. "We've been waiting for your call."

"Mr. Epstein made a few small changes–shortening our inspection time frames and stating you are to take the property in As Is condition."

"What does that mean?" asked Rex.

"With an "As Is" clause, the seller is saying up front he will not give us a credit for whatever is found in the contractor's inspection." I noticed I used the word we a lot. I felt protective over my clients, like a Mother Hen with her chicks, and wanted them to feel fully taken care of. "However, if we find something about the property we don't like we can always back out. Just so you know, I already checked with the Planning and Zoning Department and the property is a legal two-unit building. All the appropriate permits have been filed. Just be aware that no building is perfect–the contractor may find a few things here and there."

Rex said, "Well, we really like the property and will be reasonable, so don't worry. Minor fix-up items don't bother us."

"Well, you know what they say–third time's the charm," I chirped, feeling confident this deal will go through.

"Okay, then. Let's move ahead. Can you come over now? We'll sign those changes."

"Of course," I said, trying not to gush. "I'm only a few blocks away." I turned up the stereo in my car on the way as Sly and the Family Stone belted out–*I want to take you higher! Higher! Higher!* I sang along. One more sales success story–a double end sale representing both the buyer and the seller at a full 6% fee!

Lessons Learned from Chapter 5:

- ACT AS IF YOU ARE WHO YOU WANT TO BE What you think about yourself will project outward and influence how others treat you. If you have doubts about yourself, pretend as if you are confident. When you project confidence, people will want to work with you.
- BUILD YOUR STRENGTHS Each snowflake, each starfish and each flower is unique–as it is with each one of us. Take the time to determine what special strengths you have and concentrate on enhancing them.
- FOCUS ON THE PRIZE Sales is a profession in which you need to accept delayed gratification. If your clients are motivated, support them the best you can through their indecisions, whining and frustration, remembering there are big rewards at the end of the rainbow.

6

DISCIPLINE

Controlling Your Mind

Nurturing the Sale

I was getting smarter about sales, so when I received a call from someone who had gotten our office number off a For Sale sign one Saturday, I was fully prepared. The caller identified himself as Joe Phelps. He explained that he and his partner, Mark, had found a property they might want to buy. (Business partner? Lover? I was experienced enough now not to ask until we knew one another better). He wanted to know the asking price of the signed property. Even though he was eager to give me the address, I asked him to get a pen and paper first. I spelled out my name and gave him my telephone number, in case we got disconnected. Only then were we ready to do business.

Before I gave Joe the price, I asked, "What is it about this property that you like?"

Joe told me that this particular house was close to his work, public transportation, and shopping.

"One hundred and seventy-nine thousand," I said and quickly followed it up with another question. "Is that the price range you had in mind?"

I have learned that the person asking the questions was in control–not the reverse–contrary to what one might think.

"Yes," Joe answered, sparking my excitement.

I explained that there were other houses in the same neighborhood which also met his criteria. I was careful not to give him the exact addresses, however, because I wanted him intrigued and in need of my expertise. I next asked if he knew what they wanted to pay per month, because that would tell me whether they had given serious thought to buying. When a prospective buyer said it did not matter and they were open to all possibilities, they were not far along on their decision making process. Joe told me that they would like to pay no more than $1800 a month, so it appeared they were real buyers. I had all the information I needed to set up an appointment. (Later on in our relationship I would get into the details of financing).

"How about meeting tomorrow? I think I might have an opening." I told Joe to hold while I looked at my calendar. I had nothing planned, but I made it sound like I was fitting them into a packed schedule. We agreed to meet at the property after work. I would have preferred to meet them at my office, but sensed reluctance when I suggested it, so I dropped it immediately. This was common–they had not met me yet so they were more comfortable on neutral ground.

Although they seemed like serious buyers, I did not want to take anything for granted so the next day I called Joe to confirm. His partner, Mark Philips, answered. We were still on. Even so, I was as nervous as on a first date–wondering if I would be stood up. Twenty-five minutes late, they arrived. I feigned confidence as I shook their hands and introduced myself–a lesson I had learned from Mary and Dr. Maltz.

I made sure I did not point out the obvious in the house, like saying, "Here's the kitchen and this is the dining room." Instead I said things like, "This breakfast nook is really charming, don't you think?" and "Take a look at this cabinet–perfect for spices–although it originally contained a built-in ironing board."

"We don't iron or do much cooking. It's dry cleaners and take-out for us, but an extra cabinet is always good to have for something." They started to laugh and I joined in. I felt myself relaxing, knowing I was making a connection with these young men. Joe was a speech pathologist and Mark was a hairdresser. They were a great pair.

After a quick tour, I could tell from their demeanor that they were disappointed in the interior of the house. Their polite comments reflected no enthusiasm. I was prepared for this, even if they were not, since typically the property a client called on was not the one they eventually bought. I gave them a sunny smile and ushered them into my car.

"Why don't we go back to my office and let's see what else is available? We'll drive back here later to collect your car." Before they knew what was happening, Joe and Mark were listening to me chatting away about neighborhoods and possible loan options.

Before opening up the Multiple Listing Service book, I helped them figure out what they could afford. "Most lenders will want your monthly payments covering principal, interest, taxes, and insurance–PITI–to be approximately one third of your monthly income. However, with good credit, banks may go as high as forty percent." I gave them the names of three lenders to call to get the loan process started. "It is good to get the prequalifying done now, because once you find a house you really like, you do not want to be wasting any time putting in an offer," I advised. I told them 20% of the purchase price was the typical down payment. I also remembered to explain the 3% closing fees (Alan Davenport's jaw had practically dropped to the floor when he learned he had to pay me an additional $5,000 at close).

"What are closing fees?" they asked in unison.

"Well, the bulk is for lender's charges, because interest does not cover the bank's cost of lending money. Plus there is title and property insurance."

Mark interrupted, "I don't mean to sound ignorant, but what is title insurance for?"

"There's no such thing as a dumb question," I said. Since I no longer felt uncomfortable if I did not know an answer, I welcomed all questions. I had learned to simply reply, "I don't know, but I'll find out." In this particular case, however, I did know.

"Title insurance is good because it protects the buyer by confirming that the seller's title is clear and properly in his or her name and that the seller has the right to sell the property. Should a problem later arise with the title (such as an inaccurate description) the insurance company will pay the damages to the new buyer or secured lender, or take steps to correct the problem."

Joe was scribbling notes as fast as he could. I assumed he was figuring out what they could afford. He looked up briefly, admitting they might be a bit short of cash to cover the 20% down payment in addition to all the closing costs.

"Sometimes," I said, "a seller will agree to pay your closing costs or give you a small second loan to help make the deal. I can negotiate all this for you, of course," I paused, "That is, if you decide to choose me as your agent." This was the perfect opportunity for me to explain that real estate agents worked only on commission. "Not only will I negotiate on your behalf for the house of your choosing, but I will also preview houses beforehand–which will save you a lot of time. Plus, through my network of real estate connections, I can find properties fast to help get you a better deal." I lowered my voice, "Sometimes–I may even find a house that is not available on the open market." I hesitated, noting their reaction. Their faces were open, their shoulders relaxed and they both appeared to be listening intently. "I will do all this groundwork for you–provided that you work exclusively with me." I looked them squarely in the eyes as I said this. I pushed a Buyer Retainer Form in front of them and asked them for their signature.

Joe glanced at Mark, who nodded in agreement.

I remembered to tell them that if they saw an ad in the paper or a sign on a property they liked, they were to call me directly. I would find out all the particulars for them. This would help to ensure they remained more loyal and committed to me. I had a real buyer! Now my job was to preview houses in their desired neighborhood and price range. A short three weeks later, we were ratified–meaning our offer was accepted–on a two bedroom Victorian in the Ingleside District. It was a small transaction, but it gave me a boost of confidence. We were just about to close when Nettie Dieves, one of my previous mentor hopefuls in the office, approached my desk.

"That really should be my deal. I know Mark. He works where I get my hair done. He never told me he was buying a house," she said.

I gave her a weak smile, but said nothing. I had only been working here six months. I certainly did not want bad blood between us.

"So what are you going to do about it?" Nettie gave me

a menacing look. When I did not come up with an answer, she said, "You can get back to me tomorrow."

I was so new I did not have any firm allies in the office yet. Nettie could mess my wonderful new job up for me. I liked my office, loved my manager and felt I was close to success. After a sleepless night, I changed into my jogging shorts and headed for the streets. Whenever I started to get anxious about Nettie, I pushed the thought away and ran harder, concentrating on my breathing. If I wanted to stay in this business, exercise would have to be part of my routine. No more excuses. After a good sweaty run I was feeling better, but still unclear about what to do next.

When Belief Systems Collide

I noticed that ever since Nettie confronted me, painful memories of my childhood kept popping up: Being punished for getting a "C" on my report card, being scolded for not smiling when we had our class picture taken, and being grounded when I lost a library book. I started reliving all these past negative experiences. Remembering all this agonizing stuff made the whole situation with Nettie even harder. I wanted to sob, but caught myself. But the more I contemplated this situation, what I came to realize was that I was wallowing in a field of negativity. One of the very basic concepts I had learned from Maltz and other thinkers on the human mind, and also, in part, from Tommy Hopkins' seminar, is that thoughts are powerful things and, right now, my negative thoughts were a fundamental part of my problem.

What we need to understand is that past memories, their attached belief systems and accompanying fears don't just go away. They lie dormant in our subconscious. Nettie knew I was new and naïve. She may even have observed my susceptibility to criticism. Not yet as expert at reading people as Nettie undoubtedly was, I could nevertheless surmise (from my observations) that she probably had a belief system that people owed her somehow, and, very possibly, it was a strategy that had very likely worked for her in the past. Conversely, as I examined my own belief system as best I could, I realized mine could be summed up as believing that people took advantage of me–and I let them do it. I certainly felt my parents did. My mother, in particular, took advantage of my need for love and acceptance by placing unfair, sometimes impossible, demands on me to earn those things from her and, then, often withheld them anyway.

Thus, with Nettie, our two belief systems were, in effect, colliding with each other, and hers was in the dominant position–unless I changed my thinking right then and there.

What makes this difficult for us, however, is that these belief systems are seated in the subconscious, not the conscious mind. To understand this, you might begin by picturing an iceberg with only 10% of its mass showing above the water. That 10% represents the conscious mind–it is analytical, logical and rational. It handles our everyday tasks by coordinating our intentions with actions. The 90% submerged part is our subconscious–a huge database which gathers information with no discerning abilities. That is, the subconscious mind does not know the difference between a dream, the present or the past. It understands only images and emotions. It is impressionable and indiscriminate, and it can be irrational–or more accurately, *rational*. Remember, we are talking about belief systems here, not necessarily factual systems.

The way that it was explained to me, and in which I had

come to understand it, is that there are four states of brain activity: Beta, Alpha, Theta and Delta. In order to access the subconscious, we need to either be in Theta, characterized by dreaming, or in Alpha, when we are in a very relaxed, meditative-like state. The theory is that Albert Einstein, Thomas Edison, Alexander Graham Bell, among many others, developed their cutting edge theories and inventions when they were walking in nature, taking catnaps or being alone and quiet. It was from their subconscious that they received their inspiration, creativity and innovative ideas. When we are in these states, we can also let go of old, limiting thought patterns and substitute for them new, healthy ways of thinking. In a sense, it takes more than just working hard cognitively to become successful; we also need to relax so we can get through to, and have an impact on, our subconscious minds.

As an entrepreneur in real estate sales (and certainly in other fields as well), one has to live on the edge, constantly adapting to changing circumstances and challenging situations. We need the power of both the rational conscious mind and the creative subconscious. It might be unnerving to realize that our subconscious minds have such a pervasive hold over us, over our ways of thinking and our overall belief systems. Yet, what I came to realize is that, in this situation, my subconscious mind was merely connecting my past experiences with Nettie's assault on me. While the subconscious may be powerful, it is not time sensitive, and therein lies its diabolical aspect.

In my case, once I realized that I was laboring under the thought or belief system that people take advantage of me (and again, that I let it happen) I would be able to recognize this when such thoughts came welling back up again. The truth of the matter was that I was no longer a helpless five-year-old girl at the mercy of my parents; I was a smart, savvy, ambitious businesswoman just starting to taste the sweetness of entrepreneurial success. However, if I was going to continue on that path, I could no longer allow past negative images to affect me now. To be the highly successful agent I wanted to be, going forward, I would have to control my thoughts, and in particular the way that I would think about myself.

I remembered Tommy Hopkins's suggestion of using the subconscious mind to solve problems that the analytical mind could not explain. Tommy said when you combine feeling with visualization you could start creating the reality you wanted. He suggested we put all of our positive feelings into our thumb by recalling any past accomplishments like acing a test, excelling in a sport or winning a card game. Then, whenever you find yourself in a challenging situation, press your thumb and–voilà!–you feel confident, positive and ready to handle any situation.

I was taking no chances in the matter of Nettie, so I did this subconscious ritual right before I went to the office the next day. I visualized Nettie approaching me. I imagined me smiling, being calm and collected as I told her that her claim was bogus. I visualized her walking away, never to bring up the subject of Mark again. Sure enough, after my visualization, the following day I walked by Nettie projecting a self-assurance I did not know I had. "Hello," I said.

With her hands on her hips, Nettie approached. "Well, have you thought about what percentage you plan to give me out of your commission, since you stole my client?" she asked.

"I didn't steal your client, Nettie." My voice was calm.

"I had no idea you even knew Mark until you told me on Friday."

"Well, I do."

"Just because you know Mark does not mean you are entitled to a commission," I said, astounded at my matter-of-fact composure. "I showed him and his partner property, found a house they liked and got them a loan. It was a two-month long process and Mark never once mentioned your name. Are you sure he even knows you work here? He's been to the office many times, but you never came up in the conversation."

"Really? How did you get them as a client?" she asked, moving closer.

I felt it was none of her business, but answered anyway. "They called inquiring about a property."

"Well, maybe they first asked for me."

I paused a moment and thought well before I answered. I made sure I spoke slowly, enunciating each word with emphasis. "Nettie, Mark did not ask for you. In fact, it was his partner, Joe, who made that first call."

"I bet that's not how it happened," Nettie said, hissing through her teeth.

"Nettie, if they wanted to work with you, why would they make an appointment with a real estate agent they never met?" I was putting the onus on Joe and Mark now.

Nettie gasped at my response. "You are just trying to weasel out of this," she said, narrowing her eyes. "And I am not going to let you get away with this. I am going straight to Tim Brown and tell him what you've done."

I turned to face Nettie directly. "Fine," I said, finally believing in my heart of hearts that I had done nothing wrong.

My visualization that I would keep my full commission had sustained me through this uncomfortable encounter. Tim never called me into his office. I collected my full commission when escrow closed. I stayed at Saxe Reality for another two years and made sure I said hello to Nettie when I saw her, but never said anything else.

Self-Doubt Can Still Eat You Alive

Getting along with clients is always sticky. I had to learn to draw the line with Dr. John De Palma and his wife, Alicia, when they bought a Victorian in a *crème de la crème* location near Alta Plaza Park. It was in the midst of the quaint Fillmore District of Pacific Heights with trendy shops and restaurants. Even though it did not have a garage, it was on a major bus line and there was plenty of street parking along the park. The high ceilings, crown and picture moldings, rounded arched windows and large chandeliers hanging from cherub adorned rosettes captured their imaginations. As soon as the De Palmas saw the sheltered walk-out English garden, deeded exclusively to their unit, they were smitten. I led them through several rounds of negotiations to win this house of their dreams. A short year later, John was transferred to Boston and had to sell.

Disappointing for them. Fortunate for me.

The house, which was beautiful to begin with, was even lovelier now that Alicia had lavishly decorated it with custom finishes and priceless Eastlake furniture. John was eager to set a price so that he could sell and move on, but Alicia was insistent on listing way over market because of all the money and time she had invested. I appealed to her reason by showing her comparable sales in the neighborhood. She tossed the listing sheets in the trash, believing those houses were not nearly as special as hers. I suggested we lower the asking price she had set so that we would increase our chances of inciting a bidding auction. "Then you will be able to get above your listed price," I advised.

Alicia was not convinced, but I implored her, at least, to make her decision quickly, to get the property on the market before April. I emphasized that there were plenty of buyers looking then, being driven by their accountants' recommendations to get tax breaks.

"Most sellers mistakenly wait until the better weather to sell. Historically, in the early spring, we have a limited supply of inventory with lots of pent-up buyer demand. Selling in March will put us in the perfect position of getting the best price with the best terms."

Alicia took a long time deciding so it was not until mid-June that she agreed to put the house on the market, begrudgingly. By now, the market had shifted. There were plenty of beautiful condos for buyers to choose from and the demand was not as strong. We got an offer, but only one. The good news was that the buyers, a middle-aged couple living in Japan, were highly motivated. Their son would be attending college in San Francisco so they had only a week to find a place for him to live. Renting was out of the question for this financially savvy couple. They wanted a prestige neighborhood, good enough for their only son. I was hopeful that they would be able to accept Alicia's high asking price, because they just lost a bid on another house. Alicia, convinced her house was worth even more, insisted on countering their offer for over the list price.

I understood that often sellers have inflated visions of

what their homes are worth, which often gets in the way of making transactions come together, but as her fiduciary agent it was my job to get the parties to agree. Fortunately I had a good relationship with my fellow agent, Jim Caldwell, and explained that the wife wanted a bit more than our asking price. I also let him know that another party was looking at the property closely, which was the absolute truth. (I was not willing to succumb to lying as some disreputable agents would to procure a higher price.)

"If your clients accept a bigger price now, it would get them the property. If they wait, they could get into a multiple-offer bidding war which might result in their not getting the property. Is it worth the risk?" I asked. Jim conferred with his clients and his clients countered our counter with a price slightly better than the original asking price, but not what Alicia expected.

"If only we asked for more money to begin with," she wailed. "I am sure we would have gotten it!" Alicia's voice was brittle as it hit my ears. "Why couldn't we have done it my way?"

What was most aggravating to me was not Alicia being angry at me, but the negative thought avalanche that was going on inside my head: *I should have–I was wrong–I didn't do it right!* It felt like I had a gigantic searchlight coming out of my forehead, reviewing all my mistakes–with Alicia, with past clients, with my ex-boyfriends. This was not quite the throwback to childhood that Nettie's attacks inspired, but still that dangerous self-doubt was coming back. My mind was like one of those airport scanners going back and forth–looking, looking, looking. It would not let me off the hook. *I could have agreed to Alicia's higher listing price. Maybe Alicia was right. If we asked for more, maybe we would have gotten more.* It became a never-ending tape going round and round in my head.

I turned to face Alicia. In the sweetest voice I could muster, I said, "Alicia, your condo has been on the market for almost two months. You know yourself that we have advertised in all the top journals and magazines. I have had it open every weekend and on numerous brokers' tours–everyone in San Francisco knows it is for sale. If we were going to get a better offer, we would have gotten it by now." "Look at the comparable sales," I added, doing my best to win her over with logic. "You are getting the highest price of any home without a garage in the Fillmore District."

"That doesn't mean anything and you know it! I don't care what other people got–I just care what I get." She started to sob. "You just don't care about how I feel. I put my heart and soul into that house to make it special and you don't give a damn. It is just another sale to you."

That evening I was still haunted by what Alicia said to me. Why couldn't I have been more empathetic? Why hadn't I thought to say something like, "I understand your disappointment, especially when you were expecting a much higher price." Or, "It must be very difficult to move from a home you love." As I went over what happened, the scathingly critical part of my subconscious emerged like an army drill sergeant, yelling and screaming at me about how I did not handle Alicia's concerns well enough. I understood now that these pictures were brought to my consciousness for a reason, but I also knew that the army sergeant image was in part because of my highly critical parents. I counted on my rational conscious mind to sort through all this, knowing that the submerged part of my brain was trying to teach me something.

It suddenly dawned on me that Alicia probably did not want to leave San Francisco, and, more than likely, she resented anyone who, in her mind, represented the move. My listening more and talking less could have yielded a better outcome. Yes, next time I would be more empathetic to clients who were deeply attached to their homes. At the same time, I accepted the fact that I make mistakes once in a while and planned to do better with the next opportunity.

My mind continued to beat me up. I kept bringing it back to what it was I wanted–a good connection with my clients–all the time being patient with myself as one would when disciplining a small child. Each real estate situation was unique, so I would always be learning on the job. No matter what problem I was facing, I could use the power of my mind to solve it. Sometimes the conscious mind came to the rescue of the unconscious mind. Sometimes it was the other way around. But there was always an answer, even ones I thought were impossible, like the situation with Leeza O'Reilly.

Why it Pays to Rely on Your Subconscious to Help

Leeza came to me through her friend, Roy Jackson, a mortgage broker in San Jose. I met Roy at a real estate conference and we exchanged business cards. I was delighted when Leeza called a few months later to ask me for help in finding a loft in the up and coming South of Market District. From the moment I met Leeza, I was stuck by her exotic beauty. She was not what I would call movie star beautiful, for she had a prominent nose and a figure too curvaceous by current Hollywood standards. Yet Leeza had a femininity about her which I found appealing. When she opened her door, she flung it open wide and, in her lilting Irish accent, welcomed me inside as if I were one of her dearest friends.

I thought it was the combination of her deep-set green eyes and the lusciousness of her wavy shoulder-length auburn hair that reminded me of a mermaid. My first impression was confirmed when I noticed the many aquatic wildlife photos lining her hallway walls. When I asked her about them, she told me they were taken during her various scuba diving adventures in Bali, Fiji and off the Great Barrier Reef. She switched gears to the business at hand, confessing she did not have a lot of money to spend, but thought a one bedroom loft would suit her perfectly.

"Just give me a basic amount of living space and I can do the rest," she assured me. As I looked around, I believed her. She had turned an unimaginative sixties box into a warm and luxuriant home. Right now I had a full schedule. I really didn't have time to work with another client, but I was enchanted by Leeza–her charm, her lifestyle and her beauty. I decided I could take her on.

Soon we were in escrow on a loft with an interesting urban view of a red and white neon lighted Coca-Cola sign which, strangely enough, gave the unit the uniqueness Leeza was seeking. Leeza had only ten percent for the down payment, so Roy Jackson, her old friend, had to obtain the typical 80% loan. Then he had to find a 10% bank loan for the balance. Sometimes the seller was willing to loan to the new buyer the 10% balance in order to make the sale, but alas, the seller was not willing to do so in the case of Leeza's loft. Because the additional loan for the balance of the down payment would be recorded behind the first loan, it was riskier. As a result, the interest rate would be higher. Roy assured me that Leeza's income to debt ratio was still sufficient to qualify.

We got approval for the 80% loan early, so we were half-way there, but it was not a home run–we still needed to get approval on the 10% second loan to bring the down payment up to 20%. I stayed on top of my game by inquiring about the status of the second loan every time I talked to Roy, and each time Roy told me, "No problem." I worried nonetheless. By this time I was getting emotionally close to Leeza–she was as beautiful inside as she was out–and I so much wanted her to get The American Dream of owning a home. Close of escrow was only a few days away when I got the disastrous news. Leeza did not qualify for the second loan. All of Roy's declarations of No Problem were false. I called Roy to ask for an explanation. He sounded weary. "I submitted the loan to every conceivable lender out there, Paula. There are just no takers."

"Have you told Leeza yet?" I asked.

"I just told her before I called you. She was pretty upset," Roy said.

I gave Leeza a call. She picked up. "Leeza, I heard the news."

"Paula, how… how could this happen?" She was choking on her words. I could tell she had been crying.

"Can you borrow from your family?" I asked.

"You mean my mother? She can hardly make it financially herself. I have been on my own since I was sixteen. She can't help me. My brother has two little kids and can barely make ends meet. What am I going to do? I already gave notice to my landlord. I am all packed up with no place to go. I'm essentially homeless."

"How about any distant relatives–an aunt or uncle? Grandparents?"

"No one," she said, starting to sob.

"How about a good friend? A work colleague? Someone who trusts you. Someone who has some extra money to invest. You can give them a good interest rate–a good return on their investment. We'll make it all official and record the loan against the property. Isn't there anyone in your circle of friends who might be able to do this?" I asked, desperate to come up with a solution.

"None of my friends have any money–they're worse off than me."

"Anyone at all you can think of?"

"No one," Leeza was in full crying mode now and again asked the question: "How could this happen?" I knew why but could not say that Roy was not doing his job. He should have at least warned us there might be a problem with her qualifying. But Roy was her friend.

"Go for the solution," I told myself, remembering to use the power of my subconscious mind. By thinking outside the box, I might be able to come up with a way to make this right.

I called Roy back. "Say Roy, would you be willing to kick in your mortgage fees and the referral fee I am giving you to give Leeza the down payment she needs?"

"That's a lot to ask, Paula," He was subdued, but not sorry enough to help Leeza out.

"I was thinking that I would put in my commission to make this work. If you do the same, the combined amount would be enough to cover the ten percent Leeza needs."

He was silent.

"I rarely do this," I added. "But you know Leeza will pay us back as soon as she can. Besides–she's given notice to her landlord and now she has no place to live."

"I just can't," he said.

"Even if it means you won't get anything at all out of this sale?" I was surprised at his answer. I took a few deep breaths, knowing I had to proceed carefully–Roy was one of Leeza's closest friends.

"I'm a little overextended financially myself, Paula. I took on a lot of debt to buy my mortgage company. Hey, why doesn't your company lend Leeza the money she needs?"

"That is an impossible request," I told him. "Hill & Company is not in the business of lending money. The only way it would work is if we all pooled our money."

"Like I said before–I can't." *Or won't* was the way I felt about his refusal.

We were due to close in three days. I needed to think of something else. When I checked in on Leeza to see how she was doing, she kept asking the same question over and over: "How did this happen?"

"Don't give up," I told her. "Keep picturing yourself inside that new loft. Meanwhile, I will think of something, I promise."

I tried to get myself past the stress of this sale with my dance classes, Advil, and the worry dolls Bette Mae gave me for my birthday. I found the small patterned pouch where I kept them in my dresser beneath my gold hoop earrings. There was a legend among the highland villages of Guatemala that if you had a problem, you could share it with these dolls. Here again, I used another ritual to access the powerful subconscious mind. I took one doll out from the quilted pouch and, closing my eyes, I placed all my concern for Leeza into this tiny object. After I was done I laid this doll underneath my pillow and asked God, the Universe, and my subconscious for help.

The next morning my headache was gone, but I still needed to replace my galloping, runaway thoughts with a solution. I took my meditation pillow and went to sit outside on the deck amidst my potted plants. I luxuriated in the briskness of morning air and delighted in the occasional ruby-throated hummingbird buzzing around. Maybe nature in its divine wisdom could help. I sat for twenty minutes when suddenly the face of a woman in my office flashed through my mind.

Stephanie Ahlberg, like me, was one of the top ten producers, and had had an incredibly good year. Maybe she would be willing to lend Leeza enough money for a second loan. I made the call. No dice. All her money was tied up in other investments. Before I hung up the phone, I asked, "By any chance, do you know anybody else in the office that might be willing to lend some money to my client? Leeza O'Reilly is really trustworthy and will pay back the loan no problem–I can assure you of that. Plus, she will agree to a good interest rate. If you know anyone who might be interested, Leeza and I would be eager to meet with them today." I was acutely aware of how little time we had.

Stephanie said she did not, and wished me good luck. As she started to hang up the phone she stopped short and said, "Wait a minute–maybe my mother would be willing to invest some of the money Father left her. Of course, the property would have to be appraised so she would be secure in her investment, but I could check it out for her. Let me find out if she would be willing to do it."

"Great," I said. "When do you think you can get back to me?" I hated to put the pressure on, because Stephanie was doing me a huge favor, but wanted her to know the parameters of the situation. "We're supposed to close in three days."

"Today–I'll call her today. When can I see the property?"

"Whenever you say–this is top priority."

"This afternoon?"

"This afternoon–just tell me what time works for you."

When Stephanie saw the property, she admitted South of Market was a bit marginal for her taste. I brought the comparable sales data and convinced her it was a good investment. With Stephanie's stamp of approval, her mother agreed to lend Leeza the money. I asked for a two-day extension to complete the paperwork. The seller was happy to work with us and we closed the following Tuesday. Leeza was there with two beautifully arranged flower bouquets–one for me and one for Stephanie. I still remember the vibrant orange color of the tiger lilies as if it was yesterday. I so appreciated Stephanie for helping that I made a donation to her theatre company (she had been an actress before she started in real estate) and I still attend her fundraisers.

I had worked my magic! But was it really? I thought about what had happened. Stephanie Ahlberg was one of the top agents in the office. It made perfect sense for me to call her and ask if she or someone she knew would have some money to lend. And if she did not, I could have asked other top producers in the office. But what was it that caused her face to appear in my consciousness? Who really knows exactly how our creative subconscious and rational conscious mind communicate with each other? What I now knew was that, if I stilled my mind long enough, I could achieve phenomenal results.

Lessons Learned from Chapter 6:

- MONITOR YOUR THOUGHTS The mind creates a reality by aligning the external universe with internal beliefs. Think of your thoughts as images being projected onto a big movie screen. The motion picture show is your life drama in which you are the writer, director and star actor—a reality show in which you can change the course of events at any time.
- COMBINE VISUALIZATION WITH DESIRE Before you begin a task, define the goal you want to achieve. Place all your energy, all your willpower, all your desire and all your passion behind that goal. Do you see it clearly? Now visualize the goal accomplished.
- LEARN TO FAIL EFFECTIVELY Use Criticism to Your Advantage. The Critical Inner Voice—or perhaps someone else's criticism—can be your friend, providing that it is not so critical that it hurts your self-esteem. Acknowledge that this inner critic is trying to help. Learn the lesson and then move on.
- ACCESS THE POWER OF YOUR SUBCONSCIOUS Rituals, being in nature, meditating, writing in a journal, or taking up a relaxing hobby, such as painting, gardening or cooking, can help you still your mind and access your subconscious. The creative subconscious mind can give you solutions that your rational conscious mind has not considered.
- GET OUT OF YOUR BOX We all want to hit the jackpot, win the lottery and make it rich quick, but life does not operate that way. Understand that success means having the courage, tenacity, self-confidence and discipline to do tasks that are difficult, inconvenient or uncomfortable.

7

OPTIMISM

Looking at the Bright Side

Pink Elephants in Purple Polka Dot Tutus

I was back in Tim's office doing my best to be positive while being surrounded by negativity. I kept repeating my mantra, *Short-Term Pessimism Long-Term Optimism,* whenever I started feeling blue, but it wasn't working. No, it wasn't Nettie this time–I stayed away from her–it was one of my clients. Henry Clemens was upset because the house I listed a few months earlier was not selling. Henry had been calling all hours of the day to complain. I confessed to Tim that my client was swearing at me and I was at a loss as to what to do.

Tim leaned back in his chair. "Did you show him all the ads we've been running and everything you've done to promote his home?"

"Of course, I've done all that," I bit my lip, trying not to cry. "But the house is a pig-sty and he won't clean it up. I guess he doesn't understand the importance of *'Showing a Home.'*"

"Well, I'll be happy to talk to him if you want. I want to tell you, though, I won't put up with any sort of abuse, and I am prepared to give him back the listing. Dealing with this type of personality is draining. How can you possibly be productive in your current state of mind?"

"You mean you may tell him we don't want to work with

him anymore?" I was feeling so distraught that such an approach had not even occurred to me.

Tim was surprised that I had not considered this alternative. "Personally, I feel your time will be much better spent promoting your other listings rather than working with a nutcase. You have business. It is great to be tenacious, but there is a point at which you have to set boundaries." When I didn't respond, he asked if I had ever heard of making lemonade out of lemons. "Why not look at this whole situation as a learning experience? Work only with those clients who understand that selling a home is a team effort and avoid these soapy dramas." Tim paused then added, "...which you seem to be involved in on a frequent basis."

"Well, isn't that the nature of real estate?" I asked, wondering if I was the only one with problem clients.

"It is, to some extent, but you seem to thrive on turmoil." Tim gave me a smile, but I could see the edges of his mouth beginning to quiver. He was losing patience with me.

It was hard to sell when feeling down in the dumps. I needed to do something to regain a sunnier outlook. Before I went to Tim, I had complained to Ted Johnson, a colleague, about my difficulty in dealing with the ups and downs of real estate. Ted suggested I take the Erhard Seminars Training (EST), which was all the rage in San Francisco at this time. As an experience-centered workshop, the purpose of "the Training" was to show participants how to achieve a sense of personal power in their lives–to be the best they could be.

"But aren't EST and all those human potential movements, like Lifespring and Actualizations, just cults?" I asked.

"Some people call these trainings Fast Food Enlightenment," Ted laughed. "But Paula, you can make it into whatever you want it to be. The experience of improving your psychological outlook belongs to you. Just take the EST teachings that you relate to and leave the rest behind."

I knew that EST had enabled Ted to leave a tedious nine-to-five job and get into sales, or so he claimed. That, coupled with Tim's disappointment, was enough to catapult me into action. I signed up for a two-weekend seminar. If EST could help change my dismal view of what was happening, I figured it would be worth the time and energy I spent.

Sure enough, as soon as I arrived, a middle-aged man with slicked back hair introduced himself as William Reese and gave us a long list of rules to follow: no eating, drinking, chewing gum, cross talking or unauthorized breaks. This might mean sitting in the same chair for four hours at a time. Anyone who disagreed with these rules was allowed to voice their case. Several did. Some people resisted being told what to do. Some had issues with trust. Some had medical problems and were asked to see the support people in the back of the room.

The whole process seemed to be going along at a snail's pace. I checked my watch. It was already past noon and we were still dealing with logistics. Getting restless, I wondered when this seminar would ever get started. I was thrilled when a gray-haired gent asked if we could please move on, because we were wasting valuable time. Mr. Reese, the seminar leader, explained we all needed to be in agreement for this process to work.

"But I'm getting bored," the man said.

"So?" Mr. Reese said. "Boredom is just a passing emotion. Stay with it and you will notice it changes into something else."

The man continued, "I was promised this seminar would change my life and nothing's happening."

"That's an interesting perspective," Mr. Reese said. "From up here it seems a lot of stuff is happening out there." He pointed to the audience. "Are any of you feeling bored?" About a third of us raised our hands.

"Who is feeling angry?" Another third.

"Sad?" A few hands went up.

"Resentful?" More hands.

"Joyful?" Amazingly, a few more hands went up.

Who could be happy, I wondered, when we had all been sitting here since nine in the morning in rigid metal-backed folding chairs talking about dumb logistics? It was another hour before all of us agreed on the rules of how the seminar would be run. We finally broke for lunch in small groups. We were sent to neighborhood places to get to know one another. Our only instruction was that we were to speak honestly. I ended up with a couple who whispered together all through lunch about scoring some marijuana. Not being a toker myself, I smiled and nodded now and again, but felt left out. As we left the restaurant, I told them how ignored I felt.

"I made several attempts of including you in the conversation," the woman said, "but, Nooooo, you just sat there."

This was not the first time I had felt excluded. I wondered, why couldn't I belong? All I wanted was to be included in the conversation. An endless tape of how I was not good enough began playing over and over in my mind. I remembered Henry Clemens and how badly I had allowed him to treat me. I felt like a doormat. I was feeling uncomfortable and wanted to get up and leave. Instead, I reminded myself about why I was here–to be more positive as a sales person and as an individual. I turned my attention back to Mr. Reese at the front of the room.

"Just be aware that thoughts and feelings are going in and out of our consciousness all the time, but it is not who we are," Mr. Reese said.

A girl in the front in a bright yellow top said, "You instructed us to feel our feelings. Now you are telling us feelings are not important. It doesn't make any sense." My sentiment exactly. I took time from my hectic schedule to listen to this nonsense?

"I never said to ignore your feelings, because if you do, they will surface one way or another–usually at the most inappropriate times. What I said was, 'Your feelings are not *all* you are.' For instance, if you have a feeling that people are out to get you, that's all it is: a feeling. If you feel you don't belong, that is all it is–a feeling of not belonging. I repeat–a feeling is NOT all you are. You are bigger than that. Change your feelings and, voilà, your reality changes. It is really that simple."

Hmmm. I leaned forward in my chair now, my ears perked, ready to listen. A short muscular man with tattooed arms asked for the microphone. "What about all the bad things that happen to us? Are you saying all we have to do is change our feelings about what has happened to us?"

"Yes. Once you are able to change your feelings about your experiences, your reality will change."

The man interrupted and was beginning to sound angry, "What about poverty, war and injustice? We're just supposed to feel okay about these things?"

"What I am saying is that we all see the world through our own filters–and whatever we focus on becomes our reality." Mr. Reese cast a long lingering look outward, sweeping his gaze to include everyone in the room, "Focus on what you want. Let go of everything else." So we just accepted the bad things in life? That didn't make any sense to me.

"Let me explain this concept another way," he said next. "Don't imagine a pink elephant in a white tutu with purple polka dots doing a belly dance. What do you see?"

"A pink elephant in a white tutu with purple polka dots doing a belly dance," the audience yelled back.

"Exactly. The mind cannot decipher the negative. It ignores the Don't and hones in on the elephant in the tutu. So focus on what you want to feel, not on what you don't want."

"But I don't know what it is I want," the girl in the yellow top said.

"Well, you better figure it out. You only have one life and you are the rudder of your ship. Only you can change your life."

I decided to concentrate on all the people who appreciated me, such as Tim, Ted, Bette Mae and Mary Moeller. I decided not to waste energy on people like my whining client, Henry Clemens, or the woman at lunch who would not acknowledge me. With this new attitude, I felt more in control of my life. My emotion of despair changed almost instantly to one of hope, excitement and anticipation to find new, more cooperative clients.

Because of my EST transformation, I decided to be captain of my ship and focused on remaining positive, upbeat and optimistic. One night a handful of us were working late when Tim Brown emerged from his office waving a piece of paper in the air. "I just got a call from a couple in Nebraska who read *The Real Estate Times* and say they want to buy this house they saw advertised. Since they haven't even seen the property, this could be a waste of your time, but does anyone want this lead?"

Jumping Back In With Both Feet–Firmly Planted

Since I had let Harry Clemens go, my schedule had freed up. I was ready for a Hot New Buyer. I was not the same pessimistic person I was a few weeks earlier. My hand was up in a flash and, before I knew it, I was taking the paper out of Tim's hand and walking back to my desk. Surprisingly, none of the other agents were the least bit interested.

Dan and Kathy Plunket arrived in San Francisco five days later. I picked them up at the airport. They were a middle-aged couple with middle-age spreads, dressed in polyester with a matching sunny but naïve disposition. They had booked rooms at the YMCA in the Tenderloin District of downtown and wanted me to take them there.

"Are you sure that's where you want to be?" I asked. The Tenderloin, as I described earlier, was one of San Francisco's poorest and most crime-ridden parts of town. "I don't think it's that safe there," I added.

"Listen Pauline–your name's Pauline right? You seem like a nice young lady, but my lovely wife and I have traveled to lots of cities. We always stay at the YMCA. It's affordable, they have good facilities and the people there are always helpful to new people in town."

"The name is Paula, actually." I paused.

I was proud of my city, but not all parts of it. The Tenderloin, in spite of it being in the theatre district, was the ugly underbelly. "I'm afraid you'll be disappointed with our YMCA's location."

"Don't worry. We're savvy travelers, Pauline… er… Paula."

"Fine," I said, dropping the subject, I knew I could not win. "So when do you want to see this property you called in on?"

"You mean the property we are going to buy?"

"Well, you haven't even seen it yet."

Kathy, the lovely wife, piped up. "Dan has an uncanny sense of intuition. He is confident that this is the home for us."

"Really?" I said. "How long have you lived in Nebraska?" I asked.

"Our whole life. We are ready for a change."

"Hmmm," I said.

"Why don't we take a look at it tomorrow? Today we want to get situated and do some sightseeing."

"Fine," I said. "I'll call you tomorrow morning at nine."

"Why don't you make it eleven? We like to sleep in."

"No problem," I said, wondering if these people were real or what. Be positive, I told myself, give them a chance.

It was still dark outside when my alarm went off the following morning. Damn! I must have set it by mistake. I wiped the sleepiness out of my eyes and reached for my clock, realizing it was the telephone–not my alarm–that had gone off. I answered. "Hello?"

"Pauline. It's Dan Plunket."

"Good morning, Dan," I said, muffling a yawn. "What can I do for you? I thought you said you like to sleep in? What time is it anyway?"

"It's six in the morning and the place has bedbugs."

"What?!" I said. Now I was fully upright, sitting in bed.

"You need to find us another hotel, Pauline, and fast!"

"Oh, sure. Okay."

"And we don't want to pay more than $70 a night."

"Okay, yeah. I'll see what I can do." I hung up the phone, took a shower and started planning. Too early to call anyone for recommendations. I'd scour the yellow pages instead.

Several frustrating calls later I found a modest hotel which was clean and located in a better neighborhood.

"You'll have to cough up another $15 a night," I said when I called them back. Dan and Kathy agreed. That was a hopeful sign. Maybe they had more money than it appeared. Maybe they were just frugal people. I picked them up and got them situated at their new hotel. They were hungry and wanted to stop for breakfast.

"My treat, Pauline," Dan said.

I didn't correct him, figuring with these clients I'd just have to accept my new name. After breakfast we went to take a look at the "deal of the century"–the property they called on. I did not have much hope that this property was the one for them, but that was something for them to determine, not me. I did want to prepare them, however, so before we reached our destination, I said, "For this price, it must be a tear down."

"Don't worry," the lovely wife said, "Dan is real handy."

The house needed a new foundation, smelled of mold, and was in Visitation Valley, a less than desirable location bordering foggy Daly City. Not a region I would ever consider selling in. But I held my tongue. This was something for Dan and his wife to figure out.

"This isn't it," Dan said firmly. "What else can you show us?"

The Plunkets had not been financially qualified, so we headed to my office, where I started calling lenders. This was the best way I had learned to separate the flakes from the real buyers. Blake Roberts agreed to meet with them, but at his office, as he had a busy day packed with appointments. Fortunately, it was just a short drive away. We hopped in the car again. Meanwhile, Dan was perusing a copy of *Homes and*

Land magazine and has circled several properties he wanted to see. I noticed one of the homes he had circled was in Crocker Amazon–again in the south part of San Francisco. However, unlike Visitation Valley, which had some hardcore projects, it was a close-knit, community-oriented neighborhood with decent weather, charming bungalows and low crime statistics. Most of the locals didn't even know it existed, so it was more affordable than most other districts in San Francisco.

"The Plunkets qualify, no problem," Blake said after going over the numbers. "Plus, they can go up another $20,000."

"That is great news," I said and we were off–back in the car again, heading to the house Dan circled in the magazine.

The Mission style stucco house was a two bedroom, one bath home with a basement room behind the garage. It had not been lived in for several years and had lots of deferred maintenance–loose door knobs, a leaky roof and windows, and cracked plaster. But the house got great light, had a big backyard, a huge lower level that could be developed, plus it was on a great pride-of-ownership street.

"Okay, then," Dan said. "Let's put in an offer."

"Are you sure? You just got here and saw only two properties."

The lovely wife smiled. "When Dan says 'Go for it' he means it. I trust his judgment completely."

We wrote an offer $15,000 under asking and it was accepted by the heirs without a counter. We closed in a record fifteen days. I would not call the Plunkets difficult clients, but they certainly were quirky. My ability to not judge them (and the staggering temptation to do so!) in spite of all their weird behavior made this a smooth and rewarding transaction. Because the Plunkets bought so quickly, it was easy for me to remain upbeat and positive. However, real estate got much more challenging when I had to hold onto a cheerful attitude with a difficult client for months on end. Like the time Tosca Giorgi and I represented Jack Krimpton in the sale of his beloved Victorian in Haight-Ashbury.

The Truth Can Hurt, But It's All You've Got at the End of the Day

Tosca worked in my office and, as luck would have it, we both were referred to Jack. I could have looked at this situation as a glass half empty, but after EST I saw it as an opportunity. Instead of competing for the listing, we joined forces. Tosca lived in the Haight-Ashbury neighborhood and knew intricacies about the area that I did not know. She was also much more laid back in style than I was. I found her softness to be complementary to my high energy. Because of our balanced partnership, Jack chose us as a team out of all the agents he interviewed.

Jack Krimpton was a jolly, rotund sort of fellow, almost as wide as he was tall, with full cheeks and a large jowl that jiggled when he laughed. After several months without any offers, Dania Bellington, a buyer's agent, told me her clients were considering writing an offer. Dania cautioned me that it would be a low offer since the house needed some cosmetics. I encouraged Dania, thinking a low offer was better than none. I was taken by surprise when my jovial seller reacted so negatively.

I showed Jack the MLS statistics on the houses that had sold over the last six months, as well as the printouts of similar houses currently listed in the neighborhood. "Look here at the house you mentioned on Ashbury Street which sold for one million, five hundred and fifty thousand," I explained. "It was remodeled with a new custom kitchen and double paned windows, refinished hardwood floors..."

"Are you saying that the house on Ashbury is a better house than mine?"

I continued. "No, what we're saying is..." Tell-tale sweat began to collect on my forehead, "most buyers want something that is more in style right now...like granite countertop kitchens with Viking stoves and Subzero refrigerators and marble baths with Grohe fixtures..."

"So you're saying my tiled kitchen is passé?"

"That isn't exactly what we're saying... what we're saying is... " My mind was working in high gear to rephrase the facts in a manner that would not offend Jack. "... people's tastes change. Right now buyers want a more modern, sleek look than what you have here."

"All that may be true, but my house is much bigger than theirs," Jack said.

"So you think your house is much bigger?" Tosca asked.

"Yes," was his firm reply.

"The tax assessor lists your property as the same square footage of the house that sold," I said, looking up from our file, which stated the number of rooms, year built, and the square footage of Jack's house. Jack still insisted his house was bigger.

"During your ownership did you add on?" I asked. I did not think he had, because this was a typical Victorian floor plan with a double parlor, dining room and kitchen on the main floor with the bedrooms and baths on the second floor.

"No," Jack answered. "Why do you ask?"

"That could be the reason for the discrepancy," I answered.

"Well, perhaps, the tax assessor information is just incorrect," Tosca said, adding fuel to Jack's argument.

Not saying anything would have been a better approach. As I learned years back–do not automatically agree with clients, because then it will be hard for them to see the whole picture. As a seller, Jack had his perspective, but to come to an agreement, he would need to see the buyer's point of view as well. But Tosca and I had a partnership and I could not go against what she had just said.

I gathered my composure and tried another approach. "Six months ago, the interest rate was also 1% less than it is now," I said.

"That should have nothing to do with it," Jack responded, his cheeks flushing a bright red.

"But to a buyer it makes a difference in their monthly payment." I pulled out my Hewlett Packard calculator and running the amortization formula, I showed him the difference. "Right now the payment on $1,200,000 at 8.5% was $9,583. Six months ago it was only $8,338 which was a difference of $1245 a month." I now multiplied the last figure by twelve and then by thirty. "So a buyer will have to pay almost $15,000 more a year and over thirty years that amount is $450,000."

Jack shook his head, claiming his property was worth every cent of the asking price.

Tosca, playing the good cop, asked, "So what do you want us to do?"

"I think I've heard enough for today." Jack answered. "Let's talk tomorrow."

I made my way to the door and said something light and funny. Jack did not respond nor did he shake my hand, which was our custom. Out of the corner of my eye I noticed him offer his hand to Tosca. On my way back to the office, I reviewed how things went–certainly not as well as I had hoped. Giving Jack facts and figures should help him, or any seller, make a sound decision, but it was not enough. Facts did not address the emotional turmoil he was feeling on leaving a home he had lived in for almost thirty years. Jack just could not see all the deferred maintenance his house needed and wanted to believe that his house was every bit as good as the house with improvements that sold for a million and a half.

Not feeling in the mood to talk to anybody, I turned the car around and headed home. I needed some downtime. Once home, I made a long list of everything I had accomplished so far that year. I posted it on my refrigerator door:

- *Closed Escrows*:
  1. *222 States*
  2. *345 Locust*
  3. *601 Van Ness #1130*
  4. *924 Church Street*
  5. *260 Ripley*
  6. *25 Medau*
  7. *1220 Jones #601*
  8. *2077 Jackson #107*
  9. *831 Mason*
- *Bought 3 Series Convertible BMW with leather seats*
- *Came in First in Tango, Waltz, Foxtrot and Second In Quickstep and West Coast Swing in Winter Ballroom Dance Festival*
- *Landscaped my backyard*
- *Dating Wayne Roberts, my sexy dance teacher*

Whenever my mind started acting up, I looked at the list,

reminding myself that, overall, things were pretty good. Later that evening, Tosca called.

"I noticed you weren't in the office this afternoon. Is everything okay?" she asked.

I told her I was fine–just a bit tired.

"Is it okay if I offer a suggestion?" she asked. Her voice was tentative.

"Of course," I said, preparing myself not to become defensive.

"You looked hurt today when Jack didn't shake your hand. You didn't take it personally, did you?"

"I tried my best not to, but it did hurt my feelings," I said.

"Paula, you know it has nothing to do with you. Jack is upset because he knows he is not going to get the price he wanted. Since you were the one who presented the offer, he is trying to find fault with you."

"I know, I know," I said. And I did know.

I thought about other instances when I had taken a professional situation personally. Just the previous spring I was working with a couple who put an offer on a house that everyone else was vying for. We did not win the bid and the wife was brokenhearted. I sat with her for over an hour and, remembering EST, suggested she envision a new house that was just as nice–or better–than the one she lost out on. The couple eventually moved past their disappointment, but it was a tough go for them and for me. Five weeks later, they were out looking at property with me. But when we lost out on the second house as well, the couple told me they wanted to start fresh with someone else. It did not matter that I explained it was a fast-moving market and that it might take several attempts before we consummated a deal. They still blamed me.

After all my hard work, I was devastated. But then I did what all good salespeople do–I focused on the next client.

After the phone call with Tosca, I realized that telling the truth to clients was necessary but, at the same time, clients wanted you to be hopeful, positive and optimistic. Sure Jack was disappointed, but I would not let his attitude affect me. The following morning I was prepared to jump back into the real estate melee. It was a good thing, too, because my day was packed with appointments. When I got stuck in traffic, I called Jack. Hopefully, a relaxing evening and a good night's rest would have given him a chance to process the offer.

"Have you thought about what price you'd like the buyer to come up to?" I asked, assuming he wanted to negotiate.

"Paula, this buyer has no idea how special my house is," Jack said, sliding into his usual diatribe. "I've decided not to counter–the price is way too low."

"Really?" I reminded myself that to get Jack's cooperation he needed to feel like he had been heard. I rephrased what he just said into a question. "So you think the price is too low?"

"Yes."

"Jack, what makes you think the price is too low?" I asked, hoping he would reexamine his reasoning.

He did not answer and I did not answer for him. Silence was golden. An old but very useful negotiating tool. I remembered what Tosca told me once–the reason we had two ears and one mouth was because we were supposed to listen twice as much as we talk. When I arrived at the office, I called Dania, the buyer's agent. "Jack is considering your offer, but he is still digesting the low price," I told her.

"When is he planning to counter us?" she asked.

"He's just not ready to respond to you yet," I replied,

knowing this was what happens when buyers' offers were too low. She asked me if Jack was upset with them. I didn't like to set up either party as "Bad" or "the Enemy" so I explained that Jack was hoping for a better price than what they offered, adding, "Dania, realize that he is having a hard time letting go. This may take some time. Let's give him a few more days and I'll do my best to get him to respond."

"Truthfully, Paula, I don't know if my buyers will wait that long. They may start to cool."

Time is of the essence, as it said in the contract that Paul Newell had shoved in front of my face so long ago (or so it seemed) back in my Laguna Beach days, and Jack was stalling. However, I also knew these buyers were desperate for a home, having just had a baby. On the off chance that these buyers simply had to have this house, I suggested to Dania that they put in another offer.

"Why should we do that? The seller is supposed to respond to us!"

"You're right, that is how it is usually done, but Jack is being a bit slow in reacting. I don't want your buyers to get discouraged. If we could just keep the communication lines open–even if you come up only ten thousand dollars–maybe it will be the push Jack needs. Just because his ego is getting in the way of this sale, does not mean you can't do something."

"I don't think we'll do that," Dania answered curtly. "My buyers don't want the property that badly."

It bothered me when agents answered for their clients without consulting with them first. One never knows what clients will do. "It doesn't hurt to ask," I said, hoping she would reconsider. She refused. Her unwillingness to explore other options gave me only one choice. Go back to Jack and beg for a counter. In spite of all my pleading and sound arguments, Jack would not respond–even with no other potential offers on the horizon.

"I've moved on," he said. "You should too."

I broke the disappointing news to Dania and she delivered the *fait accompli*–the buyers were putting an offer on their second choice. Tosca and I still had six weeks left on the listing. We made an appointment with Jack to discuss what was next. I was not afraid to ask the direct question to Jack–which both Tosca and I wanted to know: *Are you sure you want to sell?* If Jack continued to be unreasonable, we needed to focus on other clients who would use our help and expertise to bring a sale to fruition. Jack assured both of us he did indeed want to sell. We met with him and brainstormed how to get more agents and their clients to come take another look. We had already held Sunday open houses, broker tours and placed plenty of ads in local newspapers and magazines. We decided to host an afternoon twilight tour with wine and cheese.

"We'll put up plenty of signs to get people driving home from work, and send out invitations to all the top agents," was my suggestion.

Jack was caught up in our optimism and had forgotten all about the past few days. "Now you're talking! I have a magnificent watercolor of the exterior, why don't we use that for the invitations?"

Tosca suggested that the attendees sign in a guest book. There would be a place for them to put comments about whether they think the house was a possibility. "That way, any negative feedback will be coming directly from the prospective purchasers so Jack can't get mad at us," Tosca whispered to me while we were alone.

"That's a great idea," I whispered back. Now it would be hard for Jack to deny the truth of what we had been telling him all along.

The wine and cheese preview did not bring a buyer, but it did show Jack that we were on his side. We left the clients' remarks with him, deciding it was best for him to review their comments in private. In that way, he could absorb what the buyers were really thinking, save face and not put the blame on us. What to do next? We had done extensive marketing for four months with only one low offer. Anyone who was looking in the million-and-a-half price range had already seen the home.

"We have given Jack the reasons why his house isn't selling," I said to Tosca, "but he has trouble hearing the truth. Both of us have been patient and listened to his concerns, but wishing and hoping won't change the facts. The market has spoken. We need for him to agree to a significant price reduction."

We had had the listing with Jack for four months now and it was about to expire. We asked for a three-month extension with a ten percent price reduction. Anything less would have no effect. Multiple Listing Statistics showed buyers felt comfortable offering no more than 5% lower than the asking price. It was the rare case when they would come in with a greater discount. We had no expectation of whether Jack would agree, but we remained positive, knowing if this transaction did not come to pass, another one would fill its place.

Jack was tired of keeping his house spotless, annoyed that he had to be gone every Tuesday and Sunday afternoon for open houses. He was just plain anxious to move on with his life. "Maybe I should have taken the first offer," he said when we told him our plan to reduce.

"First offers are often the best," I said, "and at the same time we understand your reluctance. You wanted to be absolutely sure that we had fully marketed the house. The best scenario now would be if we reduce the price significantly so that the Broker community will take notice. Then hopefully we will get multiple showings and maybe even multiple offers."

"Meaning," Tosca added, "we may get you a higher price when two people start bidding on your home."

"Why don't we call all the agents who have toured the property about the price reduction and tell them you are really motivated to sell. That way maybe a previous buyer is still out there who saw the property, but felt he couldn't afford it."

"Will you also carry a small second loan?" Tosca asked. "That will also help some buyers who don't have the 20% down payment."

"Well, I don't need all my money right now," Jack said. "If it helps me sell, I'll do it."

I took out my Hewlett Packard calculator. "If we reduce to $1,350,000, a ten percent second loan at 9% with interest only payment would be $12,150 a year. Over ten years it would be a total of $121,500 in your pocket."

"Hmm," Jack said. "You are two smart gals. That would mean I would be getting just about what I wanted in the first place. Fine. Sign me up for the extension and price reduction. Just promise me you'll call all the agents and let them know we reduced."

Both Tosca and I answered at once, "We promise!"

That week we got several showings. An agent who had shown Jack's home twice to the same client told me she might be bringing in an offer. On a whim, I called Dania

Bellington, the agent who brought in the first offer. I knew her client had to sell a property before they bought one–so maybe this buyer was still around. Once they heard that someone else was considering buying, that might spike their interest. My hunch proved to be correct. Their second choice fell through, because Dania's buyer couldn't sell their home in time. Knowing another party was interested geared them into action. They offered $100,000 more than their initial offer and, to counteract the sting of the higher price, asked Jack to carry a ten percent loan. Jack ended up getting more than he expected and was one happy camper. He still sends me referrals to this day.

Lessons Learned from Chapter 7:

- CHOOSE A NEW PERSPECTIVE The way we look at things affects our reality. If you are excited, hopeful and motivated, that is a perspective which will bring good results. Recognize you can change the way you view an event at any time.
- ACCEPT PEOPLE'S IDIOSYNCRACIES Remember that decisions involving money can be stressful and you may witness weird behavioral styles. Remain positive, gracious and accepting–and nonjudgmental.
- DO NOT TAKE THINGS PERSONALLY People view events from their own belief systems such that what they think and say, and how they react, is much more about them than it is about you. Talk about your hurt, disappointment, resentment or whatever other feelings you may have with a supportive person in your life in order to let go of the negative and focus on the positive.
- PUT THE ZING BACK INTO BUSINESS If you are feeling bored, depressed or unmotivated, do something different. Do not settle for familiar routine. Instead, think outside the box, taking advantage of opportunities to make your dreams a reality.

8

EMPATHY

Understanding Others

In Real Estate Surprise is a Four-Letter Word

At the end of my first year of real estate in San Francisco, I was the number one agent in our office. Confronting my fears, disciplining my mind, keeping positive and developing a strong sense of self helped me change destructive patterns into success stories. No one cared that I was driving a Chevette and, not being from California, didn't know anyone.

Tina Linstrom, a part-time agent in my office, wanted me to represent her and her husband in the sale of a house they just built. Tina was a tiny woman in her early forties, perky and upbeat. Her husband was a handsome, big Swede with thick, wavy blonde hair and massive hands, reminding me of Paul Bunyan. He was a licensed contractor and appropriately nicknamed Butch. Despite the fact that she was a third his size, Tina was the decision maker so I easily got the listing. They were a fun and outgoing couple. I was excited, thinking this would be an easy, slam-dunk transaction.

A few months into the marketing, we obtained an offer on a cold, rainy night in November. Tina asked if I could meet them at their home. It was better to meet clients at the office, but wanting to please her, I agreed. Besides, I told myself, this was a spec home (a home they built for profit) and Tina and Butch Linstrom were sophisticated sellers.

Because it was the first heavy rain of the season, the roads were slick and there was a prolonged traffic backup. Running late, I was beginning to regret my decision. Not only was her house in an inconvenient location, but I wouldn't have access to a copying machine and any forms I might need. Through the pouring rain, black night and dimly lit streets I strained to find the house number I had jotted down in my planner.

After circling the block several times, I found their majestic contemporary home in Golden Gate Heights with spectacular views of the famous bridge. I glanced at my watch as I grabbed my umbrella. I made a hasty dash for the door, but still got drenched. Dripping wet, I rang the doorbell.

Tina answered and ushered me inside. While taking off my raincoat, I could hear talking in the background. The other agent had arrived before me. Damn! Tina introduced me to Ming Le, whom I had spoken to briefly over the phone that morning. Shouldn't it have been the other way around? Me introducing Ming Le to my clients?

We gathered around the dining table as Ming Le described her client–a young Asian family for whom the newly constructed home was perfect for their three children, and it was close to their family business, a Laundromat in Noe Valley. Since the buyers were not salaried employees, I was a bit concerned over whether they could qualify. However, Ming Le handed us each a copy of their prequalification letter, and all appeared to be in order. I noticed Tina and Butch shifting in their seats. I needed to move this process along. I extended my hand and asked for the contract. Ming Le handed it over as she explained the minor contingencies. My eyes scanned downward, searching for the purchase price and was as unprepared as Tina and Butch were when we saw it.

Tina, unable to hide her disappointment, gave Ming Le a cold hard stare. "How could you be a guest in my house and insult me like this?" She started to tear her copy of the contract in tiny pieces and threw the ragged shreds on the table. I was speechless, unable to comprehend what was happening to my good-natured colleague. Butch put his arm around his wife and gave me a reproachful look. Starting to sob, Tina pointed to the door, asking Ming Le to get the hell out of her house.

I followed, whispering a hollowed regret with a promise that I would call her tomorrow. I hesitated in the entryway, taking a deep breath to calm myself as I turned around to face the Linstroms, wondering what awaited me. I was in a foggy haze as I made it back to the dining room and sat down.

Tina had put her head in her hands and wouldn't look at me. Butch shook his head as he left the room. I did my best to remain cool and collected, all the while feeling my blouse clinging to my back with sticky perspiration. Surely, deep circles of water stains were forming underneath my armpits. I took a tiny sip from my water glass, passing the time in deadening silence. Tina looked up at me with a tear-stained face. "How could you have allowed this to happen? Butch spent two years of his life designing and building that house. What do you take us for–fools?" I mumbled a few words about how I was so excited to have received the offer that I did not think of asking for the details. My excuse had little effect on Tina. Her face was squished up in pain as if she just got hit by a fast volleyball.

I remembered what Paul Newell told me when I first started. Give clients a good war story of what happened in the past and what you learned. People learn from stories. But I could not think of any. I was too new in the business. There's also the three F's that work well in negotiating. The three F's are... are... I'm a freaky', f—- failure! *No, think positive,* I told myself. All was not yet lost. I racked my brain. What are the three F's? Something about *feeling.* That had always been the hardest part for me–the empathy–understanding how other people felt. Feeling... Feeling... aah! Now I remember! *Feel, Felt, Found!*

"I understand how you must be feeling," I said, still groping for what to say next. "I've felt that way before."

"What do you mean you know how I'm feeling?" Tina's voice sounded accusatory. Maybe she knew I was just reciting some sort of sales script. "Exactly what is it I'm feeling?"

"Well... aah... you must be feeling hurt and aah... betrayed... Yes, betrayed." I'd hit a deep core truth. Tell the truth–even if it makes you look bad–something Dad preached as well as the EST trainer. "Because... because... I didn't take care of you well enough." There. I said it. The truth was now out in the open. "I should have prepared you for the low offering price."

Tina's face softened slightly, but her words did not. "It's over and done. I'm going to bed now." She stood up.

Feel, Felt, Found. What's the found?? I'm about to lose her. What's the found?

"I've found that... " I hesitate, "it's... aah... not good to... aah... give up too quickly." Yeah, that's right... "Let's not give up quite yet. Let's give them another chance."

Tina turned sharply around. "Paula, are you crazy? We're miles apart–Miles!"

"Yeah, I know," I said, forming the words slowly as they came to my head. "You're probably right–these buyers probably won't come up to our price–but what if we're wrong? That's right, Tina. What if you and I are wrong? What if they really want the house and have to have it? We will never know unless we ask."

"Goodnight, Paula."

I stayed glued to where I sat even when she motioned for me to get up. Tina glared at me in amazement. "Whose side are you on anyway?"

"One thing we know for sure is if we don't give them a counter, we definitely won't have a sale." I continued, knowing I was on to something. "Some of this is my fault. I should have spoken to the agent ahead of time and found out more about the offer so I could have prepared you. But, Tina, let's not take my mistake out on these buyers. It won't cost us anything–just a couple of minutes. It is worth taking the time to write something up, don't you think?" I sat with my hands folded neatly in my lap and waited.

Tina sat back down. The room was so quiet that I was tempted to fill the space with more talking, but that would interrupt the process that Tina was going through–trying to figure out what to do next. I stayed with my uncomfortable feelings, knowing that this was one of the main reasons salespeople were paid so well. Butch looked in from the kitchen where he had escaped during his wife's tirade. He was also waiting.

"Okay. I'll do it. Just hurry and write it up. Butch, you can come in now. We're giving them a counter."

The next day I delivered Ming Le a verbal apology and a written counteroffer. After waffling back and forth for a few days, her clients finally agreed to all the terms we asked, giving proof that *it's not over till it's over.*

After this experience, I now made it a point to explain to sellers that when a buyer's agent presents an offer, they must try to focus only on the terms of the offer. If price is mentioned, they should not take what the agent says personally. "We can discuss value between us when the agent leaves," I would tell them. "What we do not want to do is verbal volleying back and forth with the other agent, who is only trying to represent her buyers in getting them the best possible price."

I also no longer made presentations at sellers' homes where they were liable to get too emotional. Even if the homeowners were motivated to sell, they were letting go of something that had a lot of meaning to them, often for a long period of time. Who knew if they would be as happy in their new homes, or in their new cities if they were relocating? Maybe they had to prematurely sell for financial reasons. Or maybe they were getting a divorce. Or their children had grown and left. Whatever their reason for selling, sellers would most likely have conflicting feelings.

In addition, I made light of the bidding process, comparing it to a game of poker–one party makes a move, then the other, and so on. Simply put, you've got to know when to hold, when to fold and when to walk away.

Minimizing the Seller's Stress

Cindy Wilson was pretty, personable and smart, yet she had a hard time making enough commissions to pay her bills. She had been selling real estate for over fifteen years and read all the positive thinking books she could get her hands on, took all the newest seminars, and understood the basic principles of selling. But Cindy just couldn't seem to close the sale. In my eight-week training session, I observed that

Cindy talked too much and too often, appearing desperate. Coming from a strict traditional Greek family, Cindy confided to me that she had a strong need to be liked, but sales was about focusing on clients' wants and interests and not about what we needed. When she got a floor call from a man who wanted to sell his home in the Inner Sunset near Golden Gate Park, she asked me to help. It was a Marina Style, built in the twenties, and showing the beginning signs of wear and tear. In other words, it needed a paint job and maybe a new roof. Mr. Chase greeted us at the door with a quick handshake. My guess was he was his eighties and now needed a retirement home. We started in the garage first and worked our way up. He showed us the burglar alarm system, the circuit breakers and the washer and dryer. We both nodded our heads as he explained when they were installed and their warranties. Realizing we needed to connect with Mr. Chase on a more personal level, I made my way past packed cardboard boxes to the oil paintings stacked along the sidewall of the garage. "Mr. Chase, did you paint all of these?"

"My late wife, may she rest in peace, was the artist of the family." He gingerly picked up one of the paintings and showed it to us. "This is one of the many bridges in Shanghai. Notice how Rose was able to catch the shadows of the afternoon sun. Just look at the detail. Every time I study this painting I see something new. She was quite a gal, my wife."

Cindy was the first to speak. "One of my girlfriends is a flight attendant and she raves about her visits to Shanghai. What is it about the city that people like so much?"

Perfect! Even though Cindy had never been to Asia, she came from curiosity and asked an open-ended question to establish rapport. With eyes bright and shining, Mr. Chase showed us a few more paintings as he described the background story of each one. When there was a lull in the conversation, I pointed to the large bolts in the mudsill partially hidden by the boxes.

"I see you have had some seismic work done recently–a buyer is going to love to see that! And look at how close the studs are–they just don't make houses like this anymore."

Mr. Chase continued to expound on the many virtues of his home as we took notes and listened for the reason he was selling. Since he also had a rental unit, I asked if the house and apartment were separately metered.

"Oh, yes, and we have 220 amp service to the kitchen and laundry room. Both units also have their own hot water heaters and forced air furnaces, which are periodically checked and maintained."

Realizing that the conversation was becoming too serious, I glanced around the garage until my eyes landed on a tennis racket. "So, I see you play tennis?"

Mr. Chase's eyes brightened once again. "It's such a great exercise running up and down the court–even though I don't play that much anymore." He went into detail about the technicalities of the game.

I found myself nodding, recalling the time in the seventies when Billie Jean King beat Bobby Riggs in that famous challenge match. I made a joke about it and Mr. Chase laughed, outwardly pleased that I had taken an interest in his much beloved sport.

"Any place close by where you can play?" I asked, thinking this might also be a selling point.

"Yeah, by the high school–near the new Starbucks."

I jotted down both these items as Cindy described her morning walks around Stern Lake, which she found exhilarating. They continued talking about their exercise routines as we made our way up to the main part of the house. Although neither Cindy nor I were artists, had ever been to

Asia or played tennis, we were well on our way to forming a bond with a man whom we just met.

During the rest of the tour, I made sure I asked four critical questions in between our casual chit-chatting:

Why are you planning to move? This question weeds out the Not So Motivated Sellers from the Real Ones.

What's your timetable? This also helps to qualify how motivated a seller is.

How many agents are you interviewing? If I felt that a seller wouldn't be offended, I asked who they were. If they didn't want to share the name, they would usually share the name of the company. Then I would know who my competition was and how to better strategize.

What qualities are you looking for in an agent? I did not understand why more salespeople didn't ask this important question. When asked, most clients would tell you what their expectations were. Then in the second meeting you could mirror back what they told you.

Before we left, we sat down at the kitchen table and showed Mr. Chase samples of our company's advertising and history as well as background information on ourselves and a pricing and staging video. "We'll leave this for you to review at your leisure," I said. This accomplished three things–it informed him of our qualifications without boasting, educated him on how to get the highest price, and gave us a reason to meet with him again, if only to pick up the video. Of course, Mr. Chase asked the inevitable question every seller wanted to know–"What do you think my house is worth?"

I hesitated to give him a number. Almost all sellers have a price in mind. When you came in too low, it was hard to backpedal. Even though sellers typically claim they do not choose an agent on price, they often do. I had lost many sales being right instead of listening to sellers' expectations. I rephrased his question and tossed it back to him. "Well, Mr. Chase, do you have any idea what your home's worth?"

"At least what the neighboring homes are selling for plus some. So a million three is my guess. But what do you think? You're the expert."

One meeting was usually not enough time to establish a bonding rapport. We were just getting to know each other. If we gave him a reply right now, we might not have the opportunity to meet with him again. I thought carefully before I responded.

"Mr. Chase, your property is a valuable asset and this question deserves some thoughtful consideration. Why don't Cindy and I go back to the office and do a market analysis for you?" To soften my response I made sure I put my reply in the form of a question.

"Just give me an estimate." He smiled sweetly as he said this.

I decided to use an approach I learned from Mary Moeller years back–paraphrasing what clients told you. So I said, "What I hear you saying is that you feel your duplex is more special than the neighboring homes which sell for a million three–is that correct?"

"Yes," was Mr. Chase's response.

I wanted to get to the root of his thinking, so I needed to ask why. "Because?"

"My property has income. Plus, I think it has more square footage."

"I see. So you think your property has more square footage and people prefer to have some income?"

"Well, maybe not all people, but I think some might." Already Mr. Chase seemed to be softening on his position.

"We will definitely take that point into consideration when we compile our data as well as checking the square footage. To be 100% accurate we can get a bank appraiser to measure." I then took out my calendar and using the Alternative Assumption Close, asked, "Would Tuesday at 5:00 work or is Wednesday better?"

He told us Tuesday worked just fine. Like most sellers he was going to want to know two things:

What we think his house is worth.

What we are going to do to sell it.

If we could convince Mr. Chase that we were capable of getting him a high price, plus eliminate the high stress of selling, we would have an excellent chance of getting the listing.

On Tuesday, we presented our three point plan–Pricing, Marketing and Staging. I knew he was expecting more than a million three, but the data did not support that. I had a few choices: I could skirt the truth and list at a price he expected and hope later he would lower the price; or I could suggest he do some changes to the property to bring a higher price. I chose the latter–paying close attention to Mr. Chase's body language and letting him guide us to how much detail we gave him. If he started to fidget and look away, I knew he was losing interest and I needed to speed things up. If his eyebrows crunched closely together, he was probably getting confused. Then I either needed to slow down or not go into so much detail. If his body was relaxed and he asked questions every so often, my pace was just right.

"You really don't have to do much," I assured him. "We'll organize everything. We just need to paint a little bit here and there, rearrange some furniture and store away some of your personal belongings." I pointed to family photos prominently displayed on his fireplace mantle. I did my best to present the changes he needed to make in such a way that he wouldn't feel overwhelmed.

Mr. Chase had the typical reaction and started to object. "Why is all this so necessary? I enjoy my things and house just the way they are."

"I understand you want to keep things just as they are," I said.

His face morphed from being stern and angular to soft and open. I made a big arc with my arm, pointing outside. "Your house is going to belong to some buyer out there soon and once you decide to sell, you begin the process of letting go."

"This is still my house now, though."

"Why not think of your home as a means to getting onto your next phase of life? A place which better suits your current and future needs." Remembering to use what he had previously told us, I asked, "Did you say that you wanted the highest price possible for your home, Mr. Chase?" He nodded. "Depersonalizing your home will get you a better price. Prospective purchasers can better imagine themselves living in a house that has a neutral yet warm atmosphere. We can help you create that feeling by doing some minor modifications. Keep a special photo or two in your bedroom if you like, and if there is something else you really don't want changed, just let us know."

Mr. Chase took his time to answer. "I don't have to remodel a kitchen or bathroom, do I?"

If we were talking with a young, energetic couple who wanted to make the most of their house investment, we would say, "Yes." The stress it would cause Mr. Chase would be too much, so we told him we didn't think anything that ambitious was necessary.

"We'll simply hire a professional interior decorator to place the furniture–using mostly yours, of course. She may bring in a few pieces of her own, such as bed linens, pillows and maybe a chair or two to tie everything together. If you agree, maybe we could replace the rusty bathroom cabinet and the hallway sconce, which are a bit dated."

He agreed, providing we did all the coordinating. He also insisted we leave one of the photos of his wife and all the paintings in the dining and living room exactly where they were. It was not the perfect scenario, but feasible. It was now time for us to go in for the close once again. "I feel we have a good rapport going on here, don't you agree?" I asked, watching his face as I spoke. He gave us each a smile.

"Do you feel comfortable in making those small changes we recommended so that we can get you the highest price?" He agreed to that as well.

I purposely built up agreement on the smaller items first to get him used to saying "*Yes.*" "With those agreed changes, then we would recommend a list price of $1,300,000 to $1,400,000. Is that in the price range you were thinking, Mr. Chase?"

I always liked to give a range and then asked what price other agents gave. If I could get that information up front, so much the better. In any case, I did not write the price range on the market analysis I gave clients. If the market changed, or if I was overly optimistic, it was easier to get a price reduction later. He confided to us that one agent came in much higher, but four other agents were in agreement with us. "So

I'm not sure what that means," he said.

"Do you want my opinion?" I asked, knowing I was on sensitive ground.

His facial muscles were relaxed and his voice soft as he said, "Yes, I'd be curious what you think."

"Well, the agent who came in higher probably hoped you would go with the highest bidder, but that is not the best way to choose your agent," I said. I gave him the Multiple Listing statistics which showed that the majority of activity occurred over the first six weeks a property was on the market. After that the chances of getting the list price or higher were greatly diminished. And if a property was listed too high initially, the seller would probably get less than if he had listed more realistically in the beginning.

"That makes perfect sense," he said.

Now Cindy and I needed to follow up with all the positive reasons for listing with us. "As I'm sure we've proven to you, we're knowledgeable in your area, have an aggressive marketing plan, and a good name behind us with a trusted client base. We also have the contacts to help you spruce up your property and stage it so it shows to its best advantage."

I pulled out the Exclusive Right to Sell Agreement from my briefcase and asked, "Why don't we start this process and move forward?" Mr. Chase said nothing. Cindy started to talk and I shot her a look that closed her mouth so fast she almost bit her lip. Thank goodness–she remembered that the person who talked first loses! Several more seconds passed. It felt like forever. Mr. Chase appeared as if he was deep in thought, pondering what to do. Cindy shifted uncomfortably in her chair and fiddled with her purse. Meanwhile, I pretended I had all the time in the world.

Mr. Chase finally spoke. "I'm not ready. Let's wait."

I knew I had to proceed cautiously. "What's there to think about?" I asked as I lifted my eyelids to see how he was handling the pressure. I noticed he had folded his arms neatly over his chest and his mouth was curving downward. He was withdrawing. I needed to change tactics–and try a more subtle approach.

"Mr. Chase, I understand your hesitancy. Selling a home is a big decision. Just know that we love your house, and we want to represent you. Fortunately, we came prepared and filled out the paperwork ahead of time. Why don't we leave it with you and you can go over it at your convenience?" I leaned back and gave him some physical space. His austere expression softened as he took the paperwork. Cindy and I got up from where we were sitting and gave him a warm handshake. "Please feel free to call us if you have any questions."

That afternoon, Cindy sent Mr. Chase a handwritten note thanking him for considering us as the representatives for his lovely home. She took the letter to the post office herself, knowing that we needed to keep our name in front of him as much as possible while he was making his decision. We called him a few days later to reconnect. He had a long list of questions. We were helpful, but not too much so–we wanted him needing our expertise. We also needed another face-to-face meeting. Rarely could one close a deal over the phone.

"Mr. Chase, we can answer these questions better in person," I said, talking slowly so he could hear over our speaker phone. "Every home...in fact, every sale is different. We are going to be in your neighborhood this afternoon. Why don't we stop by?" There was a long pause. It was probably obvious to Mr. Chase that we would be asking him to sign the listing, but there were other agents calling him. We did not have the luxury of being overly patient. Persistent yet patient pressure was what was needed now. He agreed.

I had another appointment, but rearranged my schedule. Something could always come up to prevent him from signing with us and I did not want to leave anything to chance. He welcomed us inside with a strong handshake. I returned the handshake with an equal amount of pressure. He showed us into the dining room and asked if we would like a cup of coffee. Normally, I was not a coffee drinker, but when I saw he had a cup, I said yes.

"I take sugar, no cream," Mr. Chase said, handing us the sugar bowl. "How about the two of you?"

"That is perfect, thank you," we answered in unison.

"Do you plan to hold open houses?" Mr. Chase asked as he crossed his right leg over his left.

"We were planning to have both Broker Opens and Sunday Opens, if that's alright with you," I said. I made sure I did not speak too quickly or loudly, wanting to follow Mr. Chase's speech pattern.

Mr. Chase leaned closer as he said, "I'm concerned about security, especially the paintings I have stored in the garage."

"We can always keep the garage door locked and interested parties can make an appointment to come look at a later time. That way we will be able to determine the serious buyers from the Lookie Loos." I slowly crossed my right leg over my left, mirroring his posture.

"Explain to me how your marketing will be different from other salespeople's." Mr. Chase held a pen ready to write.

I told him that either Cindy or I would personally accompany all showings and follow up with a phone call to the agents. "That way we will know right away their feedback and communicate with you after each showing. Most agents will just put on a lock box, hand out a key, or have their assistants show your home. With us you will have two full-time agents working for you 24 hours a day, seven days a week. We will be 100% available."

Cindy added, "Who knows? That one person we accommodate which other agents can't because of their heavy schedules could be the perfect buyer."

I was feeling confident, optimistic, and determined, knowing we could sell his property, no problem. "Shall we start the paperwork?"

"If you're this persistent with me," Mr. Chase said, "you're going to be persistent with buyers. I like that. Yes, let's get started."

Cindy and I let out a cheerleading-like whoop of happiness. It paid to be clear, tenacious and optimistic. Once the formalities were concluded, I asked why he chose us instead of the five other agents he interviewed.

"All the others told me about how great they were and what they've done, but you and Cindy were different. I felt you really cared about me and would not only get me a high price for my house, but also would support me throughout this whole selling process. That was more important than any Million Dollar Club or how long I knew someone. One guy, who is the top agent at Prudential and lives down the street, will be very disappointed, but I felt I had to go with my gut instincts."

We shook Mr. Chase's hand, assuring him we would take excellent care of him. Establishing rapport had gotten us his trust and in turn, a successful outcome.

Sales might not be that academically difficult, but it is challenging in a more significant way–emotionally. Being successful requires that you develop a firm anchor of who you are so that you can handle a parade of situations. That was why I liked real estate so much. It was not the typical nine-to-five, but required constant learning.

If it Sounds Too Good: A Case Study from the Mortgage Crisis.

I was putting away my exercise mat when my Pilates teacher, Deborah Knox, approached me. "Paula, I heard you are in real estate."

"Yep. Been doing it for almost thirty years now," I answered.

"Do you ever sell in Oakland? My daughter, Roberta, needs some real estate advice. She bought a condo there nine months ago and she and her boyfriend are breaking up." Deborah looked up at me, doing her best to steady her voice. "She needs to sell yesterday."

Oakland did not have the best reputation, because of all its crime statistics, unemployment and high school dropout rates. On the upside, the hills were beautiful, they had a great mayor in Jerry Brown, and better weather. Plus, it was much more affordable; when clients got discouraged with the high prices of San Francisco, they often decided that the short commute–in spite of the congested traffic on the Bay Bridge–was the answer. Alternatively, there was the Bay Area Rapid Transit system (BART), the usually efficient subway system to the financial district, Union Square, Civic Center and airport.

I put my hand on Deborah's shoulder. "There's a woman, Dona Fuller, in my office who lives in the East Bay and sells in Oakland. She can help me do a market analysis."

I usually did not sell outside the area of my expertise, San Francisco, because I did not think it was fair to the client. Not only that, but it was immensely time-consuming to learn a whole new market. I found that specializing in an area was best. However, from the tone of Deborah's voice, I sensed that her daughter had gotten herself into a difficult situation and I did not feel comfortable passing this off to someone else. I wrote down the address of Roberta's condo as well as her phone number. As soon as I got home, I called Dona. "How busy are you these days?" I asked. "I have a lead for a listing. Roberta Knox, a daughter of a friend of mine, bought a new condo with her boyfriend less than a year ago and now needs to sell. They're breaking up."

"Uh-oh. I know the market is still streaming along in San Francisco, but in Oakland it is not quite so rosy. Especially if these clients just bought and even more especially if they bought in a new development. You know what the developers are doing over here, don't you?"

"No," I said, not trying to get alarmed. "What are they doing?"

Dona spoke with an authoritative tone in her voice. "They are offering people these phenomenal terms so first-time buyers can qualify. You know, no money down and a 4% interest rate for the first year. It is probably the only way these developers can sell all the new condos that have glutted the marketplace recently. So although people can qualify, they cannot afford to own long-term, especially if something unforeseen happens–loss of a job, a pregnancy or divorce. And let's face it, in life, shit happens."

Call me conservative or old fashioned, but I was very skeptical of the 100% financing that mortgage companies had been offering buyers the last few years. There was a good reason why lenders used to require 20% from buyers–they wanted some of their cash in the property so the buyers would be a committed partner in their investment. It would ensure that they would make their monthly loan payments so as not to lose their down payment. I never understood why, all of a sudden, their strict rules of qualifying changed. In many cases, lenders no longer required a credit report or payment stubs. People could just state what their income was and they would lend. It seemed so shortsighted and irresponsible on their part.

"I hope Roberta didn't agree to a negative amortization loan too," I said, "because then this will most likely be a short sale."

A negative amortization loan arose when the mortgage payment was less than market rate, which caused the loan balance to increase rather than decrease. These loans were also called "teasers," because the buyer was not paying the full amount of what he or she owed. A short sale was a sale in which the lender allowed a property to be sold for less than the amount owed and took a loss.

I had *almost* been involved in a short sale years before. One of my clients put a large second mortgage on their home to pay for their son's college. She was a nurse and her husband a civil engineer, but they knew nothing about finance. They probably would have been able to pay the loan back had it not been for the back-breaking 17% interest rate. Perhaps their credit was not picture perfect, or their combined income too low, or they were simply naïve and got the easiest loan offered to them–from one of those telephone solicitors. But whatever the reason, now they were stuck. Although taking out this second loan solved their short-term problem, the exorbitant interest rate ended up being a major problem. A big portion of their monthly payment went to interest and not to principal, so they were essentially like indentured servants working their asses off for this greedy home equity lender.

Ten years later, my clients were forced to sell their home. They had to rid themselves of their crushing debt, which felt like a weighted boulder on their shoulders. After two months on the market, we got an offer which was $25,000 short of their closing costs and the balance of their two mortgages. I did my best to negotiate with both the first and second loan holders. Both banks insisted my clients made plenty of money so they would not help. I went over the numbers with them, because it was crystal clear they did not. Over the next several weeks, I begged and pleaded, but neither bank would budge. Bankers tended to be very conservative and, although knowledgeable at lending, they don't know much about real estate. In this instance, the buyer got impatient with waiting and bought something else. I put my clients' house back on the market, but received no more offers.

My clients, who were respectable people with good values, became disillusioned and no longer felt an obligation to make their mortgage payments. Instead, they started saving money for a new rental which they knew was inevitable. Four months later the second lender called, ready to take our offer, but the buyer was long gone, the real estate market had softened, and both my clients and I were exhausted by the whole process. The lenders had to foreclose, fix up the house, which my clients left in a state of disarray, and take a price much less than our original offer. My clients were forced out of a home in which they had raised two children. I received no commission for eight months of hard work and the bank got a house they did not want, not to mention inheriting the ordeal of trying to sell it. That experience taught me to be leery of short sales.

"Why don't I do a market analysis and I'll get back to you?" Dona said.

"No matter what the answer–and it doesn't sound good–I owe it to my friend to meet with her daughter," I said.

Dona called me the next day with the news: the development project in which Roberta bought still had brand new condos up for sale–at a price lower than what Roberta and her boyfriend paid.

"Yep, she's in trouble. Want to come with me when I deliver the bad news?" I asked.

"Sure," Dona said, "glad to help."

Dona met me out in front of the condo the next day. It was a bright and sunny afternoon, but on this particular block of MacArthur Avenue, I found myself looking over my shoulder. I would not want to be here at night, I told myself. Why did people make these dumb decisions? I shuddered. Walking up to Roberta's unit, we noticed large alluring signs pointing to the sales office, claiming no money down, phenomenal interest rates, and no homeowner payments for a year. The whole manipulating scenario made me want to gag.

We rang the doorbell and were buzzed inside. There was a long narrow staircase which led us to the top floor where we shook Roberta's hand. She was a beautiful young woman with coffee-colored skin, short dark hair and almond shaped eyes. She was dressed in an expensive business suit and told us she was on her lunch hour. She showed us around the ultramodern condo with its eye-popping granite, cherry cabinet kitchen, sky lighted living/dining combo area, and marble bathroom boasting European fixtures. So this was how the developers hooked them.

One of the bedrooms was filled with toys. "Don't worry,"

Roberta said, "we'll clean all this up."

"You have a child?" I asked incredulously.

"Oh, I guess Mom didn't tell you. I have a seven-year-old daughter from my first marriage. The light of my life and the reason I want to quit my corporate job. I just don't have the time to be with her."

So, here we had a situation in which there was a relationship falling apart with a child involved, a mother who wanted to quit her job and both adults being overextended financially in an area of which I was not an expert. This was going to be one big headache. I suggested we go over the comparables. Dona laid them out on the sleek stone counter while Roberta and I got comfortable on the bar stools. She described the current listings and recent sold properties. She pointed to prices hovering around $640,000–$10,000 less than the price they paid.

Roberta was visibly upset. "What about all the curtains I put in? And the washer/dryer? They are brand new."

"Yes, they are–as are the two units on the market in your development which are still being sold by the developer." I softened my voice when I added, "Buyers like new. That is why they will buy the never before lived in units the developer has on the market before yours. For a buyer to buy your unit, your price will have to be lower than what he is offering–especially because you cannot offer buyers the terms the developer is offering."

"You mean I am going to have to come up with money to sell this condo?"

"It looks like it," Dona said.

"Do you have your closing papers and mortgage information I can look at?" I asked. I had told Roberta we would want to see this paperwork to help advise her. I looked them over. "It appears you only had to put down $6500 for closing costs," I said.

"That's right," Roberta said. "Buying here was about the same as renting. Plus," she waved her hands around, "you can see for yourself how beautiful it is."

I smiled softly. "It certainly is and you have done a wonderful job of making a lovely home."

Breaking more bad news was going to be painful. I reviewed her promissory note, which stated the terms of her loan. "Who was your real estate agent?" I asked.

"We didn't have one. We just walked in here one day and the person on site showed us how we could afford this new home. We jumped at the chance to finally own."

"I see," I said, "*–the American Dream.* That explains it then."

"Explains what?"

"Are you aware that your payment is going up $570 next month?"

"What?" she screamed as she reached to grab the papers out of my hand.

"The first year's monthly payment is what they call in the business a teaser rate. It was just a way to help you get started in owning a home."

Roberta thought a moment. "Yeah, now I remember. They did mention that the increase of appreciation and the fact that our salaries would be increasing would make everything all work out."

"Unfortunately, they sell you on only the best-case scenarios," Dona said.

Roberta started talking again. "The truth is neither of our salaries has increased and, like I might have mentioned, I am tired of the corporate world. The hours are killer. I never get to see my baby girl and Ralph is not into taking care of a child who is not his. Plus, we're fighting a lot." She seemed wistful and withdrawn. I wondered if there was some domestic abuse going on. Not unlikely, especially when there were financial woes thrown into the mix. I was in a thoughtful mood when Roberta asked, "Well, do you think you can sell it?"

"Sure," Dona piped up, "but not at the price you need. I don't see you getting the price you paid for it–you will probably get $20,000 less in spite of all your upgrades. Plus, you need to pay commission and transfer tax. Even if we lower our commission to 5% to help you out, you will still have to come up with another $20,000 for a total shortfall of $40,000."

Roberta looked down at her hands folded neatly in her lap. She didn't say a word.

I was the first to speak. "Since your monthly payment is going up another $570 this month, I suggest you talk to your lender. Unfortunately, they are not that fast-moving. So you need to be prepared for another six months of staying put while we market and try negotiating with your lender. Does that work for you?"

Roberta fidgeted in her chair and took a long time to answer. "Probably not. Ralph, my boyfriend, does not want to talk to the lender about our problems. He and his family are big into responsibility and paying back what you owe."

"Even if it's just impossible to do so?" I asked incredulously. "The truth is you were naïve first-time buyers, who were not represented by an agent and you fell victim to developers' and lenders' greed. And it doesn't sound to me like anybody fully explained the ramifications of obtaining a negative amortization loan."

"No, they did not. They kept emphasizing all the appreciation we would get in owning."

As Realtors®–meaning we were a member of the National Association of Realtors®–we were trained not to speak of what the future brings, but just what had happened in the past. One could never predict what the economic climate would be in a year or two years from now, and we certainly could not predict the future fortunes of our clients. Whenever my clients asked what I thought their property would be worth in the future, I told them I was not a fortune teller with a crystal ball. A property's worth could vary depending on supply and demand and economic conditions. San Francisco is a rarefied special case because there is high demand and short supply–a city of only forty-nine square miles. I also advised buyers to be prepared to hold on to a property for at least five years. Speculators who wanted to flip and make a fast buck, I didn't want to work with.

I picked up the closing statement. "You have only put in $6500 besides twelve months of mortgage payments. Think of the latter as rent. Plus, you got some tax breaks. I know it will hurt your credit if you take the route we are suggesting, but what is the alternative? Stay in a relationship and job that are not working? Attempt to pay back a loan that will eventually require one of you to take a second job? What about your health? Your baby girl?" I wanted to throw in the word, *safety,* but thought it best not to. "If I were in your situation, I would walk. You made a bad decision buying this condo, but I do not see any sense in paying for it the rest of your life. Sure, you won't be able to get a substantial loan or buy a house for seven to ten years... "

Roberta interrupted, "I don't want another house–ever. This one has been one big problem. I would agree to what you are saying, but Ralph will not. His values are such that he will feel obligated to pay off his debt–even if it ruins him financially."

She looked so stressed, I felt compelled to ask the question that had been looming in the back of my mind since we got there. "Can you move in with your mother while you sort all this out with Ralph?" I asked.

"Yeah, maybe that's for the best."

She shook our hands as we left. I would not want to be in her shoes for anything. I turned to Dona. "I wouldn't feel comfortable having an open house here, would you?"

"No way," she said.

"We'll have to do some research and find a Realtor® who specializes in short sales," I said.

"Yeah, a big, brawny, broad-shouldered guy who has taken a lot of karate would be helpful, too." We both laughed and got back into our cars. I headed home to my beloved "City by the Bay."

A few weeks later Roberta and her daughter had moved in with her mother. Ralph wouldn't sell and lose money so for a few months Roberta sent him half the mortgage payment, telling him she could not do it forever. She also told him he would have to cover the increase in loan payment. He eventually got a roommate and Roberta asked to be removed from the title.

Roberta and Ralph's situation was not an isolated case; they were just one example of the 2008 mortgage crisis. But, folks, let's call it what it really was–a mortgage scandal. Unscrupulous developers, bankers and some agents sold houses to people who should not have owned one in the first place. They all got their money up front and left the poor home-owner holding a loan which they could not afford to pay off. The bankers made double-digit profits by selling their loans to Wall Street, who wanted in on the sweet deal, but then it all crashed. Does Bear Stearns ring a bell? Why not look up what their profit was in the second quarter of 2007—a whopping $2.5 billion. And Merrill Lynch's profits upped nearly a third. Some of these companies have since been banned from lending money, but our government had us, the taxpayers, save others, which, although they participated in this scandal, were supposedly too big to fail.

Well, I digress. This book is about sales, real estate and the American dream and not about greedy corporations, self-indulgent CEOs and a disempowered government failing to act on behalf of its people.

Lessons Learned from Chapter 8:

- BE ACCOUNTABLE Actions, not words, are what accountability is all about. To keep clients coming back to you, be sure you listen to what they want and deliver what you promised them. When you make a mistake, own up to it and correct it, doing your best not to let it happen again.
- FIND COMMON GROUND People want to do business with people they like and trust. To connect with clients, find some similar interests that you can talk about. In other words, make business more personal. The emotional bond will help you create a more solid relationship with them.
- BE COMPASSIONATE Since you are the conduit between buyer and seller, who will, in all likelihood, not meet each other's expectations, people may misdirect their disappointment–even their anger–at you. You need to be understanding during the selling process as well as a supportive sounding board and their voice of reason.
- PARAPHRASE WHAT PEOPLE SAY When you repeat what people say back to them, it will do two things: (1) show them you are listening carefully, and (2) force them to rethink what they just told you.
- REALIZE IT IS OKAY TO SAY NO It is important to know your priorities and what you do best. Sometimes the best advice is to refer clients to someone who is a better match for their needs.

9

CODEPENDEDNCY

HONORING YOURSELF

When Your Clients Think They Know Better Than You

In real estate, as I am sure it is with other people-centered service occupations, I eventually learned that there was an emotional cost when I inevitably became immersed in other people's lives. I especially remember the referral I got from management on a four-unit building in Pacific Heights. Blayne, a well-known San Francisco attorney, was selling. Recently married, his new wife, Angela, had just been diagnosed with breast cancer. Her wish was to move back to St. Louis where her family lived, and she was currently undergoing chemotherapy treatments there.

As soon as Blayne opened the door, Puccini's bittersweet aria, *Un Bel Di,* from *Madame Butterfly* flooded into the entryway. Being an opera aficionado wannabe, I was entranced as Blayne invited me in to join him for his afternoon tea in the library. He and Angela lived in a two-level, lavishly decorated penthouse above three other rental units.

I passed through a customized Italian kitchen with ruby-rich cherry cabinets, a large black granite center island and tall glass doors opening to a wraparound deck. I heard songbirds and bubbling water and was immediately soothed. I took a quick peek outside. The Japanese-inspired garden was a magical vision with fountains, tall bamboo, rock garden and a koi pond in the center–a serene respite from the hectic pace of the city. The library had a British flair with floor to ceiling bookcases, oversized coffee-colored leather chairs and dark mahogany paneling. A serving tray was already laden with elaborate petit fours, dates and cucumber sandwiches. Everything around me was well-designed, impeccably placed and expensive. Blayne was as fastidious about his person as he was about his beloved house, wearing a black turtleneck cashmere sweater and freshly pressed slacks. He spoke in the matter-of-fact, clipped way which many attorneys did.

This was the early nineties, the economy was in a recession and real estate, even in San Francisco, was depressed. In addition, we had the added problem that this was income property located in one of the most prestigious areas of the city. I explained to Blayne that most of the homeowners in this area were into status and did not want the label of being a landlord. Blayne, however, was not deterred; he was determined to get an astronomical price for his property. Partially, I thought, for his wife, Angela.

Nine weeks into the marketing, Blayne decided that he wanted me to meet with Angela, who, he thought, had some great ideas on how to get their property sold. Angela was a petite, fashionable woman with a pretty face, pointed chin and painted, pouty lips. One would never guess that she was in the midst of the fight of her life until she spoke in her soft, wispy Jackie O voice. I got tired of saying "What?" and "Pardon Me?" so I did my best to get the gist of her whispering. She recited the many special amenities of the home–all of which I had listed on the statement sheet–yet I listened, giving her lots of eye contact while she talked on and on. She picked fault with my marketing plan, wanting more advertising. But I had come prepared. I took out the many sample ads from my briefcase and showed them to her.

"Obviously, it's not doing the job now, is it?" Angela whispered. "We still don't have a buyer."

"What other periodical do you suggest I advertise in?" I asked, making sure my voice was neutral and calm. I did not want to give into the common trap of defensiveness.

Blayne's response was sharp as a knife in my chest. "It doesn't matter to us. Just advertise in one that works."

"Well, it is a bit hard to track exactly what ad will bring in the buyer for your property," I said, knowing price–not advertising–was the reason for their property not selling.

Angela gave me an overly expansive smile while her eyes remained narrow and piercing. "How about the *Nob Hill Gazette?* Surely they will have a buyer of the caliber we are looking for."

Of course, she would want an ad in the super exclusive *Snob Hill Gazette* where all the pages were filled with stories and photos of San Francisco socialites. "I really don't think a four-unit building is appropriate for that magazine," I said. "Why don't we advertise in the *Marina Times* instead?"

Angela clasped her hands together. "Paula, what a fabulous idea to advertise in both! Don't you worry, when those buyers come in and see all the custom designs we have put into this house, they will be sold. Blayne, don't you agree?" Of course, Blayne agreed.

Taking in a big breath of air for courage, I said, "It really is pricing–not advertising–that is the biggest determining factor in getting a property sold. We might want to reevaluate… "

Angela interrupted in her ghost-like whisper. "We do not want excuses, Paula. We want solutions." I got a coldhearted stare. "We have a special property and we want it presented as such."

"Of course, I understand." I recognized that right then was probably not the time to talk hard truths. Instead, I took out my new color brochure, omitting the high asking price so as not to discourage potential buyers. "Well, what do you think?"

I was confident they would like it because I made sure to include Blayne in the decision process. He was there the day the professional photographer did the photo shoot, helping me place the colorful flower arrangements around the house, adjust the blinds to get the best light, and light the wood in the fireplaces.

"Mediocre," Angela responded as she gingerly picked up the glossy booklet, staring at it at length, scrutinizing for any mistake she could identify as the reason their property had not sold.

"Yes, I agree–mediocre is the right word," Blayne, the traitor, replied, not once mentioning he controlled the whole process, including editing the photos and the verbiage in the brochure.

Angela looked at me with her eyelashes all aflutter. "Why didn't you show the beautiful etched glass shower door we custom designed for the master bathroom?" Her voice was soft and melodious in high contrast to the icy coldness radiating from her.

How could I tell her that the majority of buyers were not into having naked etched wood nymphs in their bathroom? I hesitated for a moment and then replied, "I thought the other amenities of the home were more important."

"How unfortunate. I think that was a big mistake on your part," she purred.

Not knowing what to say, I said nothing. Then, sensing a lull in the conversation, I turned to the comparable sales chart underneath the brochure. As I began to speak, Angela stopped me short with a flick of her wrist. "Let's hope this meeting has been fruitful, giving you some good marketing tools to get our house sold. We really are anxious for a buyer."

"Well, more marketing may not be the one and only solution," I said as I slid the recent sales statistics across the table.

Angela pushed them back to me and stood up, offering her hand to me like she was a member of royalty. I had no choice but to stand up and take part in this ritual. "Thank you so much for coming," she said. "Don't forget to take everything with you." She was speaking so softly I could hardly hear her.

As I was being ushered out the door, I made another attempt to address the tough competition and what we were up against in a down real estate market. Angela interrupted in a firm voice I didn't know she had. "We are done now, Paula. There is nothing else to talk about. Blayne and I do not need to hear any negativity. What we need is a strong marketing effort on your part." She gave me another sickening sweet smile. "It has been lovely seeing you again–just lovely." In spite of all her elegance and social etiquette, I felt like I had just been kicked out.

Weeks went by and still there were no showings and no interest, with Blayne calling me every other day. Most agents would just shrug their shoulders and understand there was nothing more they could do. I forgot all about disciplining my mind and being positive and instead felt depressed for Blayne and his situation. The least I could do, I ruminated, was sell his house. Desperate, I convinced a close friend to preview the property and pretend he was a potential buyer.

(So much for telling the hard truth!) Of course, this plan did not work either, because now Blayne was pestering me about Ernie.

"Paula, I think we have a live one here and I want you following through. Did you prequalify him yet? What did you say he does for a living?" And on and on as I got deeper and deeper into my white lie. My inability to come clean made me realize that I needed some professional help. On the recommendation of a colleague, I made an appointment with a psychologist. The night before the first session I had a vivid dream: *A group of people approached me while I was walking my dog and pointed to a pile of feces lying on the ground, demanding that I clean up my dog's mess. I immediately agreed and apologized—without assessing the situation first. As I started cleaning it all up, I realized these droppings were too small—no way could these be Nikko's, my Old English sheepdog.*

Dr. Black's office was in Mill Valley, so I had to travel over the Golden Gate Bridge to get there. I was doing the reverse commute and had plenty of time to reflect. I soaked up the spectacularly sloped golden-orange frame contrasted against the cloud-speckled sky and rolling blue bay below. I looked for the weather-beaten lonely tree on the ridge of Sausalito's coastline. I was always inspired by its resiliency to stand there alone day after day in spite of the heavy winds, pounding rain and incessant fog. I sneaked another look as I drove, careful not to cross the white cylinder cones separating me from the oncoming traffic. I rolled down my window to take a gulp of the fresh, moist air as I pondered what I wanted to get out of today's counseling session.

It was with high hopes and some trepidation that I entered Dr. Black's office early that misty morning. She was not what I expected. Jeanette had shoulder-length bleached blonde hair, a full buxomly figure, and a gay bubbly voice. Flashing me a wide-open grin, she extended a warm hand and shook mine soundly. It would not surprise me in the least if she gave me a big bear hug at the end of this session. It was just the type of person she was, and, after all, she was from Mill Valley–the land of milk and honey and idyllic dreams.

She glanced at her schedule, pulled from underneath a pile of scattered papers on her desk. "So Kathy Trapani referred you?" I had no idea how she could find that piece of information so quickly. Some special inner radar system, I guessed.

"Yes," I said as I shifted in my chair, searching for a comfortable position in a challenging situation. I was about to expose my vulnerable underbelly of insecurities.

"Just so you know, I have heard just about everything so don't be shy. Tell me what's going on."

I stuttered at first, not knowing if I could trust this person with my ridiculous drama. I started off with last night's dream. "Isn't it odd that I should have such a disturbing dream right before our session? I realize the subconscious is powerful. Do you think it is giving me some clues to what's going on?"

"What do you think the dream means?"

I sat with her question for a moment. "Something about people blaming me for messes that are not mine?"

Dr. Black grinned as her whole body bobbed up and down. "You got that right! So how does that tie in with the problem you're bringing me today?"

"Well, my clients, Blayne and Angela, keep implying that the reason their building is not selling is because of me, but the facts show that their price is too high. But I blame myself anyway. What's up with that?"

Her demeanor turned pensive. "In the dream you believed that the accusations were true when they were not. It appears to me you are repeating the same scenario with Blayne and Angela. You mentioned you have been a top agent in San Francisco for ten years. From your demeanor and what you've described to me, you seem extremely conscientious–almost to a fault. Would you agree with that assessment?"

I nodded my head with a definite Yes, adding, "I have done extensive marketing for over four months with few showings and no interested buyers. My clients keep calling me every day or so and insist I spend more and more money on advertising. In this difficult real estate market, I am getting deeper and deeper in debt. Every time I give them the pertinent housing and economic statistics, they tell me not to be so negative. To relieve all the pressure, I even showed the property to a friend, pretending he was a real buyer, which just made matters worse."

"So they won't listen to your expert advice?"

"That's correct," I said.

"Does that make sense to you?"

"No, it doesn't make any sense, but I cannot seem to stop blaming myself for their property not selling. That is why I need your help."

"By pretending you had a serious buyer, you prevented your clients from learning the hard truth–that there is no one interested in their home. Don't protect them from the truth." Then Dr. Black asked me about my relationship with my family.

"What does that have to do with anything?" I asked. "We are talking about business–this has nothing to do with me and my family." I certainly didn't need to go into that shitty mess.

"Really?" Dr. Black asked. She sat back in her leather armchair appearing eerily pensive.

Oh, great. Here the analysis began. She wanted me to spill my guts–get right to my deep, dark secrets. Well, I wouldn't! I was not going to into any of those long forgotten painful parts inside of me. I only needed help with Blayne and Angela. I gave Dr. Black a blank look, waiting for her to talk first. After all, I was in sales. Dr. Black gave me a warm welcoming smile. A typical psychological trick. Since I could not look at her without saying something, I moved my hands to my lap and studied my nails. Moments went by with neither of us speaking. I glanced at my watch. We were wasting valuable time here. I had lists of things to do.

"We still have thirty minutes," Dr. Black said.

I glanced in her direction, hoping she would say something else, but she seemed perfectly content just sitting there. This was going to be a test of wills. Since she was the professional, I probably was not going to win this game.

"I only want to deal with my client situation," I said.

"Fine–this is your session. I need to point out though, that the roadblocks we encounter in life are often because of early established childhood patterns. It would be extremely helpful to address your behavior style rather than one isolated situation. And you must have had a compelling reason for you to share your dream."

I remained firm. "Let's just deal with my business," I said.

"All right then. Blayne and Angela hired you, because you are the expert. Give them advice, but it is not your responsibility what choices they make. You cannot make decisions for them."

"It's confusing to me, because they keep calling me, wondering why there are no showings. I have to tell them something."

"Like I said, you can only advise them. They may agree to reduce their asking price and they may not. Let them feel the frustration and pain of their house not selling. You have other clients, don't you? Focus on them. Don't be so invested in saving Blayne and his sick wife."

"I guess I put up with Blayne's intimidating behavior and Angela's aloofness because I feel sorry for them."

Dr. Black swiveled back and forth in her chair a couple of times before she spoke. "Have you ever noticed that your life gets entangled in other people's drama? That you have a hard time separating their problems from your own?"

I felt like someone just punched me in the stomach. I was lost in my own confusion when I heard an echo of someone in the back of my head talking, but I was having difficulty focusing on who it was or what was being said.

"Paula, are you all right?"

Dr. Black's question brought me back to the room. I nodded my head up and down, still unable to talk. Once again, I was that nine-year-old girl doing the housework, taking care of my baby brother and sister, while my mother was out on the porch having a few afternoon cocktails.

"Your relationship with Blayne and Angela is a classic case of a codependent."

"That sounds great to me," I said, relieved that someone knew what was going on, because I certainly didn't. "What is a codependent?"

A Primer in Codependency, and How to Deal with It

My homework was to read *Codependent No More* by Melody Beattie. I could still hear Dr. Black's words as I left her office–"Realize that your job as a real estate agent is only to guide your clients. You are not responsible for their decisions."

On my way back to the office I stopped by a local bookstore. A thin rail of a woman directed me to the Self-Help section. The selection of books was vast, addressing a multitude of issues. I spotted the title I was looking for and practically tore the book off the shelf. Melody's definition of a codependent: "*A person who has let another person's behavior affect him or her, and who is obsessed with controlling another person's behavior.*" Hmmm... That made sense. In the past I had certainly focused on other people's needs rather than my own, such as Mother's, Daddy's and those of all my loser boyfriends. Now it appeared I was doing the same with my clients.

While I was at the bookstore, I also picked up a set of audiotapes, including *On the Family,* which I listened to on the way home. The author and reader was John Bradshaw, a current leading psychologist on family dynamics. Bradshaw explained that codependency often starts when, as children, we are forced into caretaker roles in response to emotionally unbalanced parents. Since our survival depended on them, our focus shifted from our own needs to theirs. I identified with a case study of a baby girl, who at only nine months, would start comforting her mother whenever she became hysterical. Hadn't I done the same with my mother as a mere toddler? Soothing her whenever she ranted and raved–desperate to make everything all better. "The first step in changing the dynamics of codependency," Melody Beattie wrote, "is to set boundaries by separating your feelings and needs from others." I read the book cover to cover, taking notes.

When I saw Dr. Black again, she stressed that I could only change my behavior–no one else's.

"So if they don't want to listen to my advice, I just stand by and do nothing?"

"Yes."

"But they keep blaming me for their house not selling."

"Again–you are responsible for your feelings. Do not take on the blame because of bad choices they are making."

"So when they criticize me, I say nothing."

"Of course not. You need to start setting guidelines on how other people treat you. Have you ever heard the phrase, *'We teach other people how to treat us?'*"

"No. How do I do that?" I asked, my lower lip beginning to tremble. This information was so foreign to me that it felt like I was groping in the dark.

"You need to be aware of your feelings first. As soon as Blayne or Angela start interrupting, criticizing, blaming or avoiding you, tell them. In other words–*Name What is Going On* as soon as it starts to happen."

"Can you give me an example," I asked, trying to find my way out of this forest of confusion.

"The next time Blayne interrupts you, stop him by saying, 'It feels to me that whenever I discuss price, you want to change the subject.'"

"Yes, that's exactly what he does! So you want me to actually tell him that? Won't he get angry with me?"

"Probably not–if you use *I-statements* so as not to put him on the defensive. It is hard to argue with someone else's feelings. Then ask for what you need."

Oh, no, here I was in the scary dark forest lost again. "So how do I do that?"

"I find the phrase '*What works best for me*' to be helpful. '*What works best for me* is if I can finish explaining my marketing strategy. After I'm done, then you can make suggestions.' Or if Angela is ignoring you, say, '*What works best for me* is if I could have ten minutes of your undivided attention. If right now does not work, tell me when a good time would be for us to get together.'

"And what if they won't cooperate?" I asked. "What do I do then?"

"You will need to set up some consequence for their behavior, such as, 'When you are willing to discuss *all the factors* of why your property is not selling then we can reevaluate our marketing plan. Without looking at the full picture, I won't be able to help you come up with a solution.'" Dr. Black took a long pause, then added, "What you are doing is setting boundaries– teaching people how to treat you. And realize it is much easier in the beginning of a relationship. Hopefully, your changing will be enough to shift the dynamics of your relationship with Blayne and Angela, but it may already be too late."

With much trepidation, I set up a face-to-face meeting. Although I usually liked to have both decision makers present, Angela was back East again. I was relieved. Learning this whole new way of communicating and having two against one would be too hard. Best to start with smaller steps. I compiled all my ads and the comparable properties sold and available in the surrounding area, using visual tools would help support me. Plus, everything was more powerful in written form. I then went over the four steps of how to set boundaries:

BE PRESENT – Stay with your own feelings, needs and wants instead of focusing on other's needs.

NAME WHAT IS HAPPENING – When someone transgresses your boundaries, tell them.

ASK FOR WHAT YOU NEED – What works best for me is…

CHOICES HAVE CONSEQUENCES – If the same behavior continues, tell them to stop or face the consequences.

At our meeting, Blayne was, of course, opposed to lowering the asking price. "Which properties in the comparable listings sold are you using to support your price?" I asked, making sure I looked at him directly.

Blayne shoved the chart aside, ignoring my question. Instead he picked apart the new ad I had written for an upcoming open house. "It doesn't fully describe the Japanese garden with the waterfall and fountain. Look here–you abbreviated garage. Not everybody is going to understand what that means."

I reminded myself to stay in the present moment and feel my feelings–even if it was painful. As Blayne kept talking, I felt my body posture slumping–a sign that I was not taking care of myself. I took a deep breath and said, "Blayne, I don't think you heard what I just said." He looked at me quizzically. Gaining momentum, I continued. "We are not talking about the ads right now. We are discussing our current competition and the sold prices of other similar properties–information which any potential buyer will review before putting in an offer. Afterwards we can discuss advertising."

He paused a short moment, then started off again, pointing to the Open House Ad.

I needed to honor what I'm feeling. "This isn't working for me, Blayne."

"What isn't working for you?" I could hear irritation in his voice.

"The direction this conversation is going. It doesn't feel like a discussion."

"What are you talking about?" His voice was getting louder.

I reminded myself to use *I-statements*: "I feel intimidated when you keep interrupting me. I know you have some good ideas as I do, but I feel my suggestions are not even considered."

"That's ridiculous!" he said.

I tried another approach. "You did hire me for my expertise, didn't you?"

"All I want you to do is to sell my house and it's not selling! I'm just trying to help!"

I made every effort to steady my voice. "It works better for me when we can discuss things calmly." There! I said it. I asked for what I needed. Step Three.

He picked up the ad again and started restructuring my sentences. Since Blayne was ignoring my request, I needed to set up a consequence for his behavior. This was the fourth and last step. I was almost there. "Blayne, if you continue focusing on just the ads, we might as well end the meeting. Like I said before, I am open to any suggestions you might have, but before we go over marketing, we need to talk about what's currently happening in the marketplace. Otherwise, we are not addressing all the concerns of why your property isn't selling."

Blayne sighed as he looked at his watch. "I don't have much time. Here's the ad with my notes. Please make the necessary changes." He got up from his seat. Now he's using the ploy at which Angela was so adept.

"I will leave the comparable sales statistics with you," I said, doing my best to remain unaffected by his behavior. "Please go over them so we can have a discussion about pricing."

"We won't reduce the price."

"Well, that's certainly a choice you can make." I was beginning to understand profoundly that I could not force him or Angela to do anything. In the following days I did not hear from Blayne or Angela, and I realized that I was starting to feel depressed again. I listened to the codependent tapes some more and got a massage to help me through this rough spot. Changing patterns was stressful. I was treading on unfamiliar territory. It was time for another counseling session.

"Guilt," Dr. Black said, "is merely a nagging fear that you have done something wrong. You are not operating in the present moment, but dwelling on the past. Worry is the flip side–a fear that you will do something wrong in the future. You seem to be doing a bit of both."

"So, how do I stop feeling badly?"

"Remember to separate your feelings from your clients' emotions. It is okay to feel empathetic with what they are going through, but do not become enmeshed with them. As soon as you start wanting them to do things your way, know you have regressed into your controlling codependency behavior. *Remember: whenever we do things for others at the expense of our own well-being we have crossed the line into the world of codependency.*"

My homework was to find something I loved to do and lose myself in the moment. "When we are 100% occupied with what is happening in the present," Dr. Black said, "our mind does not dwell in the past or wander into the future." She suggested I engage in a form of physical exercise that required mental concentration. It would keep my mind occupied plus release those happy endorphins to help me feel more positive. I chose ballroom dancing. Now not only did I have a hobby I looked forward to three times a week, I also learned to stay in the present. When my partner took a step, my body needed to listen so I could make that split-second-later counter motion. I did not have the privilege of worrying about my real estate deals or my financial woes, because I had to focus on what my partner was doing. If I didn't do my part, we were not in sync and we ended up tripping over each other.

I became so involved in dancing that even if I had a bad day, I was able to have a good night's sleep and start the next day feeling positive. I realized that my life was no longer dependent on what was happening with Blayne and Angela. When they tried to pull me into *their* drama of *their* house not selling, I kept reminding myself that I was not responsible for *their* choice of overpricing. The only thing I could do was to give them my professional advice and then let it go. I started focusing on prospecting and developing new business.

Lessons Learned from Chapter 9:

- TELL THE HARD TRUTH Although it is important to be empathetic with your clients, they also need to hear the hard truth–no matter how uncomfortable it is for them to hear or for you to say.
- ALLOW CLIENTS THEIR PROCESS You are the expert that can guide your clients, but you cannot make decisions for them. They are independent beings and will make their own choices. They may have to make a few bad choices before they are ready to move on.
- SET BOUNDARIES As soon as you notice a person projecting their negativity on to you, tell them. Then state how you expect to be treated by using the following phrase: "What works best for me is.... " If he or she continues, follow it up with a consequence for their behavior.
- DETACH FROM THE OUTCOME Present your clients with the facts and then let them make their decision. You cannot force anyone to do something they do not want to do.

10

FRUSTRATION, ANGER AND VICTIM MENTALITY

Managing Your Emotions

Of Betrayal and Loyalty Restored

I slammed the phone down so hard it almost broke. I continued unpacking the groceries I just bought–putting the fresh organic produce in the hydrator, the meat in the freezer, and the dry goods on their appropriate cabinet shelves. I looked at the dozen eggs and decided not to unpack them individually as I usually did. I just didn't trust myself. Not right now anyway. Instead, I paced back and forth across my living room, recalling the conversation I just had with my neighbor, Dr. Larry Kessler.

I met Larry several years ago when he moved into his home on the top of our cul-de-sac overlooking downtown. He and I would walk our dogs together. It did not matter that he had a punctilious Pug and I had a sappy Old English Sheepdog. As a Jewish doctor from Manhattan, we had New York, a medical background and a love of San Francisco in common. He had traveled three thousand miles, as I had, for the adventure and the promise of milder weather. Sure, we also liked the eclectic attitude and diversity of San Francisco, but what we really loved was the architecture. And San Francisco certainly offered a variety of that, whether it is Edwardians, Victorians, Tudor, Marina Style, Arts and Crafts or Modern. Our houses, which were built by the same developer in the mid-eighties, were inspired by the narrow Stick Victorians they mimicked. Yes, they were narrow like sticks, but they actually got their name from the exposed trusses or "stickwork" on the exterior.

We chose our houses because we liked the charm of a bygone era, but wanted all the modern conveniences of newer homes. These homes had the high ceilings, but not the cold draft coming in from the creaky old wooden windows. They also had good practical floor plans–not the tiny rooms with big parlors which Victorians were known for–but generously-sized bedrooms with walk-in closets. We enjoyed spacious bathrooms with plenty of room to navigate getting in and out of the shower, and we loved our gourmet kitchens with all the bells and whistles. Plumbing had not been introduced into houses until the early 1900's, so the kitchens and baths of the earlier homes were awkward, back-of-the-house additions. They did not have cars back then either, so these Victorians had no garages. But we did. Yet we still loved the older homes. I got my fix by selling real estate. Larry got his fix by drooling over the mansions in Pacific Heights during Sunday open houses. He told me he had compromised when he bought in Noe Valley. He just was not able to afford what he wanted in the more prestigious North of Market neighborhoods, so he settled for the next best thing–to his constant regret.

Since the first day I had met him, Larry had been compulsively saving until he could get into his first-choice neighborhood–even if it meant downsizing to a condominium. He had approached me three months earlier and asked for my help in finding him something in the trendy and upscale Cow

Hollow area near Union Street. Not only was he compulsively searching for his ideal home, but also his ideal mate. I would have fixed him up with one of my girlfriends, but he was not into women. After he and his partner, Scott, got together, he was more determined than ever to find his ideal home in the most prestigious neighborhood. And now he told me he found it–with another real estate agent! Of course, I immediately asked him for the address–3282 Filbert–and, of course, I knew the property. In fact, it was our company who put the condo up for sale! So naturally, I had already previewed the property. Granted, it was on a special block, utterly charming and spacious, but it was certainly not a match for Larry. Larry could not fix a thing and this condo needed tons of work. Tons!

"Larry, you looked with another real estate agent after all the real estate advice I've given you over the years, after all the times you've been to my house for dinner…"

"Paula–Stop for God's sake! I didn't do this on purpose!" I said nothing, waiting for him to explain. "I just asked a guy I knew at the gym that's in real estate, too. He had been offering to give me a free appraisal of what my house was worth. Then one thing led to another."

"But Larry, I told you what your house is worth. I gave you all the comparable sales in our neighborhood, plus what is currently for sale." My knuckles were turning ghostly white, because I was gripping the phone so hard. I switched the phone to my other ear and shook out my cramped fingers.

"I just wanted to be sure–that's all." Larry lowered his voice–as if that would make all this easier for me. "Then when I told him what I was looking for, he told me he had the perfect place. You know, we've been looking for over three months now, Paula."

"But you told me you could only spend up to a million," I said, trying not to panic. "The asking price is $950,000, plus all the work it needs will bring it up to a million plus."

Larry let out a long sigh. "I really wish you had told me about this property. Then we wouldn't be having all these problems."

Well, at least I have the listing on his house, I told myself. But my ears perked up at Larry's last comment. "What do you mean problems?"

"Well, H and L Realty also offered to list my house at a much lower commission if they represented me on both the buying and selling end, so I agreed. I can do a lot with an extra eight thousand dollars in my pocket."

I felt like I had just been hit by a 40-ton tractor trailer. That was the point when I said goodbye and slammed the phone. Now I kept pacing the floor, wondering what to do next. I opened the refrigerator door and looked at the carton of eggs sitting placidly on the middle rack. Underneath my professional exterior and need to help others, lay another person, ready to leap into a rage when I felt someone had taken advantage of me. The voice in my head was getting louder and louder, repeating over and over *After all I've done for you!* I imagined throwing the dozen eggs one by one against his new tri-colored paint job. I pictured the yellow yolk oozing down the front of the building, making a terrible mess. It gave me some satisfaction, especially since Larry was such a compulsive neatnik. Would he figure out it was me who did such a dastardly deed? I slammed the refrigerator door. I lifted the telephone up from the cradle to call him back and tell him what a creep I thought he was. But I couldn't do that either. I flung the receiver across the wall and watched as it crashed. I still felt frustrated so I battered the plastic earpiece into the floor until it was smashed. Wires were sticking out all over the place. I sat back on my heels and started to cry.

After my knee jerk reaction to Dr. Kessler's betrayal, I spent most of the day in bed. That evening I was feeling better and, not wanting to be without a phone, I went shopping for a new one. I was ashamed, but I did not know how to stop breaking things when I got upset. Despite my impulsive reaction, I knew what I needed to do next. I relinquished my hurt feelings and reminded myself that real estate was a service business. I called Larry back.

"Sorry, if I seemed abrupt when you called me yesterday," I said.

"Hmmm… " is all I heard on the other end of the line.

I continued, knowing to get reconnected to Larry I must tell the truth. "My feelings were hurt." Silence. I persevered. "If you want the name of a few contractors whom I trust to check out the condo you are considering buying,"–I tried not to choke–"I can give those to you."

"That's nice of you Paula, but we had the contractor's inspection today."

"And?"

"I hate to admit it, but you were right. The place needs way too much work and money–money I do not have."

"I'm sorry to hear that," I said with genuine concern as well as a wave of relief. I paused before I asked him the question I needed to know. "Will you still want to continue looking with me then?"

"To tell you the truth, Paula, I'm pretty wiped out by this whole process. I think I need a break."

"But what if I see something really special–can I still call you?"

"Well, you know what I'm looking for... okay... sure."

Larry was no longer on the top of my client list, but if I happened upon something that met his needs, I would call him. I wouldn't let this incident stand between me and a sale. It was mid-summer before I found that special property. I was brimming over with excitement when I placed the call.

Larry was ambivalent about looking. "I just bought an expensive couch and loveseat for my living room as a consolation gift to myself," he said.

"So? Bring it to your new home. This condo is one in a million, Larry. Right on Vallejo Street. It's a charming Edwardian with all the wainscoting intact, original light fixtures, and a renovated kitchen with one of those center islands. And you know, Edwardians have more practical floor plans than Victorians. Instead of narrow triple parlors and tiny bedrooms you get wider, larger rooms with bigger closets and a good size kitchen with plenty of pantry space."

No reply.

"Plus, the bathrooms are all located throughout the house, not just in the back, because these homes were originally built with plumbing. Sure, the outside of the Edwardians do not have all the intricate gingerbread molding like the Victorians, but inside they kept all the charm–the wainscoting, hardwood floors, high ceilings, the crown and picture moldings. They also added box beam ceilings, stained glass and built-in china cabinets in the entertaining rooms."

"Well... "

"Not only that," I said, "but this condo has already been renovated. The kitchen has Caesar stone counters and top-of-the-line appliances, including a Subzero refrigerator, wine cooler and cherry wood cabinets–the cherry wood is smooth as silk. You are absolutely in heaven when you touch it." I waited to hear his reaction. He appreciated fine quality and good taste and this condo had both.

"I don't know… "

"It has a formal dining room with built-in leaded glass cabinets, space for your hutch and a window seat. The two bathrooms are Italian marble and when you glide your hands across–just take a look–you owe it to yourself."

Larry acquiesced. "All right then. I'll go take a look."

I brought a measuring tape to see if the new furniture would fit in the living room. The couch would, but the love seat would not. "What if we put the loveseat in the den?" I suggested. We measured it together. It would fit, but it was going to be tight. I waited for his response.

"I'm not sure," he said. "Can I have Scott take a look?"

"Sure," I said, and the next day the three of us were back looking. "It's not perfect," Larry said.

"Is it because of the loveseat?" I asked. "Is that the only objection?" He did not answer. "Life is not perfect, Larry, and houses aren't either. Even millionaires do not get one hundred percent of their wish list," I said. "If you get 80% of what you are looking for, you are doing well."

I could tell from the glint in Scott's eyes and his wide smile that he loved the place. I tried to enlist his help in bringing Larry around. "What do you think, Scott?"

"I like it," he said. "I *really* like it." He touched the smooth Brazilian cherry wood cabinets in the kitchen with the palm of his hand, admiring the workmanship. This was good; now I had an ally.

"I'm just not sure," was Larry's answer.

I continued showing Scott the special features and did

a lot of oohing and aahing–all sincere, of course. This was a great condominium at an affordable price. I knew in my heart of hearts it was perfect for Larry. As we headed down the stairs, the listing agent whispered in my ear, "You have the patience of Job." If only she knew the whole story.

"We need to make a decision before the Sunday open house," I said, as we got into our respective cars. "After that it will be a free-for-all and this flat will get multiple offers."

The following day Larry decided to pull the trigger. He wanted the property. He offered at the asking price and the offer was accepted.

The Things You Cannot Change (Part A):
How Not to Handle a Client with Cold Feet

Frank Woods was one of my favorite clients. He decided his current house was too small for him, his new fiancée, Linda, and her five-year-old son. Frank was bright, witty and charming with a high profile job in the insurance business. He also had plenty of money and such an easygoing personality that it was a real joy to work with him. We had become good friends and even saw each other socially. He was a great source of referrals. He sang my praises and lauded my merits to his influential circle of friends.

In the span of a few months, I had found him a magnificent (and very expensive) home in Pacific Heights. To make sure we won the bid (it was a seller's market at the time), we got our inspections done before the offer date. As I was driving to Yosemite to celebrate my birthday, I got a call on my cell phone. I was in high spirits, thinking our non-contingent over-asking offer was a sure thing. It was Darlene, the listing agent, on the phone.

"Frank just called and withdrew his offer."

I gasped, searching for what to say. "He did what? What reason did he give?"

"No reason. You better call him and straighten this out. I am meeting with my sellers in an hour. You still have time."

I called him immediately. Although Frank was an astute businessman with a prestigious job, he was nervous. I felt exasperated. I expected much more of him. All the time we spent looking was for nothing. He was about to miss out on a great house. He told me he could not sleep at all the night before. Instead of recognizing his buyer's remorse, I got irritated.

"We've done our inspections. The house is in perfect condition and in your most favorite neighborhood. It is such an opportunity," I pleaded.

"I just can't go through with it," he said.

"But this is your dream house."

"I'm not ready," was his answer.

I started to get forceful. I reminded him how prestigious an address it was. I knew I should not be thinking of my feelings, but I let him knew how embarrassed I was letting down a top-selling agent in my own office. As a professional, I should be detached, but I could not contain my disappointment. I felt the anger collecting at the bottom of my throat. Instead of throwing the phone, I did something worse. I attacked him where he was most vulnerable.

"Did Linda put you up to this?" I could almost hear the venom in my voice.

There was silence at the other end of the phone. I had made a huge miscalculation. My bitter words hung like drawn daggers in the air. Cruel words which I could not take back.

He did not answer, but rushed a goodbye. I wondered if it would be goodbye for good. Would I ever be able to amend the hurt I just caused to my friend and client?

When I returned from my vacation, Frank avoided all my phone calls. A few months later I noticed his home listed with someone else and wondered where on Millionaire Row he lived now. I still wrote and called him occasionally, but never heard back. I could feel like a victim and beat myself up after ruining my relationship with Frank, but I chose instead to move on and help my other clients. I got past my frustration, although some agents often could not get out of their victim mode and seemed to wallow in self-pity for too long.

The Things You Cannot Change (Part B):
A Fellow Agent Wallowing in Self-Pity

Herbert Hubbard wasted a lot of time by acting as a tour guide for "Lookie Loo Buyers." In other words, he did not qualify his buyers financially or emotionally. He did not ask the five basic questions which every agent needed to know to determine a buyer's motivation:

1. *"Are you currently working with another agent?"*
2. *"Why are you buying?"*
3. *"Have you been preapproved with a lender?"*
4. *"When do you intend to move?"*
5. *"How long have you been looking?"*

Instead, as soon as Herbert encountered a live body, he shoved them into his car, hoping for the best. This sloppy business practice was always getting Herbert into trouble–and he seemed oblivious. More than once I overheard agents in our office warning Herbert about Sarah, a client they saw him counseling in the conference room. Agents who had worked with Sarah in the past knew she had been looking for property for years, but could not make a decision. Herbert shrugged off their concerns, insisting he had a special relationship with his new client, and felt he would succeed where they had failed. After several unsuccessful months, Herbert came to me for business coaching. He shared his disappointment that Sarah never purchased a home. Herbert told me that he had written three offers, but each time they were accepted Sarah backed out. When I asked Herbert why he did not listen to the other agents, he became defensive. I continued, explaining why I saw his effort with Sarah as a big waste of time. "Wouldn't your time be better spent prospecting?" I asked.

I reminded him of the popular saying–*if you really want something, you need to let it go.* "Trying too hard to force an outcome rarely works. Maybe Sarah needs some space to sort things out for herself." I gave him the example of Russ, a well-to-do client of mine from Beverly Hills who bought a probate on the top of Nob Hill, a block from the Mark Hopkins Hotel. It was a premium location for sure, but also a four-level home with no garage and no yard–not a typical choice for most people. Russ considered himself an innovative marketer and felt he could turn this property quickly and make a tidy profit. After six months with no offers, he still was not willing to reduce the price, so I needed to let him go. He listed with another top Realtor® in the city. When the other agent was not able to sell it either, Russ came back to me, ready to reduce his price. Why? Because he trusted my advice–that hard truth again–and now was ready to do what was necessary to sell.

"Herbert, from what you have told me, you've done everything you can to help Sarah. It is time to let her go. Sarah may never be ready. If she is, then, like Russ did with me, she will come back to you."

Shortly after our counseling session, I noticed that Herbert was no longer attending office meetings. Curious, I called him at home.

"I've been in bed ill with some sort of bug the last couple of weeks."

Whenever I got sick myself I always looked for some underlying emotional cause. My scientific training taught me that microbes were around us all the time. I had also learned that when we are under stress is most often when we get sick. "Is something else bothering you?" I asked.

"Well, I think this thing with Sarah has gotten me a bit down."

"Maybe that is why you are sick. You have been working nonstop for several months, trying to get her in contract. What do you think, Herbert?"

"I have been thinking that all I need is to find the right house for Sarah, but now I'm beginning to realize it is not the house–it's her–getting in the way of a sale. She can't make a commitment." He promised me he was going to tell Sarah that he was no longer willing to work with her. He had learned a valuable lesson about being more selective in working with clients. I felt gratified. I had done my job as his coach. Not long after our conversation, I passed him in the hallway. He looked miserable, so I asked him how he was doing.

"I've been working with this couple for over a year, but the transaction fell through because of their terrible credit."

"Wait, Herbert!" I said. "Didn't we discuss how important it is to establish the three signs of readiness in each new buyer? Why didn't you have them preapproved by a bank beforehand?" Herbert shrugged his shoulders. I was not going to buy into his victim mentality. "You could be more selective, Herbert," I said gently.

"You don't have any idea of what I am going through," he said as he stomped off. "Just feel lucky that you don't have loser buyers like I do."

Lessons Learned from Chapter 10:

- BE PREPARED FOR ANY POSSIBILITY Real estate involves a lot of money. People are unpredictable, fickle beings, capable of a wide spectrum of behavior. Be prepared for your best, most loyal clients to act in ways you never thought possible.
- SELF MANAGE YOUR EMOTIONS Concentrate on your goal first and foremost. Next, when events or people drive you crazy, do whatever you can to take care of yourself: talking out your frustration with a friend, taking an exercise class or even yelling in the car, if you must.
- SAY YOU ARE SORRY There will be times that clients will frustrate you. You may say things you regret. If and when that happens, own up to it and say you are sorry. Most clients will forgive you.
- KNOW WHEN TO LET PEOPLE GO You need to qualify your clients motivationally as well as financially. Ask how long they have been looking, when they expect to buy and why they want to buy now. If their time frame is six months or less, they are motivated buyers. If for some reason they cannot go through with the sale and it happens more than twice, waste no more time and let them go.

11

JEALOUSY, GREED AND ARROGANCE

Looking at the Bright Side

Sticking to your priorities once you have set them is challenging. I discovered this as I was writing this book. At one point, I was involved in a very problematic real estate transaction with a fellow colleague of mine. What I learned from the following example was the importance of associating with people who have similar values. Doing so may very well save you time and heartache.

The Ties that Blind

One year I listed a Grand Victorian in Pacific Heights; it had no garage and was right across from a bustling medical center. It had been Jerry and Jesse O'Neill's childhood home and they had inherited it from their mother when she had passed on a few years before. Trustee Sales, which this was, can be tricky. These big older homes usually had not been lived in for several years, and since the owners were often either sickly or elderly, there was almost always deferred maintenance–leaky roofs, drafty windows, busted pipes, faulty wiring, out-of-date appliances and obsolete floor plans. In other words these houses were white elephants.

There was also a precise legal process and specific disclosures uncommon to the average sale. Did the person die in the property? Did the heirs have all the correct signatures and a copy of the Trust? Was there an appraisal of how much the property was worth when the person died? An appraisal when a spouse or other joint heir died? Was anyone contesting the will?

In addition to the choice of a real estate agent, determining the sales price, and evaluating how much work the property might need before it was offered for sale, there were the personal effects of the home which needed to be sorted through, dispersed, sold or given away. Decisions, decisions, decisions. What made Trustee Sales especially tough, though, was not the paperwork, the condition of the house and all the work it entailed, but the emotional baggage of a family besieged by grief, rivalry or petty grievances. The sale usually involved people who did not always agree, had their own demanding lives and did not have the time, energy or the money to deal with the mountain of details they suddenly faced.

Our homes are more than an investment, more than a place to hang our hats, more than a tax break. Homes represent family, love and security and, like many things in life, often come up a bit short. These family homes are riddled with sentimentality and the overburdening sadness of what was or what could have been. It is often a complicated, messy affair of conflicting personalities and emotions. The O'Neill's house was no exception.

Before Jerry and Jesse enlisted my help, they had made the choice of painting the exterior of the home a loud brick red with black trim, and the stone walkway and wrought iron gate an incandescent white. The combination of the three stark colors with three different textures was what I would describe as alarming. However, what could I say? They just spent $20,000 on the new paint job and I did not want to insult them.

Jerry was the younger brother who never married and lived in the apartment downstairs. He was supposedly the caretaker of the property, but with the amount of fix-up that this home needed, he had been a bit lax in his job. He kept telling me he would get this and that done, but he never did. He was all talk and, from my observation, hitting the bottle pretty heavily. Jesse was slightly older, married, and a lawyer who lived in the East Bay. He was introverted, quiet and soft spoken–not the typical attorney. He also was quite protective of his younger, troubled alcoholic brother.

A week before we planned to put the property on the market, Jesse called to tell me Jerry wanted to increase the list price from $1,295,000 to $1,595,000. "It's a historical home," his brother had said to me several times. "Mayor So and So lived here. It has three bedrooms and a view. It has got to be worth at least a million and a half." Couldn't they see that their mother's house needed at least another half million to bring it into this century and two hundred grand more to put in a much needed garage? The top floor, which claimed a city view of sorts, was really a converted attic. The deck was so dry rotted I was afraid if more than three people stood on it at one time they would fall through. The kitchen needed to be gutted. The house had only one bathroom. On and on and on....

"It's not just the money the buyer has to put into the property," I told Jesse, who was the executor and the supposed decision maker. "But it is all the hassle the buyer has to go through to get the work done. Getting plans approved by the Planning and Building Departments is not easy. Plus, this house has the added complication of having an apartment where the garage needs to be." I tried to explain to him that San Francisco was unusual in that only a third of its residents were comprised of homeowners and the other two-thirds were renters. Since politicians side where the votes were, renters had a huge say in how our city was run.

"But my parents never rented out the apartment," Jesse argued. "It was just used for our family."

"It doesn't matter," I said. "The city doesn't like it when rental units are removed from the housing inventory. They will put up a big fight to keep the apartment intact–even if it was never rented. This is going to be a big obstacle for prospective buyers. We need to give them an incentive to buy. Since we aren't investing a lot of money in the fix-up, a competitive price is essential to get this puppy sold."

Jesse understood and agreed with me on the lower price when we reviewed the comparable sales, but Jerry wouldn't budge. He stormed out of the room, hurling insults at both of us about how we were ganging up against him. It was obvious Jerry did not want to sell. He was very attached to the property. Having lost both his mother and his eldest brother in the past few years, he felt that selling was just another loss. Although Jerry's unrealistic stance frustrated his older brother, Jesse gave in. He was afraid Jerry might go on one of his binges, and he admitted that he was not up to having another casualty in his life right now. After all, Jerry was Jesse's only surviving family member. Since I wanted to make the selling process as easy as possible for Jerry, and my direct presentation of the facts was not working, maybe a slower, soft-pedal approach would. So I changed the price in accordance with their wishes and added three months on to the listing period.

Getting agents inside the property was a huge challenge. Besides having no curb appeal, there was the added drawback of a busy street with no parking. I catered Broker lunches, mailed handwritten invitations to the neighbors, and distributed an elaborate color brochure to the top agents. I advertised in every magazine and newspaper I could think of–all with hardly a response. The one thing in my favor, however, was the shortage of big houses on the market. If someone wanted a family home in a prestigious area and did not mind doing the work, this could be a definite possibility. Each month that passed made Jerry and Jesse less committed to their asking price. Thirteen weeks into the marketing of the property, an attractive preppy husband and wife, John and Muffy Winthrop, with a small child in tow, came through on one of the Sunday open houses. They were not working exclusively with an agent, but did not want me representing them since I was representing the seller.

"That's fine with me," I said, just wanting to get this albatross sold so I could go on with my life. After a long litany of questions, they assured me they would be back once they found an agent. A few days later they were back with Suzie Weinhammer and a licensed contractor. I went through the house with them once again, answering all their questions. Two hours later, I handed them a detailed disclosure package, including the presale inspections already completed on the property.

It was almost seven in the evening on a Friday when my home phone rang. My husband, Gralen, was due to return shortly from a week-long business trip. We had made plans to meet up for dinner and, since I was already late enough as it was, I had my assistant answer. Suzie Weinhammer of Sotheby's had an offer for me. I got out of the shower, still dripping, and took the call, asking if she could call me back in ten minutes. "I'm running late and have to meet my husband and a group of friends for dinner," I explained.

"No, I can't." she said, insisting I call her back instead.

"Fine," I said, thinking Suzie might be one of those prima donna egomaniacs. Realizing I was being negative, I canceled that thought and concentrated on the positive. Suzie Weinhammer was an established agent and this was the first offer we had received after several months of marketing. I looked at the clock, knowing I was late and threw on a dress, some makeup and earrings. I made sure I grabbed my cell phone on the way out, and planned to call her en route. I did my best navigating through bursts of pouring rain, and suddenly realized I did not have Suzie's telephone number. That meant I had to retrieve her number from my voice mail at work by punching in my extension, security code, and going through all my other messages. I decided it was just too dangerous to do in the car and so I drove on.

The restaurant was small and intimate and spilling over with people celebrating the start of a weekend. There was no place I could go to make a phone call. I ordered a glass of wine and relaxed, enjoying dinner with my husband and his friends. On the way home, rain was still spilling from the sky in sheets. When the downpour lessened a bit, I pulled over, but with the rain pounding my convertible top, I could not hear my messages, and unfortunately, it was also getting late. "Well," I reasoned to myself, "they waited a week to write the offer, they can wait a few more hours."

When I called Suzie early the next morning she did not

answer. I noticed a contract came through the fax machine, but it was light and hard to read. I changed the ink cartridge, read the contract, had breakfast, got dressed and waited for Suzie's call. Twenty-five minutes into my yoga routine the phone finally rang. I asked if she could meet with my sellers to discuss the offer. "The price is a bit low," I said as softly as I could so I didn't offend her.

I hardly got these words out of my mouth when she shot back at me, "Great! Now you're telling me that you have difficult sellers who aren't motivated! I don't know how thoroughly you read the offer, but you'll have to hurry because we expect an answer by five tonight!"

"How do you expect me to do that? It's Saturday and almost noon!" I answered without thinking, ready to meet her forceful energy. Catching myself in a power play, I looked at my Buddha sitting comfortably above my desk and changed my approach, remembering my Empathy Rule–maybe Suzie had a really hard week. In my softest, most understanding voice I said, "I will do my best to get a meeting with at least one of them today, but I know Jesse has an appointment in Santa Rosa. Hopefully, it is later in the afternoon and I can meet with him before he leaves." I did not want to meet with Jerry and certainly did not want this agent to know I had a difficult seller–an overly sentimental, alcoholic seller to be exact.

Once again I made a plea for her to be at the presentation, using team language and her name so she felt acknowledged. "Suzie, if you are present, you will be able to push harder for your clients than I can. I need to represent the seller."

"I really can't." Her tone was bitter and cold.

"It is a seller's market," I reminded her and lightly laughed.

"You know how tough clients can be." I then took a deep breath, waiting for her response.

Suzie got more agitated and belligerent. "Didn't you hear what I just said–I am busy."

My approach was not working. I wondered if by being direct and naming what was going on I would get her to be more cooperative. That would be Dr. Black's recommendation. In a quick ten-second analysis, I decided that telling her she was too aggressive would only add more fuel to the fire. A softer approach enlisting her help was probably best. "Why don't we work on this together and make it a win/win for both our clients?" I asked. She said nothing. Deciding to use more empathy to build rapport, I once again asked for her assistance. "I would really like to make this work, Suzie. Are you sure you can't take a half an hour out of your day to meet? You're a great agent and I'd love to sell my listing. How about at your office?"

Her voice was tight and gritty. "Aren't you listening, Paula–I am busy! You also should know that these buyers are considering another property so if your sellers aren't interested, we will just move on. You have by five tonight or we walk."

I could feel red hot anger surging up from my chest like a volcano about to explode. *How dare she speak to me like that!* I wanted to tell her what I really thought, but stopped myself. That was an old pattern that never worked. I needed to get into a more positive frame of mind before I talked to my clients. A few quick stretching exercises and I was ready. I reached Jesse on his cell phone. Unfortunately, he was already on his way to Santa Rosa.

"By the way," he said, "before I left the house, I did some checking on our buyers online."

"Really?" I never thought of doing that. "What did you find out?" I asked, impressed he had taken the time from his busy schedule.

"Both the husband and wife are from wealthy well-established East Coast families, and John is a Harvard grad with a top-notch position at a local law firm. They certainly have the money, whereas the proceeds from our mother's house are our main source of retirement."

"Does that mean you won't negotiate on price?" I asked, taken aback. "Remember, our list price is higher than we originally agreed."

"We'll negotiate some–just not much. Why don't you meet with Jerry today since they want an answer right away? The earlier the better. Hopefully, he won't have started drinking. Let me call him first."

I was frustrated that Suzie Weinhammer had put me in this position. I could not very well tell her what I was up against, because she was focusing on just her clients and did not care about my clients' needs. Definitely not a win/win situation. Instead, I was being forced to negotiate with an irrational alcoholic who did not want to sell. If only Suzie was willing to work with me, I might have a fighting chance to get a decent counteroffer for her. We could have played good cop, bad cop, or presented the Winthrops to Jerry in such a way that he would want them to get the house. Better yet, we could have waited until Monday to meet with Jesse, who would be more practical and realistic. But, no, Suzie wanted it her way or the highway.

Looking closely at the offer, it became clear that neither Suzie Weinhammer nor the Winthrops had read the disclosure packet I had given them. They did not follow the guidelines of a Trustee Sale, nor had they signed off on any of the inspections. I did my best to convince Jerry to give them a counter, but Jerry decided against it.

"What about them going to another property?" I told him what Suzie told me, but in more delicate terms, hoping it did not sound like a threat.

"Let them. They don't seem like serious buyers. Besides, I don't like ultimatums."

I typically liked to give a counter, because I felt constant dialogue was key to a successful transaction, but Jerry was adamant. I folded up my paperwork with a sigh–a low offer which did not work was better than nothing. Perhaps Jerry and Jesse would consider lowering their asking price soon. I made the courtesy call to Suzie and left her a message, thanking her for the offer and wishing her luck with the other property because we were not going to respond.

The following day Suzie Weinhammer left a message on my voice mail telling me how unprofessional I had been (the perfect compliment to convince me to want to work with her). Yet, in the next breath she said she was willing to extend the expiration time, requesting us to counter her offer. I was left to wonder if the Winthrops really had another property they were considering or not. I spent a good part of my morning weeding my backyard. I did not want to be reactive when I spoke with Suzie. With my mind clear, I returned her call, suggesting we start fresh by having the Winthrops approve the disclosure package first, and then resubmitting a new offer by following the Trustee Sale guidelines.

"No! That is not how we're going to do it! You already have our offer–you *must* get back to us. That is the only way we will work with you."

Her aggressive energy was like a cluster of angry gnats around my head. I was getting tired of all her threats. "Well Suzie, I guess that is your choice," I said.

I took a long shower trying to wash away the emotionality of our interchange, refusing to let myself get pulled into her drama any longer. I felt the pent-up frustration drain out of the soles of my feet through the tile flooring to the ground outside. I imagined the negative stream moving far away from me into the center of the earth. When I felt that I had cleansed myself completely, I called Jesse and Jerry, relaying my conversation with Suzie in a light, off-handed way. We laughed together, agreeing that none of us wanted to work with controlling people like these.

The next day Mike Greenland, my current manager, called me into his office. Suzie Weinhammer had called and complained. I dug my heels in, becoming more persistent than ever that she was not going to win by intimidation. At the same time, I knew the importance of remaining calm. Mike had seen me get emotional in the past and hated it. I thought of my yoga practice to keep my voice steady while I explained that we were not given enough time to respond. I added, "The O'Neills are reasonable people and not opposed to working with the Winthrops. We are only asking the buyers to follow the standard protocol of a Trustee Sale with the disclosure package approved beforehand. Then they can submit a new offer." Mike suggested we play the game the way Suzie Weinhammer wanted. "After all," he said in his most convincing tone, "she is the number one agent in her office."

So whatever Suzie wants, Suzie gets–while she mistreats everyone else around her? Now was the honeymoon phase of the negotiating process when the selling agent did everything possible to please the listing agent. Once her offer was accepted, I could only imagine Suzie Weinhammer's difficult behavior escalating. Why would I want to put myself, or my clients, through all that drama? It was time to start setting boundaries now–not later when she felt even more empowered to get her way through force and intimidation. I reminded Mike that my loyalty was to my clients who hired me–not to any agent–it didn't matter if she was the top selling agent at Sotheby's.

"I don't feel comfortable trying to convince my clients to counter an already expired offer, which is way below their asking price and full of loopholes, because no one bothered to read the disclosure package," I said. "Let them do their due diligence and then my clients will entertain their offer." I left Mike's office feeling calm, with my self-esteem intact. I rewarded myself by taking a long walk by the Marina Green. A week later I heard from Tracy Bingsley, an agent who worked in the same office as Suzie Weinhammer. She told me she had a new offer from the Winthrops on Sacramento Street.

"Have the Winthrops approved the disclosure package yet?" I asked. She answered that they had. "You understand then that this is a Trustee Sale?" I wanted no misunderstandings this go-around.

Tracy said she knew that too and added, "They've also been preapproved by a lender."

This was how offers should be done. I suggested to Tracy that she do a face-to-face presentation so we could start fresh, admitting that the first offer got off to a bad start. "I find it always helps if the clients know a little about each other so they can relate better during the transaction. With you present, the O'Neills can ask you questions about the buyer that

I can't answer," I said. Tracy agreed and we set up a time to meet at my office. When Jerry suggested that we meet at the property instead, I stood my ground, knowing we needed a neutral place. I used the excuse of having access to all our forms and copy machine.

Jerry and Jesse arrived a few minutes ahead of time so we could strategize. "Feel free to ask the agent any questions you wish," I advised. "Just don't get hung up on price. Keep in mind that a buyer wants to negotiate the lowest price possible, so don't be insulted. We can always counter their offer after Tracy Bingsley leaves."

"Since the Winthrops have already given us an offer, won't it be better this time?" Jesse asked.

"I would think so, but it's hard to second guess. We'll just have to wait and see." I looked at my watch. "We'll know soon enough. Tracy should be here any minute."

I offered them both a cup of coffee and got my notebook out with the counter form, thinking I would probably need it. If it was another low price, I hoped Tracy Bingsley brought some Multiple Listing statistics to show how they arrived at their offering price. Although Jerry did not want to hear what I had to say about price, he might listen to someone else if they could substantiate their figure with some hard facts.

Tracy was right on time and was dressed in a powder blue Chanel suit. Her hair was blonde and long, and she was a bit younger than I had expected. Despite her age, it was easy to see she put considerable effort into looking professional. She extended a warm handshake to each of us. She had photos of the Winthrops and a nice letter from them, which was a good idea, because Jerry and Jesse might have had some preconceived, not-so-nice notions about these buyers. She also had a copy of their credit score from their lender–another item we never got with the first offer. So far so good.

I glanced over at Jerry and Jesse. Both were alert with open body language. An excellent sign. Jerry even asked Tracy about what the Winthrops planned to do with the property, actually leaning over the table to listen to what she had to say. It was obvious he had not been drinking. I secretly applauded myself for scheduling an early morning appointment. He gave his own opinion about what he thought could improve the home, things that he always wanted to do, but never found the time. This was the perfect opening for Tracy, who had a cost breakdown of improvements that she handed out to both brothers. Maybe not what they expected, but something that they needed to hear. She then discussed similar properties that had sold recently. Since she was not representing the O'Neills, she could be more forceful than I.

Previously, whenever I talked price, I had to be careful not to offend them lest they think I did not like their mother's home. Even though the Winthrops had not changed their low offering price, Jesse and Jerry remained cordial. They asked Tracy a few more questions, and told her how much they appreciated her meeting with them. She left and I discussed the offer more thoroughly alone with them.

Although the Winthrops had already had a contractor's inspection and the disclosure package had copies of termite, geological and energy inspections, they still included a ten-day contingency period to get more inspections. Jerry and Jesse were apprehensive. "They already had their inspections. Why should we give them more time? It's just a way for them to get out of the contract." I also saw this clause as a possible escape, but I wanted to get this process rolling along. So what if this offer didn't work? Maybe the O'Neills would be more open to the next one.

I responded by saying, "The buyers have the right to do as much discovery as they wish. They want to be secure in their decision and, as sellers, I suggest you allow them to make any inspections they want. At this point, let's concentrate only on price. Remember, even if this offer does not work, I can tell other agents we received an accepted offer. Having an accepted offer will encourage more interest, because the adage, People always want what they can't, which also applies to real estate." I pushed a pen towards them and waited. Neither Jerry or Jesse picked up the pen.

"If the Winthrops ask for more money after their inspections," I said, "We can always tell them no."

Jerry spoke first. "We still want more money though." Jerry and Jesse looked at each other. Their eyes locked. Their hands were closed with an air of rigid determination.

One step at a time, I told myself. I could only persuade so much. "What's the verdict?" I asked. I made sure I was smiling.

"We'll counter only on price," Jesse said. "We'll come down $20,000, but that's it."

It was not much, but it was something. I called Tracy Bingsley to tell her we were faxing the counteroffer to her office, explaining that my sellers would be open to a response. Jerry and Jesse did not tell me that, but I wanted to keep communication lines open. The Winthrops did not respond. A week went by. I continued marketing the property. Another week. And another. We still had not heard from the Winthrops and there were no other buyers on the horizon. I waited one more week, then called Tracy to see if the Winthrops found another property. They had not.

"Would they consider submitting their absolute best offer on Sacramento Street?" I asked. "It would have to be better than their last offer, but I think the O'Neills are ready now."

Tracy came back with an offer only slightly better and still with the same ten-day inspection period. The O'Neills were disappointed, but had been worn down after almost five months of having only this offer. They grudgingly accepted it, emphasizing they would not negotiate a penny less–no matter what the Winthrops found in the contractors' inspections.

We were in contract, but the following Sunday I still held an open house. I had learned that one never knew what the outcome would be. A dowdy, slightly overweight woman in her forties rushed through, bubbling with excitement, declaring that she had finally found her perfect home. *It always happens this way,* I mused–*feast or famine.* I told her that the house was already in escrow with an inspection contingency. She ran to get her husband who was sitting in the car with two small children. He previewed the house, also agreeing that this was the house for them. Chris and Macy Remy left their number and asked me to call them if I knew of any similar properties. That week I showed Macy three other houses. She did not like any of them.

"Please promise me you will call me if the other offer doesn't work," Macy pleaded.

"It's doubtful," I said as I handed her my cell phone number. "But feel free to call me Saturday if you wish. They had two inspections yesterday and it went well. They are supposed to remove the inspection condition by end of this week." Too bad they didn't come by a few weeks earlier. It always seemed people wanted what they couldn't have.

Thursday, late afternoon, I called Tracy. She had been out of town for a few days, but was expected back later that day. I got no call back. I called twice more the following day. Still no response. I was wondering why the delay in getting me the removal of the inspection contingency. I called her manager–he was out of town. It was now time for me to contact Jerry and Jesse to ask if they wanted to give the Winthrops a Twenty-Four Hour Notice to Perform. They did. I sent the fax to Tracy's home and office and called to tell her what we were doing. This time Tracy called back in a matter of minutes, requesting an extension of the contract. I was thinking that the Winthrops wanted one more pass at the new listings open this weekend before they fully committed to buying this house. So it appeared the inspection condition was a loophole after all.

I called Jesse and asked what he wanted to do. He did not want to extend the contingency period. Why would he? The Winthrops had had six weeks to think about whether they wanted the property or not. The Twenty-Four Hour Notice to Perform still stood. Saturday morning came and went. The Winthrops had not responded to our request and were now out of contract. Chris and Macy called Saturday evening to check on the status of the house and were thrilled to learn that they had a chance. They had no agent representing them and wanted me to write up the offer. I met with them the following day, which was Mother's Day, and Macy was beside herself with happiness.

"This is the best Mother's Day present I could ever have," she said. "What ever happened with the other offer?" she asked.

"Well, the most curious thing happened. We did not hear from the buyers all day yesterday and then this morning their agent called to tell me that they wanted a $135,000 credit. Can you imagine? Of course, my clients said no."

Chris and Macy shook their heads. "You'll find we are easy buyers. We'll stand behind our contract and what we sign." They eagerly reached for a pen and signed every page without hesitation. They had brought a preapproval letter and credit report from their lender as I had requested, and a 3% earnest money deposit. Macy handed me a handwritten note to the O'Neills as a way of introduction, praising their mother's home. I could see nothing that would stand in their way of purchasing their dream home. I was just about to call Jesse to let him know the good news when my phone rang. It was Tracy. She was checking to see if the O'Neills would consider crediting her buyers half of their initial request–just $67,000. "No, they're not interested," I said, now self-assured with my hand on another contract. "In fact, we have another offer."

Tracy was aghast. "You can't do that. We had a contract. Let me call my clients. I'll call you right back."

The phone rang less than a minute later. It was Tracy. She sounded out of breath. "Okay, then. The Winthrops will stick with their original offer."

"Tracy, we can't do that now," I said slowly, choosing my words very carefully. "There's another offer."

"But, Paula, you know how hard I've worked on this. I had to come back early from my vacation in Mexico to get this done."

"But the truth is you didn't get it done. The time elapsed yesterday at ten in the morning. You received a Twenty-Four Hour Notice to Perform and you ignored it. It is now Sunday evening and there is another offer. If you want to resubmit your offer, I will present it again to the O'Neills, but you are now competing with someone else."

The next morning the O'Neills and Mike Greenland and I discussed the two offers with my manager. The O'Neills did not trust the Winthrops anymore, thinking they might find some new angle to wrangle over. They accepted the Remys' offer unequivocally. It was an easy choice.

Twenty-one days later I deposited the $75,000 commission check into my bank account–a direct result of not slipping into my usual pattern of resentment and anger, focusing instead on getting the house sold. My days were always full of surprises, sometimes very pleasant ones, like the day I held an Open House one damp, foggy Sunday afternoon.

A Return to the Joy of the Sale

The Bay Area real estate market, like the rest of the country, was deep in a recession. I had a great listing–a home in the Haight previously owned by Graham Nash–but with no activity for six months. That day, like many days before, I dressed for success, put on a positive attitude and told myself there's a perfect buyer somewhere out there, who wants a home just like this one. I was rewarded when a casually dressed, short black man appeared at the door and extended his hand.

"Hi, I'm Bobby," he said. He had an aura of self-assurance and importance that I guessed no last name was necessary.

So I answered in kind with just my first name. "Hi, I'm Paula," I said and shook his hand. Hmmm–am I supposed to know who this guy is?

After a quick walk around the first level, I took him downstairs to the sound studio that Graham had built in the seventies when he owned the home. I usually guided people upstairs to the bedrooms first, but had a hunch that this guy would appreciate this special feature. Bobby was enthralled. "Do you mind if I test out my voice in here?" he asked.

"No... aah... not at all... sure go ahead," I said.

Bobby proceeded to sing–not in words–but in varied combinational vowel sounds. I moved to one of the back rooms to give him some privacy. Who is this guy, anyway? I wondered. After about twenty minutes he was ready to see the rest of the house. Bobby breezed through it, while here and there I gave him gossipy tidbits of the home's past history to keep him interested. I showed him the hundreds of popsicle sticks on the sloped attic ceiling.

"These were supposedly glued on by the band members of Crosby, Stills, Nash, and Young," I chuckled, "after their jamming sessions." I then pointed to the huge Georgian Colonial on the double lot next door, telling him it had once been owned by the Spreckels Sugar family. "By the way," I continued, "I just sold that house to Danny Glover a few months ago. I understand he's doing a huge remodel and putting in another full level for a gym. He could have bought anywhere and he bought here." I hoped this potential buyer, whomever he was, could see the value of this location–directly across from San Francisco's beautiful Buena Vista Park.

The next day at the office I asked my fellow office mates who he could be–this short black man with long dreadlocks, who sang in weird vowel sounds, and whose first name was Bobby.

"Bob Marley has come back to the living," Kevin O'Connor answered, always the Irish smart aleck.

"Come on, really! This guy came into my open house

yesterday. He was singing in all the rooms and he acted like he really knew what he was doing."

"Sounds like some impersonator deadbeat to me," he replied. "After all, Paula, it is the Haight–all kinds of riffraff there."

"Nope–you're wrong," I answered. "This guy is someone famous–I had goose bumps just being around him."

My colleagues walked away, shaking their heads, probably thinking what a nut I was for being so gullible. Well, I thought, I would just have to wait for him or his agent to call me. He did seem really interested. Sure, enough, his agent called later that day, thanking me for taking such good care of her client and not fawning all over him because of his fame.

"And your client is...?" I asked sheepishly.

"Bobby McFerrin of 'Don't Worry Be Happy' fame."

"Oh, of course! His name just escaped me for a moment," I said, trying to save face. "You know that is one of my most favorite songs. I use it kind of like a mantra." And that was absolutely true!

"Well, he wants me to bring his wife through tomorrow. And just off the record," she snorted at her pun, "he's very excited to live next door to Danny Glover."

A few days later we sealed the deal. I secretly thanked my mind and body for clueing me in that this person was a well-known artist. If I had not taken my hunch seriously, I might not have gotten the notion of radically changing up the way I approached showing him the home, which turned out to focus on the "sound studio" and historical features that in all likelihood were what he most fell in love with in the course of that initial house tour.

Lessons Learned from Chapter 11:

- PAY ATTENTION TO BODY CUES Our bodies are like radar and can sort through confusing sensory information that the mind does not understand. By paying attention to our bodies, we can develop better communication by understanding what is happening in the moment.
- CHOICES HAVE CONSEQUENCES Every choice has a consequence. Know what your professional standards are because there are times you may have to sacrifice a sale or a friendship to remain true to what is most important to you. Integrity, fellowship and honest communication should be high on your list.
- CONCENTRATE ON WHAT YOU CAN DO. There are some things you can control and some things that you cannot. Avoid interfering with family dynamics and be as flexible as possible. Often, time, like water, will wear down the staunchest positions.
- WORK AS A TEAM Selling homes is complicated. The more people work together, the easier it will be to get the job done. Real estate transactions are best accomplished when it is a win/win situation for both buyer and seller.

12

IMBALANCE

Learning Temperance

Must the Fruits of Success Always Include Overwork?

After a ten-day span of twelve to fourteen-hour workdays, I dragged myself out of bed when I heard my phone blasting in my ear–another *Manic Monday.* I glanced quickly at my appointment book crammed with showings, inspections and offer presentations, half wishing I had gotten the few extra hours of sleep I needed instead of going out last night to see Cirque du Soleil. *But when was it that I went out last?* I could not even remember.

I prepared one of my antioxidant energy smoothies. Deciding this was a two-scoop day, I swallowed the murky pea-green concoction down with a handful of vitamins. *This should do the trick,* I said to myself–all the time wondering how I would ever make it through the week that would lead off with three ready-to-buy clients and a listing on which I had just received an offer.

After my 60-second shower, I checked the messages on my cell phone, the ones left on my home recorder, and the ones in the office voice mail. It was eight in the morning, so I called Steve Bellos, the fast-talking stock broker, to get his final signature on a counter offer–supposedly the "sophisticated buyer" who assured me he would be reachable all weekend. As soon as he picked up the phone, he told me he was thinking about asking the seller to pay for his inspections.

"I wouldn't recommend doing that," I advised. "Another agent showed 1998 Filbert yesterday and probably will be bringing in an offer."

"They can't do that," Steve insisted.

"In fact, they can. I don't have your final signature, Steve. Remember–time is of the essence when we are in the midst of negotiating." I answered, doing my best to remain calm, as I had practiced so many times before. "By the way, where were you all weekend?

"On the golf course. I work hard during the week."

"You didn't think to turn your cell phone on even though we are in the middle of negotiations?" I asked, bewildered by his lackadaisical attitude. We could lose this sale.

"Not when I play golf. What is this anyway–the Inquisition?"

Against my better judgment I returned the volley. "Gee, I wish I had some time off once in a while." Being right was becoming more important than the money now. *See what happens when I'm overtired,* I said to myself, promising to go no further. I took a deep breath, remembering when Frank Woods refused to return my calls after I made the blunt remark about his fiancée.

"Did Paul Bishop sign the counter yet?" Steve asked. Paul was the co-borrower and a past client, who brought Steve Bellos in on this deal in the first place. All the condo needed was a new kitchen and bath, and then it could be flipped in a year or two for a tidy profit. Even if the market were to head south, they could rent it out for a good price and break even, because of its close proximity to Union Street, the Marina and public transportation.

"Yesterday morning. We are just waiting for you."

After a harrowing list of questions Steve finally agreed to sign, but insisted I come to his office way across town, because he wanted to have the original.

"Fine," I said, not wanting to argue. His faxed signature sealed the deal, so before I left, I opened up an escrow with a title company, ordered the preliminary title report, and arranged to have the good faith deposit money delivered. I then coordinated what needed to happen to remove the contingencies of the sale, such as setting up the termite, contractor and geological inspections and organizing the mound of disclosures that would need to be signed. A partial list for sure, but at least it was a start.

In the midst of all this craziness, I got a call from one of my Gotta Buy Now clients who wanted to write an offer on the condo I showed them Saturday. Then the other Ready To Go buyer called to tell me he found the perfect house when he was out looking at open houses yesterday. In the olden days I would have been out of my seat excited, but I found myself getting depressed–not knowing how I would ever be able to handle all the tasks in front of me. My office phone started ringing madly, so I begged to get off the line and call him right back.

The other phone call was from the agent who had been saying he might be writing an offer on the listing I just put in escrow this morning. I then called the seller, Mr. Yang, who pressed me with why I did not present the offer yesterday. "Because I just got the call today–this minute," I answered, double-checking that my voice remained calm even though his accusation was like a knife in my gut.

Fortunately for me, the first offer was the better of the two and this second would be a backup. Still, I felt like I was on the firing line and Mr. Yang did not speak the best English. I got off the phone as quickly as possible, promising him I would call him back later to discuss his concerns. I went back to my computer to finish the counteroffer while the fax machine rang loudly in my ear and decided to jam. On this of all days? While I tried to pull out the crumpled paper, the machine let out a huge screeching noise as if it was alive and I was purposely torturing it. Then the phone rang once again, disturbing my concentration even more.

After being unavailable all weekend, Steve now had silly questions that he deemed urgent. I thought they could wait until tomorrow for answers. I explained I was swamped, but he did not understand. He got irate, because he was a Right Now kind of guy. He threatened to call Paul when I told him I would get back to him later. Sure enough, Paul called shortly after. Now I had to do damage control. This was how my day went–high stress to the max.

I was overworked, overtired and, although well-paid, I was wondering if all this was worth the money I would make. I grabbed a cup of coffee to keep me going and hopped in the car to meet Steve, hoping to patch some of the damage caused by not giving him enough attention. I looked at my watch and noticed I was running a bit late. So what else was new? An intense coal-hot heat took over my body, causing my blood pressure to rise and my heart to palpitate. If I were a car, I would be ready to blow a gasket.

I should never have drunk that caffeine-laden coffee. Too preoccupied with what I needed to do next, I ignored the police car at the intersection monitoring cars rolling through the stop sign. Looking in my rear view mirror, I saw a spinning red light. I pulled over to the curb. A square-shouldered uniformed man with a badge approached my car with brusque steps. "Didn't you see the stop sign? Let me see your license, registration and insurance."

Unable to utter a word in my defense, I gave him the feeblest of smiles.

"Come on, move it. I don't have all day." He already had a pen and a uniform violations booklet in hand. I fumbled in my purse, hoping I could locate what he needed quickly.

The officer started to preach like a pulpit priest. "I am sick and tired of people ignoring signals as if they don't exist. People these days have no regard for the law and are in their own little world. But then when they get stopped, they can't understand why. No one wants to take responsibility. But guess what? You are because you are getting a ticket!"

I wanted to go back to bed and pull the covers over my head. Add going to traffic school on my never-ending task list. *When is this hectic life ever going to end?* Yes, sales could be exciting, but at the same time, very seductive in a sinister way–taking over your whole life if you were not careful. I sometimes forgot all about determining what matters most, because I got so caught up in the adrenalin rush of being successful. Balance was a constant juggling act. I sincerely believe that we were not meant to live these frantic, frenzied lives where productivity, money and success are our only values. In choosing such a limited scope of reality, we have lost the richness and expansiveness of life experiences around us… the smile of a child, the smell of fresh-cut grass, the sound of crashing waves on the beach and the vividness of a scarlet sunset.

It was the early nineties and I had accomplished virtually everything I had set out to do. I had become a consistent top salesperson, got my Broker's License, was recognized in the real estate community by being elected to serve on both the Board of Directors for the Bay Area Real Estate Association and San Francisco Apartment House Association, and I now had all the material necessities one could ask for–my own home, an apartment building, blue chip stocks, a BMW convertible, designer clothes and five ball gowns for my competitive dancing. Yet I was yearning for something more–though I had no idea what. Finally, I got a subliminal clue when I started having dreams that I was living in Europe again. My creative side needed to be fed.

In my waking life, I then manifested a boyfriend from Poland (I met him in a health food store of all places!) We dated a few months and shortly afterwards spent the summer in his small country town near Czestochowa. Although Marek and I did not make it as a couple, I received some valuable insight from his culture about what I needed to do to be happy. Europeans took time to enjoy the small pleasures of life–casual conversation, cooking, gardening, walking in nature–instead of the American way of focusing exclusively on making money. The European attitude was: *Work to Live* rather than *Live to Work*. Embracing that idea, when I heard of *Balance for Life,* an Australian-based holistic approach to healing, I volunteered to sponsor their program in San Francisco. We learned all about the benefits of food combining, basic yoga postures, herbs, essential oils and acupuncture points. We then followed up our learning with an advanced month-long course in kinesiology and anatomy in Melbourne, Australia.

I started to get in touch with the core of me–that I was more than just my real estate and dance achievements, my travel experiences or who I was dating at the time.

During this same period, my company, McGuire Real Estate, in honor of their 75th Anniversary, sponsored four charity events. I volunteered to organize a benefit for breast cancer. Since the statistics in the Bay Area had jumped from one in nine women to one in eight for this deadly disease, my friends and I were concerned. Breast cancer was still not openly discussed in the conservative affluent circles of San Francisco of which McGuire was at its epicenter. However, that did not deter me. Through a friend, I met Matuschka, an artist who was famous for her startling self-portraits after undergoing a mastectomy. She was portraying herself, although scarred, as a woman with her beauty, pride and dignity still intact. Amelia Davis, a native San Franciscan artist and Annette Porter, a photographer from Seattle, were also featured in *The Invasive Art Show,* which I held at the Spectrum Gallery. All proceeds went to the National Lymphedema Network. It was a spectacular success. (Little did I know then that, in a few short years, my sister-in-law would be one of the statistics, dying at the young age of forty-six.)

After I sponsored the Australian-based *Balance for Life* Workshops and *The Invasive Art Show,* I started to feel whole again. I was feeling more balanced, but I could still sense something remained out of whack. What was it?

McGuire was–and still is–one of the leading real estate firms in San Francisco. It had taken me almost ten years to get there. I was proud to be affiliated with them, but lately their cutthroat competitiveness was having a negative effect on me. I could deal with the snobbery and elitism in the good-time eighties because there was enough business to go around. But the nineties were tougher financially, and the cliquish prima donnas, who were the San Francisco social set, ruled at McGuire. I was beginning to realize that selling at any cost was not my style and never would be. I liked representing first-time buyers, quirky artists and my past, true-blue loyal clients. But McGuire's main objective was to be the biggest, the strongest and the best. And, of course, to sell, sell, sell.

My projects at McGuire were beginning to go bad for me in many different ways. The previous year I had listed a great house in Jordan Park, near Presidio Heights, which was a referral, but now my contract had expired. We had planned to put it back on the market in a few months. I was surprised when one of the super agents, who sat behind me in the office, listed it two weeks later. When I had listed that particular property, she had gushed and gushed. And later when she heard the listing had expired, acted like a cat that just caught a prize goldfish in its mouth. Could she have just bypassed my feelings, thrown comrade loyalty out the window and called this seller asking for the listing? Then, shortly thereafter, one of my past clients, Doug Haskins, was being transferred back to Houston and thinking of selling. I brought a sales manager, Art Mayfield, and a few other agents through to price his home. Obviously, Doug Haskins was not happy with our price, because he ended up listing with another top agent in my office at $50,000 higher than what my colleagues and I quoted.

Next, a "For Sale by Owner," whose house I had put an offer on, promised me I would get the listing if he could not sell it on his own by the end of the year. Wouldn't you know it–when I returned from Christmas vacation, it was listed by one of the favored pets of the office. Surely the seller must have called the McGuire office looking for me. I assumed management, instead of contacting me, referred him to one of the chosen ones. Still I stayed. What was I thinking? Well, for one thing, I knew I was not being singled out. These unfortunate events happened to several of us. My closest associates urged me to talk to management–this type of business practice was demoralizing. I agreed and made an appointment. What did I have to lose? Best to get grievances out in the open. Mr. Beltham listened to the three different scenarios, nodding in acknowledgment. After I was done, he smiled, "So what's next?"

"Next?" I echoed, not understanding what he meant.

"That is all in the past Paula. It's time to move forward. What are you going to do now for business?" *So he is just ignoring my complaint?* I shrugged, astounded that he was not about to acknowledge what had transpired here. "You could always take Lifespring and get a new attitude," he suggested with a smile so broad it felt insincere.

"I've done that route," I said. "EST, Lifespring, actualizations, affirmations, positive thinking, meditation. What I think I need from you is a referral to make up for all these unfortunate situations," I said.

"Yeah, you probably do," he said and wrote himself a note. From the look on his face, I doubted I would ever get anything from him. The only referral I got in all the years at McGuire was Blayne Ritter–not the kind of transaction I would like to repeat. Yes, I finally did sell their property, but only after my commission was slashed in half to save the deal. Truthfully, these were the type of clients I would never want to do business with again.

Was the universe trying to tell me something? It was time to see Dr. Black again and get some clarity on what to do next. Still her same blonde, bubbly self with maybe a few extra mid-life pounds, Dr. Black's first question to me was: "Why aren't you with a firm that is more aligned with your values?"

I countered her argument. "McGuire is a well-respected firm with a good brand, and they represent prestige properties. I spent a lot of energy reaching the top and I am not willing to let that go."

Besides, I really did not want to move again. In the fifteen years I had been selling real estate in San Francisco, I had been with three companies: Saxe Realty, my start-up in the Mission, Pacific Union, my upwardly mobile years, and now McGuire, the pinnacle of success. Each time I made a move, I wanted a company that was more prestigious so I could sell more architecturally interesting, highly visible or even famous properties.

"But, Paula, you aren't happy. Isn't that what's most important in life?"

As usual, Dr. Black was upbeat and positive. Her ubiquitous, jovial self was beginning to annoy me. *What was she so happy about all the time, anyway?*

"Why don't you make a horizontal move instead?" she suggested. "There must be other good companies selling properties in the better neighborhoods of San Francisco. What about that company you recommended to your friend, Helen Clawsen, a few months back?"

"Oh, Hill & Company? She never went to work there. Helen decided to go to Coldwell Banker instead." I took a sip from my water glass and continued. "I know I would never be happy with a corporate franchise. I like the local independent real estate firms. San Francisco is special and those big companies just don't understand our unique city. Also, as I'm sure you've observed, I'm no corporate gal–too many rules and restrictions. I like the boutique San Francisco companies."

"Well, isn't Hill & Company one of those family-run boutique companies?"

Boy, Dr. Black sure is persistent. Why doesn't she let up? "Yeah, but"–I stammered–"not as competitive."

Dr. Black, with that wide open smile of hers gave me a playful wink. "Isn't that exactly what you are looking for? Not to be so shark-like, sell-your-mother-down-the-river competitive?"

I pondered for a moment. "Certainly, Hill & Company is as respected in the real estate community as McGuire," I said, trying my best to be open-minded, "and they're known to be team players. Like me, many of them have not just a Real Estate Salesman License, but the prestigious Broker's License–considered somewhat like a Master's Degree–so they are definitely a cut above the average. Plus, there are no prima donnas working there that I know of, and the manager, Linda Carroll, is one of the smartest real estate managers around." I felt my heart beginning to expand in my chest.

"Well, then. It's obvious. Go there." I did not say anything. I was still thinking. "Paula, what's wrong?"

"Well, the truth is, I don't know if they would take me."

Dr. Black looked at me with sincere, puzzled concern. "Why not?"

"Well, you know how I have been complaining about McGuire being a bit competitive and hard-edged? I think, in the past I have been a bit like that myself. I don't know if Hill &

Company would want me. They are all pretty team-oriented and maybe they would think I wouldn't fit in."

Dr. Black looked at me directly. "Paula, you have been seeing me off and on for five years now. I can see a change in you. You are much more empathetic and caring and would make an excellent team player. I think Hill & Company is a perfect match for you. Just tell them the truth–that you have changed. It is obvious that McGuire is no longer a fit for you."

I left her office, still unsure. Changing offices meant telling my client base I was moving again. The universe did not let me off the hook, though. The following week on Broker's Tour I stopped to view a large home in Laurel Heights. The agents were out in full force and, as usual, there was no place to park. As was the custom, I parked for a few minutes in a neighbor's driveway, making sure to put my flashers on. I barely had entered the house when I heard loud footsteps behind me.

"You just parked in my driveway!" The voice accompanying the noisy entrance was hinging on hysterical.

I turned around to see a face pinched in pain. "Yes, I did," I said. "I'm very sorry to have inconvenienced you."

I grabbed the keys out of my purse as the woman stepped forward with one of her hands raised. I stepped out of her way and made a hasty retreat to move my car. She shrieked after me. "What is your name?" Her voice was reaching a high shrill while I did my best to ignore her. "I just asked you–what is your name?"

As I opened the door to my car, I could hear this woman asking the listing agent for my business card. I prayed that Marianne Stein had enough sense not to give it to her. I was back at my desk only a few minutes when Mr. Beltman motioned me into his office. "I got a very disturbing call from a woman called Mrs. Pitts on Palm Street today, Paula."

"Oh, that. I parked in her driveway when I was out on tour today. I moved my car immediately, but she still went ballistic on me," I said, standing uneasily on my feet. Stay grounded, I told myself. This was just a minor inconvenience.

"Paula, you have to call her and apologize."

"Do I have to?" I asked, pleading with him now. "She was crazy. She almost hit me," I said.

"Paula, you have to. We cannot afford to have anyone upset with McGuire Real Estate, especially in such a high status neighborhood." *High-status? Well, maybe, but certainly no class.* I made sure not to voice that thought. I was given a stern look. "Really, Paula, you should not be parking in front of people's driveways."

"You know we all do it. How can we preview thirty properties in two and a half hours?"

"Paula, you must apologize. End of story."

I left his office with my shoulders slumped. I knew I would not call this crazy woman–no matter how much money she had. This was just the excuse I needed to call Hill & Company. I tried to sound upbeat and positive, although deep inside I was wrenchingly anxious.

"Hi, Linda," I said over the phone. "This is Paula Pagano of McGuire. I was thinking of making a change and wondered if I could come in and talk to you." I told her that Hill & Company represented the team player cooperation I now craved rather than the competitive atmosphere at McGuire. "Perhaps, you have an available desk?"

Linda answered in the affirmative. This was a good sign. At least Hill & Company was open to speaking with me.

Linda set up a clandestine meeting early one morning for us to talk. It was done this way so as to not jeopardize my relationship with McGuire. Linda, always the consummate professional, did not hold my previous edgy competitiveness against me. She recognized that I was a hard worker, had a good reputation and solid client base. At the end of the short interview, she said what I had hoped for–that Hill & Company would love to have me on their team. Losing a top producer was not something real estate companies' relished, but it was clear that McGuire and I were no longer a match. Not wanting to burn bridges, I explained to management that I wanted to cut back on my work hours and Hill & Company was willing to accept my more laidback approach. Once I made my decision, I never looked back.

The transition to Hill & Company was quick, easy and seamless. All I needed to do was get clear what it was I wanted. So here we are back to the importance of Clarity–Chapter One. We have journeyed a full circle in life lessons.

Dealing with the Millennials' Relentless Expectations

Twenty-five years to the day after I received my first Top Selling Agent Award, I sat down to write this book. I was now married to my soulmate Gralen, a friend and past client who had been circling me for years. I had been on the real estate merry-go-round for so long, I could not see the gift right in front of me. But then, once I put balance on the top of my priority list, I was able to accomplish one of my most cherished dreams.

I no longer yearned for the bigger sale, recognition as the Agent of the Month, or any of the other accolades that came with being a top producing agent. In those twenty-five years

I had shown properties to celebrities such as Danny Glover, Nicolas Cage, Michael Tilson Thomas, Bobby McFerrin, Alice Waters, Tracy Chapman, Pat Montadon, Jill Eikenberry and Michael Tucker, plus a few well-known sports stars–whose names have escaped me–and even a famous Hong Kong playwright. Some bought. Some did not. During my journey as a Realtor®, I remained a consistent member of the Top Ten Producers in San Francisco, won two trips to Mexico, one to Hawaii, one to Australia, and earned three diamond pins, a fourteen carat gold bracelet, two designer watches, lots of expensive dinners and numerous gift certificates to Nordstrom, the Ritz Carlton and wine country resorts. I even won a week-long sailing trip aboard an eighteenth century ship docked in Perth for the America's Cup! Finally, I realized the truth–that it was not the perks, but rather the people who made my real estate career so rewarding.

I realized that I could make big, significant changes in people's lives, like the day my financial advisor, Mickie Clark, referred me to a young professional couple who owned a penthouse in downtown San Francisco. They had taken two years to remodel their home with no intention of ever selling. Then Nathan landed his dream job in Chicago as the head web designer for Sears. For Penny, who was not a typical stay-at-home mom, moving close to her family would enable her to go back to work.

Mickie raved on and on about how special the unit was with its open, fashion-forward design and the 270° view, stretching from the Golden Gate to the Bay Bridge and beyond. During the day, one could see the ships sail by and, at night, Mickie said, the city's panorama of pulsating lights was an experience not to be missed. I was intrigued. Even though we were in a recession with a glut of listings on the market, I replied with an enthusiastic, "Yes–I'd be happy to help your client!" This would be one special property, except that when Mickie gave me the address, a pit formed in my stomach. Although the building was only seven blocks from the fashionable Union Square with its upscale designer department stores, it was also on the edge of the Tenderloin–one of the seedier neighborhoods in this magnificent city, with a reputation for homelessness, criminal activity, prostitution, illegal drugs and, quite sadly, generally squalid conditions.

Yet I did not have it in me to say no to Mickie. She had guided me through a difficult financial crisis and was part of my supportive team. Besides, I had previewed this building before when the full floor penthouse was sold some ten years earlier. It had gone for $2.5 million then. The Mandel's unit, although half the size of the penthouse, sounded truly special. Plus, I knew the historical significance of "The Alexander Hamilton Hotel."

The Hamilton opened in 1929 as a first class apartment hotel complete with kitchenettes, an upscale restaurant and a full-service staff. The theme was to provide luxury living combined with city convenience. Its close proximity to the theaters was the perfect home-away-from-home for many opera singers, actors and actresses. Word around town was the building had housed many celebrities, including Vivian Vance, Florence Henderson and Lauren Bacall.

Touted as an excellent example of 1920's Art Deco Moderne architecture, I wanted to get there early to have a look around. Parking across the street, I took a moment to absorb the neighborhood. It had been years since I walked this particular block, and I immediately detected two new restaurants, an internet café, and a small grocery on one corner with produce proudly displayed out front. The immediate neighborhood actually looked quite pleasant.

I grabbed my briefcase, took a deep breath and before crossing the street, looked closely at The Hamilton's eight-sided exterior. Its unusual zigzag design forced the eye to travel upward, culminating in a sleek, elegant and glamorous impression. The entry was massive, with Egyptian-inspired cartouches above. A doorman approached as I reached for my business card. With renewed wonder, I scanned the Art Deco furnished lobby with its symmetrical crystalline-based lamps, dramatic wing-backed cushioned chairs, and a sleek white grand piano in front of a stone fireplace. The lobby extended far from where my eye could see. I knew there was also a lovely garden courtyard with a center fountain on the other side where the hotel residents would have their tea. And, of course, I remembered the few times I had the delightful opportunity to frequent the famous ballroom. This "Let's go back in time, Old World Charm" with its dangling chandeliers was a feature imbedded in my memory–for I was a ballroom dancer.

"Ms. Pagano? Ms. Pagano? Did you hear me?" the man dressed in black asked.

"Sorry, I had my mind on something else," I replied, suddenly jogged from my reverie and becoming aware of my immediate surroundings.

He pointed to a double glass door several feet away. "The Mandels are expecting you. I can buzz you in now."

As I moved toward the elevators, my attention was drawn to the gilded dials as the arrow moved down the numbers, the carriage descending to pick me up. With elegant efficiency, I was on the twentieth floor in a matter of moments. Nathan swung the apartment door open wide, extending his hand to meet mine. His handshake was firm and strong to match his forthright and confident manner. I took three steps into the foyer. Directly in front of me was an elegant array of windows with the most expansive city view I had ever seen.

The ultra-modern high-style kitchen to my left had glossy gray lacquered cabinets, specialty under-the-counter lighting, luxurious Caesar stone countertops, and a Carrera marble built-in breakfast table. A cozy sitting area was adjacent to one of the windows. A matching dry bar of Carrera marble with more custom lacquered cabinets lined the opposite wall. At the far end was an L-shaped living/dining room, featuring light oak floors with dark wood inlay, a centered marble mantled fireplace and mahogany bookcases on either side. The modern media center on the adjacent wall featured a large flat screen TV. The wall had been painted black, letting the Old World detail take center stage. The ceilings were nine-feet high with recurring rectangular Art Deco moldings in the corners–a subtle yet classy detail one could easily miss. Eight large windows spanned the long north wall through which the glowing downtown lights could be seen at night. A huge mirror above the fireplace reflected the shimmering night lights. The contrasting Art Deco style of these rooms blended surprisingly well with the modern theme. Everything was open, elegant and dramatic. I succumbed to the deliciousness of the moment.

The Mandels led me back through these public rooms to the private zone of the house. The first door off the hallway opened to a thoughtfully planned laundry room with floor to ceiling cabinets, wall-mounted ironing board and wine refrigerator–important features for today's upscale clients. Farther down the hall were two master suites with several windows, all having spectacular–but different–sweeping city views. The larger bathroom was the epitome of romance with original marble floors, full length mirrors and a lavish porcelain claw-foot tub, from which one had a view of the reddish orange towers of the Golden Gate Bridge.

After the tour, we returned to the dining room. "I would like to sit between you, if that's okay," I said. "That way I can share the market analysis with both of you easily." It would also give me the psychological advantage of being at the head of the table.

Penny was the first to speak. "Well, what do you think?"

I was impressed by the avant-garde style, the abundance of views and the excellent use of space. The Mandels certainly went for it full tilt. I made sure I gave them both eye contact when I said, "It's breathtaking." Not ready to express my concern that the Mandels had probably over-improved their space, I noticed a soft shadow of bluish-green illuminating the kitchen. "Are the recessed ceiling lights tinted?" I asked.

"Oh, no. That's just the reflection off the Ann Sach's beveled marble backsplash. We had a great architectural firm and…" Penny smiled broadly at Nathan, "with both of us having a background in style and design, we had quite a team." She stood up and motioned me to follow. "Let me show you a few other features the kitchen offers."

Penny opened one of the cabinets and a mechanical arm swung out, providing more reachable storage. Next to the window, she pulled out a built-in Caesar stone cutting board which could be used while enjoying the city view. She then turned to the focal point of the kitchen: the six-burner Wolfe Range. With a mere push of a button an elaborate exhaust fan rose up from the counter. The cabinets were all soft-closing; there was a hidden appliance garage and an abundance of outlets. The under-the-counter lighting, wall sconces and ceiling spot lights were all on dimmers. The Liebherr refrigerator, Bosch two-zone dishwasher and Thermador speed convection oven were the latest, top-ranked energy savers for the new "green conscious" generation of buyers.

What surprised me most was not the modern sleek kitchen, the views or the specialty lighting. Instead it was how the Mandels were able to combine the functional modernity with the Art Deco motif. I was sure that was not an easy feat. In thirty years I had seen hundreds of renovations, but this was one of the best–certainly surpassing many of the unimaginative look-alike Pacific Heights mansions I'd viewed. (I've never been a believer that big was better anyway. Quality innovation is more my preference).

"Before we go over the market analysis," I said, "I have a quick question. Mickie said your homeowner dues are $1900 a month. Did she mean a quarter?"

"Mickie got it right," Nathan said. "$1900 is the monthly fee, which also includes all the utilities plus maintenance and reserves."

"Really?" I said, taken aback. This condo fee would be a blow to most buyers. "Does that include parking?"

"No, that's another $225."

With that added cost, I did my best not to sound alarmed. "So you don't own your parking, it's leased?"

"Yes." His face was placid when he added, "Oh, there's also a bit of a complication."

I leaned forward. "And that is…?"

"There's a waiting list to get a parking space."

I felt like the wind had just got knocked out of me. I took a slow measured breath, hoping my face did not reveal my concern.

Now Penny joined the conversation. "However, we are willing to secure a parking space from one of the other residents. The upstairs penthouse was able to do so and our unit, being the mini-penthouse, should be able to procure one as well. Of course, it will mean we will have to pay for it."

"How much?" I asked, knowing they would try to recoup that cost when they sold.

"$10,000 to $20,000 is what we figure," Nathan answered.

"It's worth it, though," I said, somewhat relieved. "You can consider it a selling expense." It would be next to impossible to market a unit like this without parking. "Besides a 24-hour doorman, what other amenities does the Hamilton offer?" I asked, hoping to hear some good news.

"We have a full-time manager, eight maintenance people, a conference room with Internet access, a roof deck, a ballroom with kitchenette for parties and a new gym."

I wrote all of this down. Most buyers were busy professionals and having an exercise room was often one of their requirements, as was having a club room where they could entertain, and 24-hour security. Having gotten answers to my questions, I was ready to review the sales data with Nathan and Penny. Usually, I set up a second meeting, because each property is unique with its own special features. Then I could go back to my office and evaluate my observations. However, Mickie confided to me that Nathan was leaving for Chicago in a week, so I did not have that luxury in this case. Learning from mistakes earlier in my career, I came fully prepared. I pulled out the statistics I had brought with me. Unfortunately, there were no two-bedroom units in the Hamilton and also no unit which had been renovated with such flair. The only other unit which had such compelling views was the penthouse above, which just happened to be on the market for $4.5 million. With more than twice the square footage, two walk-out terraces and an elevator opening directly into the unit, it was not a true comparable. I also knew little had been done to it since the early sixties when a wealthy heiress created her fantasy apartment. Unit 2100 was essentially considered a white elephant with its Corinthian columns, 18th Century French décor and Palladian style solarium with 20-foot arched glass ceilings. Add an additional million for renovation. Definitely not a comparable property.

I just hoped the Mandels had not gotten an inflated idea of what their property was worth from this unfortunate and untimely overpricing. Having them face the reality of the market would not be easy. Most owners identified very intimately with their homes, especially if they did substantial remodeling. Although, as professional people, we like to think of ourselves as logical, rational beings, the truth is most people are more emotional than we would like to admit. To tell the Mandels they made a mistake was unthinkable. On the other hand, I could not take on an albatross of a listing that would cost me time and money and might not even sell.

I opened my presentation packet. I concentrated on the last six month's sales–the Marquee at the corner of Van Ness and O'Farrell, the Mint Lofts on Jessie and only four blocks away, and the brand new Odeon development on the edge of fashionable Union Square. All these properties were selling in the mid-$800,000 to $900,000 range. I was still in a quandary though, as these prices might be overly optimistic. The Mandel's unit was saddled with the astronomical dues and potentially marginal neighborhood. I paused a moment to observe Nathan and Penny. Their proud confidence was obvious. I suspected that they believed they had a million-dollar property. I looked at the statistics long and hard, wishing something would lead me to that conclusion as well. It did not.

Nathan started talking about better-located downtown properties–not too far from the Hamilton–which were priced over a million. Surely his property was worth at least that, he reasoned. I explained that in this slow economy–listing data, that is, the properties that were currently on the market–did not mean that much, because only one in four properties was actually selling.

"What do you think for a price, then?" they asked in unison.

"A million is too much of a stretch," I said in a soft, calm, matter-of-fact tone. The Mandels needed to come to grips with the hard-core obstacles that would inevitably get in the way of someone making an offer. "Your condo has high homeowner dues and leased parking in a transitional neighborhood."

The room was eerily quiet. Again Penny was the first to speak. "But this is one special property. We spent a year with a European architect to design this space and another year of construction. We tore down walls, installed new floors, put in new windows, a laundry, and used the best quality materials obtainable in the kitchen."

I had just boldly addressed the elephant in the room. I did not want to get into a power play over price just yet. To make matters more complicated, there was no real comparable property like theirs in all of San Francisco. This would mean pricing will be more subjective and intuitive on my part. Now was the perfect time to switch tactics.

"All excellent decisions!" I said. "The grand open space with views from every window, a kitchen any chef would envy, combined with the sophisticated Art Deco details, is unequalled. This renovation is one of the best I have ever seen." The Mandels needed to feel my excitement and appreciation for all the work they had done. I was now ready to start the marketing part of my presentation.

I pulled out a chart from the California Association of Realtors® which showed that 92% of buyers find a property through the Internet. "Times have changed. Buyers prefer visual to the printed word." I showed them the long list of websites where their property would be featured.

"I'll hire a professional photographer to take both day and night photos. Plus, your property will be on the San Francisco's Multiple Listing Website, both California and National Association of Realtors'® websites and Hill & Company's as well as a new designated website for their condo. Of course, we'll also advertise in newspapers and magazines and in the office display windows at Union and 24th Street, where there is plenty of pedestrian traffic. Combining all these tactics we will be able to reach the maximum amount of potential buyers to get you your best price."

I pulled out my laptop so the Mandels could examine the different websites I mentioned along with a slew of other third party websites, such as, Zillow, Trulia, Redfin, Amazon and SFGate where their property would be featured. Penny took out a pen and paper and jotted something down.

I pushed the marketing book toward her. "What you want to know should all be in here," I said. "The only thing I ask is that you do not share my marketing information with other agents as it is my own unique marketing plan and meant for your eyes only."

Penny continued to write notes. "This is how I remember," she said.

Fortunately, I had listened closely to what the Mandels had told me earlier–that they had not completely finished decorating, were not happy with their bedroom wall color and needed more furniture.

"I can connect you with an interior decorator to help stage the property to show it in the best possible light. They will bring in some decorative accents, such as flowers, high-grade linens and towels. They will even supply dining room chairs and adjust the paint color in the bedrooms to make the views pop more–all with your consent, of course," I added. I wanted to make sure they knew they would always have the final say. "Besides sending out Just Listed Cards and creating a brochure with eye-catching photos, we will have Sunday Open Houses and Brokers' Tours where there will be fresh flowers, bottled water and soft music. I will always personally show your unit myself. I won't be sending an assistant or a new agent. You will be getting the real deal–a top salesperson with thirty years of experience."

"Anything else?" Nathan asked.

I had saved the best for last. With a wide smile, I gave them Merriam Webster's definition of a penthouse: "a luxurious spacious apartment located on one of the highest floors of a building."

"What I would like to do is market your property as a Two Bedroom Penthouse. Although your condo is only 1500 square feet, it does have fantastic views and stylish features and the new developments in South of Market call the top three floors penthouses." This would accomplish two things–soothe the Mandels' ego and get the attention of potential buyers.

"Don't penthouses start at a million dollars?" Nathan asked, puffed up by that reference.

But I was not naïve. Most value-driven buyers would buy only the very top floor: both a prestige and logical consideration. Who wanted to pay a whole lot of money and possibly still hear people above them?

I pointed to my data sheets. "Buyers like to compare similar properties that have actually sold. When you look at these figures, what price do you come up with?" I pushed the paperwork toward Nathan to let the statistics do the talking, not me.

Nathan put the paperwork off to the side. "Paula, if you are concerned about the neighborhood, it is changing. People are no longer calling this area the Tenderloin, but the Trendy-loin! There are popular restaurants here, future bars and cozy internet-friendly cafes. The Hamilton itself is a well-known San Francisco historical landmark." Nathan spoke very persuasively, doing his best to prove to me that his property was worth more than I thought–a typical seller's reaction.

I played along. "This is how you can help me market your unit," I said, once again shifting the focus away from price. "Why don't you give me a list of all your favorite haunts, what you will miss when you leave, and some history of the building so we can create a lot of interest, especially when you first hit the market? Let's also create an evening event so agents and their buyers can experience the special ambience of your unit at night. The specialty lighting and the glittering glow of city lights give your unit a unique, very special feel."

Penny wrote this down. I would have to be on top of my game–she was one detailed gal.

"I would also suggest having the grand opening before we even put the property on the market. We can send out written invitations, call it an Exclusive Event to create excitement. We will have people clamoring to come." Once again I was appealing to the Mandels' ego. I continued, getting more jazzed as I spoke, "I can hire a bartender and get some food catered from one of your favorite local eateries. We can even send out a press release."

The edges of Penny's lips were relaxing into a smile. "One of those future bars we were talking about is at the corner–*Bourbon and Branch*–a real happening place. We could have an after party there."

I did not know what a future bar was, but nodded my head in agreement. This input was good. I liked it when clients put some of their own emotional energy into getting a property ready for market–it showed they were serious.

Nathan chimed in, "Then agents can see first-hand that this neighborhood has changed."

"So do you think we can get close to a million?" Penny asked. Her voice was pleading.

Here we were back at pricing–always the main challenge. It was clear the Mandels had put their heart and soul into their renovation, never expecting to leave. Now they had to let go of their dream. "Your penthouse certainly *looks* like a million-dollar property," I said.

Waiting for that remark to sink in, I also reminded them how difficult the economy was, the huge supply of properties available, and the apprehension many potential buyers had about their job security. I noticed Nathan was having a hard time swallowing. Swallowing the truth can often be hard.

In my typical theatrical Italian-Irish manner, I flung my

arms wide, pointing to all the special features. "I absolutely adore what you've done! My Dad is an architect. I love design, and,"–now I brought my arms down to my sides and spoke in a soft muted tone the truth they needed to hear–"unfortunately it is not just your remodeling that is the factor determining price."

Nathan stood up. "We need to talk to a few other agents." He extended his hand.

Realizing this might be the last opportunity I had to sell myself, I shook Nathan's hand firmly, recognizing enthusiasm was what I did best. "I would love to represent your penthouse and I believe I can sell it for you." I gave Penny a long encouraging smile. The door closed behind me. It would seem that now all I had to do was sit and wait. Not true. I had homework to do.

First I wanted to experience one of those future bars Penny and Nathan spoke about. Didn't they say *Bourbon and Branch* was only one block away on the corner? I left my car where it was and took a walk. One corner was a grocery store, another an Indian restaurant and the two other corners appeared to be some sort of business establishments with tightly shut doors. One had a small non-descript sign hanging from the third floor which said: "Anti-Saloon League." Maybe this was it. I knocked on the sturdy oak door. No one answered. I noticed a buzzer and rang. The door opened a crack–just enough for me to see a shaggy head of auburn hair.

"Password?" a woman asked. Her voice was a whisper.

"Huh?" I said.

"What's the password?"

"Is this *Bourbon and Branch*?" I asked.

"Yes," the gal said, "but you need the password to enter."

"Where do I get that?"

"Go on our website." Then she shut the door.

This was one crazy way of doing business, but it was attention getting. Perhaps the historical theme of the Prohibition Era "Speak easy–don't arouse suspicion if serving alcohol" was part of their marketing. As soon as I got home, I googled *Bourbon and Branch*. Branch went back to the 1800s referring to pure, clean water from a tiny stream. Ah! So Bourbon and Water–thus, the name–one mystery solved! The homepage had a big banner in front which said Reservations. I clicked on it. I was given a password to get in tomorrow night at the only available time they had–6 p.m. I'd bring a friend and stop by for a drink. I wanted to get a feel for the Trendyloin, which Nathan avowed was the new and upcoming neighborhood.

I was intrigued, realizing there was a whole new world out there which, before now, I did not know existed. This trendy penthouse was unlike any property I had ever seen. Yes, it was in an edgy marginal neighborhood, but the Tenderloin was in transition. This thirty-something upwardly mobile couple was teaching me a few things–certainly about style and design, as well as the latest trends. Plus, most young people were not so focused on quality neighborhoods; instead, convenience was most important.

Learning still–after thirty years! I loved this offbeat crazy city! Suddenly I realized I *really* wanted this listing. I sent the Mandels a handwritten personal thank you note and followed it up with a cheery phone message on their answering service:

"This is Paula touching base, wondering if you have made a decision on your agent yet. I would love to represent you so *please* keep me posted," I said. "I also wanted to add another service to our marketing plan. Call me at 415-888-6478 when you can."

Give them a carrot and maybe they would bite. My ploy worked. "You must have been reading my mind," Penny said when she called the next day. "What's up?"

"Why don't we create a video and put it on all the websites as well as YouTube? A narrator can describe all the special features instead of having a buyer read through bullet points. Visual is where it's at these days, anyway. Let's spoon-feed the buyers as much as possible!" I laughed.

So did Penny. "I love that idea!" Her voice softened. "We have one more agent to speak with tonight, but we are leaning toward working with you. Would you be willing to take the listing close to nine hundred thousand? I understand that is the high range, but Nathan worked so hard on the design of this place, he does not want to give the property away."

I agreed to their new compromised price. "Provided," I said, "you will give me a six-month listing and if it does not sell in the first six weeks, you will agree to a price reduction. Also, that you agree to stage it." I had to start managing expectations right from the beginning.

"Promise," Penny said. "We'll call you tomorrow."

When Penny called me the next day and told me I got the listing, I asked her why they chose me over the other three agents.

"By far you were the most appreciative of all the work we put into this place, knew the San Francisco market well and really listened, understanding we had to get highest price possible. You had all the qualities we wanted in a Realtor®."

Okay, so I won out. But truthfully, getting the listing was

only one step in a series of steps before a sale would be consummated and we got paid. I had several more battles to win and, in each case, I needed not only enthusiasm, empathy and tenacity, but self-confidence, discipline and an optimistic attitude to help make this sale happen–which I did to the client's delight. Those are all lessons I have shared with you in this book.

Lessons Learned from Chapter 12:

- MAKE YOURSELF YOUR NUMBER ONE PRIORITY Make sure you schedule time for yourself in your appointment book. We all need time away from our jobs to recharge so we can operate at our optimum. Rest is important, because when your body and mind are well taken care of you have energy to make decisions, juice to be creative, and the pizzazz to be charming.
- CONTRIBUTE Real estate can be a very lucrative profession, but just making money cannot make a person feel rich. Giving can.
- ADJUST YOUR LIFE TO CHANGING VALUES Our lives consist of several stages. In the beginning of any career it is necessary to focus on developing the skills necessary to be an expert in your field. Once the foundation is built, you may want to shift some of your attention to other areas, such as family and friends, hobbies, spiritual practices or charitable work to help you feel balanced.
- TAKE ONE STEP AT A TIME When it comes to negotiating, each day is a new day. Each step taken–no matter how small–is one step closer to the goal of closing the transaction.

13

SELF MASTERY

Creating Healthy Habits

Unresolved Emotions can Play Havoc with Your Success

By now you are well aware that not all sale transitions run smoothly. Since real estate involves many people, each with their own unique personality, it is a very fragile mechanism. I like to compare each person involved in the sales process to the spoke of a wheel. If one of the spokes is out of alignment it can affect the stability of the whole wheel, causing the ride to wobble and even fall apart. It is an interdependent process and relies on everyone doing the absolute best job they can.

Admittedly, some behaviors are hard to change, especially if the source is an unresolved emotion. I am an adult now, but I still act like a little kid sometimes when I get frustrated. I smash and break things. I am sorry to say this is not my only self-defeating behavior. When my feelings get hurt I often strike back and say things I should not–as was the case with Frank Woods. I have endeavored–through accessing experts, taking seminars and classes, engaging in self-help programs that seemed to have merit, through extensive reading, and finally through introspection and reliance on trusted friends and associates–to cope better with life's frustrations. But things happen. People forget. People make mistakes. The truth is we all have our emotional issues and behaviors thast can get in the way of living a masterful life.

The Lessons Learned at the end of each chapter can help achieve success, but I want even more for you. It is simply not enough to just identify a behavioral problem. There are plenty of people who can recognize what is not working in their lives, but take no action to change it. One needs to dig deeper. My belief is that our unresolved emotions, such as, jealousy, greed, arrogance or victim mentality, often lead us to automatic behaviors which can become destructive. Just look around you. Notice how much we are driven by our ingrained habits. Fat people gorge on pizza; drunkards down bottles of scotch; victims cry over bad business deals; rageaholics rant, and greedy zillionaires flaunt their McMansions.

Herbert Hubbard lived in a fantasy world of thinking that somehow his deadbeat clients would change and buy something. When they let him down, he denied that his poor screening had anything to do with it. He was so attached to being a victim that he took no responsibility for wasting his time with losers. Cindy Wilson's pattern of being a people pleaser and making promises which she could not deliver got in the way of her establishing a trusting bond with her clients.

Suzie Weinhammer, in spite of her external success, was so self-centered and arrogant that most people couldn't stand her. And me? When I feel taken advantage of or betrayed, like I often felt in childhood, the anger looms so large that I will literally burst unless I am able to let off some steam–even if a million-dollar sale is at stake!

Of course, many automatic behaviors, which we commonly call habits, have helped us live successful lives, such as getting up early to go to work, exercising and eating healthy. But all of us have a few habits which have become actual liabilities. As a scientist in my former life, I think you will find it helpful to understand how our habits are formed: The brain is like a gigantic computer coordinating hundreds of intricate everyday tasks. It does this by producing feel-good biochemicals called neurotransmitters, which attach onto our cells in the same way a key fits into a lock. This locking mechanism encourages us to repeat tasks necessary for our survival, such as breathing, eating and moving. We want the pleasurable feeling these neurotransmitters produce, so we create a continuous cycle of habits. Getting our biochemical rush is our primary goal, like a junkie trying to score. We are so intent on getting the dopamine fix, which our biochemistry craves, that we are unaware of what we do to ourselves and to others. That is the power of neurotransmitters! Sure, destroying a phone may relieve stress when feeling overwhelmed, but most anyone would agree that hurling insults or throwing things is not a constructive coping mechanism.

So how do we disable an ingrained destructive neurological pathway? First of all, you may never be able to completely disable it. Although I have achieved a high level of success, I still struggle with my automatic reactions to frustrating experiences. Instead, I have set up my own personal radar to avoid situations that can trigger my destructive patterning, so that I choose who I associate with carefully. When red flags are flying high, I do my best to avoid people who display arrogance, self-centeredness or victimizing behavior. Lastly, when I cannot avoid a challenging situation, I stop and take a breath, consciously looking at my emotional reaction and then correcting any destructive behavior as soon as I can. Even as I am writing about creating healthy habits, I find myself embroiled in a power play which has escalated into a drama of operatic proportions. Since it is so timely, let me share it with you:

"Money Changes Everything" –C. Lauper

I met Carrie Mingleton, a title representative, through Kevin O'Connor, an easy-going, good-looking Irish lad and a San Francisco native, who sat across from me at work. Kevin kept me in stitches with his off-the-wall humor and endeared me to him by calling me "Honey." That he also called the other gals in the office "Honey" as well didn't bother me, because his devil-may-care attitude and charming demeanor took the stress out of the intense daily grind.

I thought he had a crush on Carrie, who came by the office promoting USA Title and who frequently chatted with Kevin whenever she could, even though she had a boyfriend. Besides being a pretty, blue-eyed natural blonde with a slim athletic figure, Carrie was poised, soft-spoken and articulate–an alluring package. I was a genuine appreciator of beauty, whether it was an antique Chinese vase, a violet pink sunset or a graceful demeanor. I appreciated Carrie's sense of style and after a few months of her politely pressing me to give her some business, I did.

Carrie steered me to only the best and most competent escrow officers, who handled the small details of loan payoffs and demands, required city documents, arrangement of fire and title insurance policies, and the fine intricacies of balancing the credits and debits from sellers and buyers with masterful precision. If they were too busy, I could always count on Carrie for following through, delivering time-sensitive paperwork and making sure the deal got done correctly. She and I made a good team. In spite of all her glamour and social connections, I thought she wanted a friend who appreciated her good work. I willingly filled that role.

I had gotten Carrie into her first real estate purchase, which, she repeatedly told me, was one of the best decisions she had ever made. During our friendship, I had been there for Carrie when she needed advice on her marriage, business pursuits and divorce. Over the years of our friendship, we had supported each other. When my sister-in-law discovered that her cancer had metastasized, I felt compelled to tell my brother the truth–that Janie was now on borrowed time. Carrie advised me against it. "Let him have hope for as long as possible," she had said. I did what she suggested and for that sage advice, I felt indebted to her.

Carrie called me immediately when she noticed a For Sale sign posted on the upper flat of her two-unit building in the desirable Marina district. She loved her lower flat and thought it would make good economic sense to own the whole building. I had introduced Carrie to Robert LeCamp years ago in the hope that the two of them could form a partnership and buy the building together. I showed them how they could own near the hip-happening Chestnut Street–a popular haunt of the twenties and thirties crowd–where they both wanted to live. I explained that after they lived in the duplex for a year, they could then start the condominium conversion process. It would mean working together with an attorney to draw up the CCR'S–the rules of the condominium association–and the subdivision map, which would specify which part of the property would be Carrie's, which would be Robert's, and which would be the common area. Once all the paperwork was approved by the Department of Real Estate, they could refinance and replace their partnership agreement with their own separate grant deeds.

Now, years later, Robert LeCamp was selling his flat because his company had transferred him to Boston. Carrie's divorce also had just been settled, which could not have been better timing. She could buy his upper unit with all cash, if necessary. Of course, I was a bit dismayed that Robert had not called me to list his condo, especially after I gave him an incredible opportunity to own in San Francisco, but I was not surprised. Robert had found me on the Internet, we did not have a particularly close relationship, and he knew Carrie and I were good friends. During their six years of co-owning and developing this property, they had had a series of disagreements and were barely on speaking terms. I am sure he wanted to keep me at arm's length during the sale.

The first scheduled showing was to be the Brokers' Tour when agents caravan the new listings, looking for a possible match for their clients. I knew the agent, Regina Holloway. She was the top agent at Coldwell Banker and, besides this condominium, which was listed at $995,000; Regina had three other listings, all in the three to six million dollar range. I also knew the real estate market was booming. If Carrie waited until after the designated tour date to place her offer, she would most likely get into a competitive situation in which the price could be bid up and Carrie might lose the property. I got on the computer to check what the Multiple Listing said. It stated no preemptive offers, meaning no bids would be taken before the customary two-week marketing schedule. This was a common practice in a hot San Francisco sellers' market. However, I was not going to let these obstacles deter me in getting Carrie the property she wanted.

Since Regina was used to dealing with the highest echelon properties, I was hoping she would not be interested in spending much time with a sale for under a million dollars. I structured an offer which was a no-brainer–all cash with no conditions and over the asking price. Carrie Mingleton was in a unique favorable position. She already knew the property, so she did not need any inspections. Accepting our offer would be to Regina's advantage. She would not have to market the condo, coordinate showings or worry whether the escrow would close because Carrie was offering to put up a non-refundable $34,000 deposit and a quick twenty-one day close. Just as I had hoped, Regina took the bait and agreed to present our offer to Robert LeCamp.

However, we were still on shaky ground. Like I mentioned before, Robert LeCamp did not like Carrie. She had expanded her lower unit into her storage space in the garage and made an extra room, enhancing the value of her condominium. It infuriated Robert that, in spite of insisting on the top unit, Carrie had gotten the better deal. It took some strong negotiating, but with Robert already relocated in Boston, and Regina, living up to her four-star reputation as one of the best agents in the city, our offer was accepted. I appreciated Regina's candor when she explained we were to follow the contract to the letter, because Robert was not willing to "give us a single inch of slack." We had only twenty-one days to sign off on all the disclosures, obtain a title report and insurance and record the grant deed. The second Robert LeCamp signed the offer, the clock started ticking. Still Carrie complicated the transaction when she decided to get a loan instead of using up all her cash. To make matters worse, she chose an out-of-state mortgage broker, one that her new boyfriend, Craig, recommended.

I explained to Carrie that a lender she had never met was not a good idea. It was easy for a lender to give the best scenario over the phone, knowing he would probably never see her face-to-face. I relayed war stories of when lenders could not deliver on their promises and pushed buyers into undesirable loan programs to get the deal closed or, even worse, became missing in action and did not return calls when they could not perform. Instead, I hoped Carrie would choose one of my lenders, with whom I had developed long, close business relationships over the years. Because they wanted my continuing business, they would do whatever was necessary to close the deal. In the rare case when a lender I recommended cannot perform, because of a low appraisal or lack of available funding, she/he would tell me immediately and not leave me hanging. Being stranded with a buyer who was already packed with no place to move was a predicament I never wanted to experience. I gave Carrie several names, but her response was unexpectedly rigid. "I really want this 90% loan at 6% interest rate which the Las Vegas lender is offering," she countered.

I was familiar enough with the current financial market to know that these terms seemed overly optimistic. "This loan sounds way too good to be true–what if this mortgage broker, who neither of us knows, does not perform?" I asked.

"Craig got a loan from him with no problems," Carrie bragged.

I felt we were taking an unnecessary risk. This guy was not from San Francisco and I am sure had no clue to the exceptionally high prices of our real estate. Only a San Francisco-based appraiser would know what properties in the Bay Area were worth. I tried the back-door approach with Carrie to soften the information I was about to deliver. "How large was Craig's loan?" I asked.

She covered the phone with her hand and I heard muffled talking in the background. "$250,000," she answered.

"Carrie, your loan is going to be much more. Anything over $417,000 is a jumbo loan and has entirely different guidelines. (The lower conforming loans can be sold in the secondary financial market and are much easier to obtain). Plus, we don't have much time. Three weeks goes by really quickly." I suggested that she use Michael Peck, one of my lenders. "He has been in the mortgage lending business for years and would know a local appraiser who could bring in a purchase value high enough."

"Paula, you are such a Nervous Nellie. Will you stop it, please?" I begged Carrie to reconsider. "Okay, I'll call this Michael Peck and talk to him, but I am telling you right now–I won't use him if his terms are not good."

Instead of getting embroiled in a power play, I remembered the Buddhist wolf parable, to give energy to the good wolf inside of us–the one that is full of passion to get the job done, the one that wants to focus on the solution–and not to focus on the bad wolf, my frustration. I ushered a quick thank you and was off the phone.

Day Two: It was time to touch base with Carrie. "I talked to your friend Michael," she said. "The interest rate is one-fourth of a percent higher so I'm sticking with Craig's lender."

I bit my lip. What if the bank required we get a termite inspection? This was pretty standard procedure for most out of state lenders. I would have to get Robert LeCamp's permission and it was doubtful that he would cooperate. After all, the only reason he took our preemptive offer was because it was hassle free. I spoke softly, "Craig's lender is not from here. What if he can't get this 90% loan? What will you do then? You could lose your deposit and even the house–is it really worth the risk?"

"Don't you trust Craig's recommendation?" was her response.

I knew there were some boundaries friends could not cross and boyfriends were one of those. Yet I also knew that if the lender did not come through, Carrie would turn to me to solve the problem. "Okay, then. Let's use Michael Peck as a back-up," I suggested, trying not to sound aggravated. Most lenders did not like to do this, because it was a lot of work on their part and little chance of reward. However, Michael was a good guy and I knew he would do this as a favor for me.

"Paula, I have not finished the first loan application. I don't have time for all this nonsense."

Put a lid on it, I told myself. I did not want my anger to blow this deal or our friendship. So, to quiet my fears, I gave Michael Peck a call myself. I had been in this business long enough to know that *Wishin' and Hopin'* did not close real estate transactions. I wanted to know if this Las Vegas lender was for real. When I gave Michael the quotes, he promised me he would call his list of banker contacts to see if anyone could match them.

Day Four: Michael called me Monday morning, telling me he could not find any lender who came close to the Las Vegas quotes–even for conforming loans under the $417,000 guideline. I thanked Michael for all his time. "Would you still be willing to help Carrie?" I asked.

"Sure. I'll offer to meet with her in person to help her fill out the loan application." Now that was 5-Star Service! Not only was Michael on top of his game, but he was generous as well. I made a mental note to myself to use Michael's services for my next transaction.

I knew the frantic last-minute stresses of closing, so I talked to Carrie's lender about his loan program. He was vague and noncommittal. I then asked him to put his quote in writing and fax it to me. A day and a half passed and I had not received anything. I called again. He did not respond. I knew from experience what this meant–that the phenomenal rates and terms were not accurate.

A value I hold dear is being truthful and Carrie needed to know the truth. When I explained the ramifications of the lender's unresponsiveness to Carrie, she did not believe me.

"Why would he lie to me?" she asked.

"It's simple. He wants your business," I said. When I told her Michael Peck would meet with her at her home, she told me she was too busy. Busy doing what? She didn't have a job. Perhaps Carrie's and my values were not aligned. I promised Regina and Robert a smooth real estate transaction and wanted to keep to my word. Carrie's focus seemed to be only on getting the best deal–even if it went against the terms of our agreement. I explained how the last-minute stress so characteristic of closings could take its toll–peace is another value I hold dear–but Carrie would not be persuaded. She was sticking to her guns. Not wanting to be the one who was shot and feeling the bad wolf waking up inside me, I said, "Carrie, you and I are done," and hung up the phone. Although my body was shaking from the outright denial, the lies and the broken promises, I had not taken out my anger on Carrie. Instead, I faxed Carrie's lender requesting confirmation on his loan quotes and then folded up my paperwork. I was going to reward myself by leaving early.

Day Thirteen: Carrie's lender had not responded to my fax, my posted letter or my four telephone calls. I was getting nervous. I called Carrie. Carrie was aggravated with my nervousness and told me–in not-so-polite terms–to back off. "Paula, if I don't get the loan, I'll pay all cash if necessary." From my many encounters with codependency, I realized I could not make Carrie do anything. I had to let it all go. I also understood that I might lose this deal.

Day Twenty: We were supposed to be closing tomorrow and the loan papers had not yet arrived. Carrie had been calling me every couple of hours for the last three days in a panic, trying to blame me. Instead of saying, "I told you so," I patiently reminded her that she could always pay all cash. Meanwhile, I was telling Regina Holloway what the Vegas lender told Carrie–that the papers were due to arrive within a day or two. (Or three? Who knew with this guy?) I assured Regina that we would close with or without the loan papers, because Carrie would pay all cash, if necessary. Regina gave us until Friday and moved on to her next transaction.

Day Twenty-three: Wednesday morning. The loan papers had arrived. Carrie was on her way over to sign them. I called Regina and told her the good news–just a few days late–but it was finally going to happen. As I shifted my attention to other business, my cell phone rang. It was Carrie calling me from the title company. She was hysterical. Sure enough, the loan terms quoted to her were not the same as in the loan papers, so she was refusing to sign.

"That's okay," I said. "We still have time. Regina has given us an extension until Friday to close so you can bring in your cash today or tomorrow."

Carrie surprised me by attacking with the viciousness of

a pit bull. "What? All my cash? How dare you even suggest such a thing?"

"Carrie, that is what you told me you would do if this loan didn't come through," I said, shocked at her line of reasoning.

"Well, do you believe everything I say?" she asked with an accusatory tone.

I answered, "Of course. Aren't I supposed to?"

"No," she said. "I must have been under duress when I promised you I would use up all my cash. Now I've changed my mind." Instead, she planned to go to the bank directly and by-pass her dishonest mortgage broker–the same guy she so vigorously defended a few weeks ago.

I told her that this would take time. I reminded her that we were three days late in closing and the seller, Robert LeCamp, was getting impatient. He took our price because it was supposed to be a quick uncomplicated transaction. If he decided not to wait, she might lose all her deposit.

"I don't care," she said. "And don't think you can convince me to pay all cash which is not in my best interest. I thought you were supposed to be representing me!" Her voice was bitter and accusing, the words harsh. To save a few bucks, Carrie had forgone truthfulness, loyalty and friendship.

I did not even attempt to answer. I had kept the bad wolf at bay in my conversations with Carrie, but that last call was sending me into my old destructive anger pattern. On the drive home I tried not to beat myself up. I told myself anger was not necessarily a bad thing. It warned me that something was amiss and that I needed to take action. I had made progress over the years. I knew when I was in danger. I could hear the wolf banging at the door before he got too out of control. That was why I got off the phone with Carrie.

I looked at my anger from another angle. Like Carl Jung, I knew that my impassioned enthusiasm and my impetuous temper were interconnected somehow. If it wasn't for my anger, I wouldn't be as successful as I'd been. My anger fueled me. It helped me pay for my college education by giving me the energy to work two jobs in the summer and a part-time job during school. It helped me find a research job right out of college although I had no guidance, no car and no money. It gave me the courage to leave the medical field and get into real estate. It gave me more courage to move to San Francisco. Anger propelled me to the top even though I had no business skills. I did not want to kill my wolf. He warned me when things weren't right. But I did not want him ruining relationships by running amok either. The trick was to notice when my bad wolf was at the door so I could avoid situations that triggered my negative anger patterning.

Day Twenty-four: I learned from Carrie that the bank was willing to work with her directly, which cut down on some of the costs, but they wanted a new appraisal. Re-enter Michael Peck. With my tail between my legs, I asked him for another favor. Did he know of an appraiser who could write up an opinion of value the same day? He made a few calls on our behalf–all pro bono–and was able to find someone to do an on-site inspection and a written appraisal in two days–a record in the fast-moving San Francisco real estate market.

Day Twenty-five: Friday morning. Regina did her best to calm her client, but Robert LeCamp called the title company directly and demanded to know the status of the transaction. When he learned that the first loan papers were never signed and we wouldn't be closing for a few more days, he wanted $5,000 for the inconvenience. Regina and I persuaded him to accept the much-reduced fee of $2,500. I personally delivered a bottle of Silver Oak Cabernet to Regina and told Carrie of the good news. Instead Carrie demanded that I pay the $2,500. Since she had already asked for a 20% referral fee–which is a highly unusual request from a buyer–because, she said, this would be such a simple transaction and I was such a close friend. So, with another tail between my legs, I begged Hill & Company Management to make this one exception. After some deliberation, they acquiesced. There was no way I would go back to them a second time. Besides, this easy deal had become one hell of a nightmare. So I refused. Hissing like a pissed off snake I had just stepped on, Carrie threatened to back out. Cool as the fog folding in around me, I told her I would stand behind her decision. Losing my self-esteem, I felt, was more painful than not getting paid.

She changed tactics, knowing that her $34,000 deposit was at risk. She now threatened a lawsuit, saying she did not understand the contract she signed. (Not only had she bought the Marina flat I sold her ten years ago, but since then, a two-and-a-half-million dollar home in Tiburon, as well as a ten thousand-square-foot villa in Mexico with her ex-husband. Oh, yes, I almost forgot–before she married she worked for a title company for eight years. Carrie was no naïve young lady.) I listened, but again did not react. "Do whatever it is that you have to do," I said.

Day Thirty: Carrie paid the $2,500 penalty and bought the condo, but a huge rift had come between us–a rift that could not be bridged. Carrie chose money over a long-term friendship, honesty and fairness. I also felt badly about how she had used my good-hearted, knowledgeable business associate, Michael Peck, with not so much as a thank you. I had previously heard her divorce to her multimillionaire husband, whom she'd been married to for only a few years, had been extremely bitter. I did not want to believe it before, but now I knew: Carrie would do just about anything for the almighty dollar.

Friendships were tricky. They could make or break a business relationship. In the case of Michael Peck, our friendship had brought both of us professional advantages. In a tough situation liked the one I just described with Carrie, Michael helped both me and my client. While we were attempting to get answers from the out-of-state mortgage broker, Michael was available for advice and direction. He got us in contact with a local appraiser who was able to give us an appraisal within two days. When we needed a copy of the appraisal, it was Michael who facilitated it. Michael confided to me that Carrie was periodically calling him to check on the information she was getting from her lender because, although she wanted this guy's rates, she did not trust him. Michael was not paid a dime, but did all this as a favor to me because of our solid business relationship. Michael was a person with whom I wanted to do business in the future. Carrie was not.

As a Realtor®, I knew when a loan deal was too good to be true. I continued to work with Carrie even though I could see trouble down the road with the financing. Some transactions were tough, but that was why we were paid the big bucks and sometimes it is not until you are in the middle of a transaction that difficulties arise. Still, one has to draw the line somewhere. When Carrie attempted to blame me for her bad decision, I refused to pay the $2500 penalty even if it meant the deal would not close. If I had to do this negotiation over again, I would make the same choices.

This transaction showed me the importance I placed on

good solid relationships, fair play and integrity. Being financially successful and being rewarded for a hard day's work were also important, but I would choose the former over money any day. I had never seen where money alone has made a person happy.

Understanding the Wolf Within

Wanting to live the best life I possibly can, I am fascinated about how we can get ourselves hooked on something that is not immediately pleasurable, such as a real estate sale–a protracted process with ups and downs, challenges and pitfalls. Good salespeople understand the importance of delayed gratification–that the pleasure of a sale depends on doing tasks we do not particularly like. We can actually become engaged in productive, innovative, problem-solving thought and behavior designed specifically, and sometimes ingeniously, to achieve that delayed success.

It seems to reason that setting up *positive constructive patterning* in our hearts, minds and lives is just as possible as our unconscious destructive patterning. Tommy Hopkins was fond of reminding people who attended his seminars that the mind is a goal-seeking device. In order to begin to set up positive patterning you need to identify your existing healthy habits–no matter how weak they may be–and consciously begin to work on strengthening them. For instance, I knew I got obsessive about details when I was making a sale. Many people found this an annoying trait, but I was just as detail-minded about people as I was about things. I sized up people very fast and recognized what motivated their behavior. That was how I was able to get Carrie's offer accepted by Regina, not depend on an out-of-town lender's promises–though it would have been easier to do so–and create a back-up plan with Michael Peck's support.

So here's the formula to set up constructive habits: If one of your strengths is establishing bonds with people, think about making a new friend when you make a cold call. This common bond will be enough to get a conversation going. If you are a curious person, interested in what other people do and how they think, do a survey. *How long have you been in your home? Have you ever thought of trading up? Is your home convenient to your work? Do you have any children at home?* Then you need to *FOCUS* on your goal.

Know the statistics: one in a hundred calls will produce a potential client. (The statistics of turning that client into a closed sale are one in three.) Think of it this way–every time a person hangs up or says *No,* you are one step closer to the person who will say *Yes.* When you get someone on the phone, you have about twenty seconds to get his or her interest. I offer clients my assistance in determining the market price of their home as well as refinancing, remodeling and relocating options. This soft-sell approach of helping rather than getting works wonders.

After focusing on your goal, the next step is consistency: *PRACTICE, PRACTICE, PRACTICE.* It takes about three weeks for the brain to start producing neurotransmitters, so that is how long it will take for your new behavior, such as making cold calls, asking for a referral or taking a few breaths instead of getting angry. It is the same twenty-one day rule whenever you start an exercise program, learn a new language or take up a new hobby.

Last and most importantly, you need to trick your body into getting your feel-good rush. Therefore, it is vitally important that you *REWARD* yourself after your hard work. The sooner the better, so the body connects this new activity with those pleasurable feelings. If I get off a particularly rude call, I get up from my seat and make myself a cup of tea with lots of honey. The honey is a good symbol for me. If I feel I need more support, I have some chocolate on hand–a sure fire way to feel better. You can do the same by telling yourself–*Aha! After I'm done I deserve a night out to do whatever my heart desires! A hike in the mountains when I'm done! A day at the beach! A scrumptious dessert!*

Whether you are creating a new habit or replacing a bad habit, it is the exact same process. For instance, I was aware that my destructive patterning of not keeping my bad wolf at bay cost me sales, friendships and peace of mind. With Carrie, I consciously observed my behavior, and when I felt the bad wolf knocking on the door, I got off the phone as soon as possible and took care of myself the best way I knew how. I was able to create a positive habit of not responding to her irrationality by focusing on my goal of getting the sale closed and then rewarding myself afterwards.

I have related my experience with negative patterns throughout this book to show how to look inside and see where you can self-manage your emotions. Be aware that whatever you do not acknowledge you cannot change. As you know, changing behaviors to achieve your goals is a lifelong process and, although the steps are simple, it is not easy to create new patterns, and one is never done.

In conclusion, just because our biochemistry can make us addicted to destructive patterning, such as anger, excessive people-pleasing, victimization or procrastination, it does not mean we are not responsible for our actions. Laziness is the common excuse thread of mediocrity. Remember: *Change requires intense focus, practice and reward.* This should be your mantra. Post a sign at your desk. Say it in the shower as you get ready for work and share this knowledge with others. Making changes for the better is an ongoing process.

My real estate journey has brought me a great deal of personal awareness, so that both my professional and personal life have changed for the better. I truly have been able to enjoy a happy, contented, heaven-like-at-times existence. Attempt to change one pattern at a time; more will be too overwhelming and you may get discouraged. Keep plugging away. In twenty-one days or so you will begin to see results. That's *every* day. You don't get weekends off.

How do you define and measure your own success? Success can be measured by the amount of money one makes, if you so choose, or the number of deals one brokers. However, it can also be measured by the serenity and joy one feels in his or her relationships. I hope the true stories and life lessons I have shared help you take stock of how you have been measuring success. If something is lacking, perhaps now, armed with these insights, you can begin to operate from a new level of interaction with colleagues and clients. And of course, first and foremost, with the most important client of all–yourself!

Lessons Learned from Chapter 13:

- BE IN THE PRESENT MOMENT By being in the present, you will become more aware of your surroundings, your client's motivations and your own behavior, and be able to circumvent or solve problems as well as communicate more effectively with others.
- AVOID SITUATIONS THAT TRIGGER NEGATIVE PATTERNS When you feel that pang in your gut, the fluttering of your heart or the sweat on your brow, you may be in the middle of a survival pattern which can trigger negative emotions. It is best to remove yourself as quickly as possible and get grounded so you can problem-solve.
- CHANGE REQUIRES FOCUS, PRACTICE AND REWARD Focus on what your goal is. If you get off track, make a self-correction and be sure to reward yourself for your good efforts. Remember, it usually takes at least 21 days for a change to become a neurological habit.

Praise for the Author's First Book

" 'Secrets of a Top Salesperson' is a powerhouse of ideas for entrepreneurs and anyone who has been hit by the mortgage/real estate crisis. It gives you a systematic and creative roadway to help you get your life back on track."

– Barbara Corcoran, Celebrity Real Estate Expert of the TODAY SHOW and SHARK TANK

"Real estate agents and the rest of us as well will greatly benefit from Paula's excellent tactical tips, perceptive relationship insights and invaluable time management advice."

– Ray Brown, 15 Year KNBR Radio Host and 30 Year Real Estate Broker/Owner and Best Selling Author.

"I thoroughly enjoyed reading "Secrets of a Top Salesperson." I received Paula's book after she gave a seminar to Realtors® on the topic of "Recession – Pain or Opportunity?", which I got a whole lot out of. I read this book in a matter of days, as I could not put it down! Paula shares her experiences and sales tips in such a unique, fun and exciting narrative fashion! I highly recommend this book to anyone looking for inspiration and entertainment–and strong words of wisdom from an incredible warm, friendly and successful person & saleswoman. I learned a ton & plan to pass this book onto my friends, family and colleagues. Great energy and passion!"

– Sara Werner, San Francisco Top 1% Realtor®

"I have read a lot of self-help books, but, boy, reading Secrets inspired me like no other. I felt like I was walking in your shoes, learning as you learn, living a day in the life of a top successful salesperson. Now I want to go out and conquer!"

– Carol Soutar, ASP Senior Stager, San Mateo California

"Highly entertaining,and useful book. By giving many real life examples, the author provides interesting insights into handling the emotions that arise during the high pressure of real estate transactions. The book takes you through her personal story and the secrets of success she has learned in real estate. I'm glad I read it."

– Michael D. Tekulsky, Realtor® San Francisco

"Author Paula Pagano shares so much in this book. Paula writes from the heart sharing very personal experiences in a most intimate way. You feel as if you are right there with her. The book flows very well and is hard to put down. 'Secrets' gives very specific instructions on successful salesmanship and how to deal with clients, both good and bad. In addition to the real estate sales lessons and what surprised me most, was the inspirational way in which Paula writes. She shares her life in this book. I would recommend this book to salespeople and non-salespeople equally to increase their success. The life lessons shared in this book alone are worth the read."

–Jean Romeo, Entrepreneur Phoenix Arizona

"Paula's story took a path I was not expecting, and I enjoyed it more than I anticipated. I was a struggling real estate agent in Southern California years ago during another recession, and I could have benefited immensely if Paula could have been my mentor."

– Ralph Dacy, Automobile Executive Chico California

"I loved reading Paula's book. Easy to read and full of great stories you can relate and learn from. I found out about this book when I saw Paula give a talk as a guest speaker. I loved the way she carried & expressed herself. The book is written as an honest story about her life, evolution & mind shift she had to make from being a scientist to become a top successful Real Estate Agent. Smart woman, that's for sure. I am also a Realtor® in the San Francisco Bay Area (East Bay) and I don't know Paula but I do admire her from a far. She is a rock-star in my mind. I recommend every real estate agent & sales professional read this book."

– Tania S. Realtor®, East Bay

"Paula has such great energy that it is contagious! My favorite chapter was on empathy. People buy from people they like and Paula has such an easy approach that it feels like she is telling you her stories just to you!! It is a fun read! Enjoy!!"

– Katey Shinn, Partner Keller Williams Real Estate

"I was pleasantly surprised by this book. I found it engaging on a general level because of its humanity, wit and wisdom. The lessons in this book can be applied to so much more than real estate, or even general successful salesmanship. I found it human, interesting and inspiring. And it's a hard-to-put-down fun!"

– Doug Wink, Graphic Designer, New Mexico

"Secrets sucked me in. I found it to be a practical delivery of healthy philosophies tied to personal convictions expressed through adventurous colorful and heartfelt stories–reminding me of a San Francisco centric Eat, Pray, Love book."

– Lisa Bass, Global Account Executive

"Beyond being a brilliant education in how to become a top producer in business, Paula's book, Secrets of a Top Salesperson, is a remarkable guide that leads you by example into being a more fully realized successful person. She skillfully takes you beneath the dynamics of business into understanding how to convert negative interactions into personal triumphs. More importantly, she teaches how to use emotional conflicts with others to determine and clear your own personal and psychological conflicts. The result is self-realization, becoming your own teacher, master, and guru in the dynamics of life."

– Frank Jordan Author, Educator, and Spiritual Counselor

About the Author

Originally from New York, Paula Pagano moved to San Francisco in 1980 and in her first year became the top sales agent in her office the first year. Shortly thereafter she obtained her California Broker's license, and over the next thirty years remained a consistent Top Producer.

Paula has served on both the Board of Directors for the San Francisco Apartment House Association and the Board of Directors for the San Francisco Association of Realtors®. Paula is a trained business coach, with a certification from the Coaches Training Institute (CTI) and is an active member of the Women's Council of Realtors®. She is also a Competent Toastmaster (CTM) and past member of the National Speakers Association and Professional Toastmasters. She is also the CEO of ClientConnect and currently teaches sales training in the Bay Area.

Paula is also the author of two books, Secrets of a Top Salesperson: How Emotions Make or Break The Sale (Booksurge,2009), and Getting the Property SOUL'D: A Breakthrough System for Successful Stress-Free Buying and Selling (New Voices Press, 2016).

As a community-conscious Realtor®, Paula has been involved in many local charities, especially with the American Heart Association and Walk to End Alzheimers, as well as politically active in protecting homeowners' real estate interests and preserving San Francisco's architectural integrity. In Paula's spare time you will find her on the dance floor--she is a proficient ballroom dancer, having won many awards in local and international dance competitions.

Proud of her mostly Sicilian descent, with a bit of Irish and Mohawk Indian thrown in for good measure, Paula believes that if she could become successful, anyone can! She still resides in her beloved City by the Bay with her husband Gralen and their seventeen-pound Maine Coon cat Cosmos.

To learn more about Paula and her secrets of success, go to:

www.PaulaPagano.com

Made in the USA
San Bernardino, CA
11 May 2016